CRYSTAL
MORPHOLOGY

An outline of
CRYSTAL
MORPHOLOGY

A. C. BISHOP, B.Sc., Ph.D.
Lecturer in Geology,
Queen Mary College, University of London.

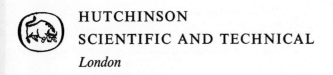

HUTCHINSON
SCIENTIFIC AND TECHNICAL
London

HUTCHINSON & CO (*Publishers*) LTD
178–202 Great Portland Street, London, W1

London Melbourne Sydney
Auckland Bombay Toronto
Johannesburg New York

First Published 1967

This book has been set in Times,
printed in Great Britain on Antique Wove paper
by Balding & Mansell Ltd,
of London and Wisbech, and bound by
Wm. Brendon & Son Ltd, of Tiptree, Essex

CONTENTS

Abbreviations and Symbols

$\mathring{A}$	*Ångstrom units* (10^{-8} *cm*)
	the crystallographic axes:
a, b, c	*orthorhombic, monoclinic and triclinic systems*
a_1, a_2, c	*tetragonal system*
a_1, a_2, a_3, c	*hexagonal and trigonal systems*
a_1, a_2, a_3	*cubic system*
a, b, c	*cell edges in the x, y and z directions respectively*
a, β, γ	*the angles between the positive directions of the b and a, a and c, and a and b crystallographic axes respectively*
C	*end-centred Bravais lattice*
d	*interplanar spacing*
F	*face-centred Bravais lattice*
hkl	*x-ray 'reflection' from a set of lattice planes*
(hkl)	*crystal face indices (Miller indices)*
$\{hkl\}$	*crystal form indices (Miller indices)*
$[hkl]$	*zone axis indices (zone symbol)*
$(\underline{hkl})$	*the twinned position of face (hkl)*
$(hkil)$	*crystal face indices (Miller-Bravais indices): hexagonal and trigonal systems*
$\{hkil\}$	*crystal form indices (Miller-Bravais indices): hexagonal and trigonal systems*
$[hk.l]$	*zone axis indices (zone symbol): hexagonal and trigonal systems*
I	*body-centred Bravais lattice*
m	*reflection plane of symmetry*
P	*primitive Bravais lattice*
R	*rhombohedral Bravais lattice*
x, y, z	*the crystallographic axes; the notation used in structural crystallography such that the morphological axes a, b and c correspond to x, y and z respectively.*
$1, 2, 3, 4, 6$	*rotation axes of symmetry*
$\bar{1}, \bar{2}, \bar{3}, \bar{4}, \bar{6}$	*inversion axes of symmetry*

PREFACE

Crystal morphology has long been taught as part of elementary courses in geology. It is appropriate that the study of our dominantly crystalline planet should at an early stage include a study of crystals themselves. The study has added point, however, for the manipulation of crystals and their projections helps to develop facility in thinking three-dimensionally; perhaps the most generally useful skill of the geologist.

This book is written for those who are starting to study crystal morphology. It has been born of teaching experience which has revealed the need of a text at this level and of an essentially practical character. No attempt is made to cover the whole field of crystallography (which extends far beyond the study of morphology): there are several excellent texts that already do this. The aim is rather to give first an outline of the principles of crystal structure and then, on this foundation, to acquaint the reader with the more practical aspects of crystal morphology that he is likely to meet in an elementary university course or its equivalent.

The concepts of atomic structure, forces between atoms and the aggregation of atoms to form crystalline solids are introduced at the outset and are treated non-mathematically. In this I would ask the forbearance of the chemist and the physicist. These topics are placed first because they are the prerequisite of a proper study of crystal morphology. They give the reasons why crystal faces are arranged in a definite and regular fashion.

Systematic crystal morphology forms the subject-matter of Part 2 of the book. The nomenclature of forms is in line with modern British practice and has been kept as simple as possible. Where several names are in current use for one form, I have ventured to express an opinion.

I am convinced of the value of the stereographic projection in teaching crystallography, and projections are used from the outset in this book. Apart from their immediate value, the manipulation of stereographic projections is of wider use in other branches of geology.

It is assumed that crystals will be available for examination and measurement with a contact goniometer and a worked example of the construction of a stereogram is given for each crystal system together with the necessary constructions and calculations for the determination of crystallographic constants.

The Hermann-Mauguin point group notation is used throughout and the symmetry symbol given in the *International Tables for X-ray Crystallography* is chosen to describe each symmetry class. Those wishing to confine their attention to the eleven commoner crystal classes will find these treated at the beginning of the appropriate chapters. They are further identified by an asterisk and by the name of the associated mineral.

The value of illustrations in a book of this kind need not be stressed. Nearly all the illustrations have been specially drawn. I am grateful to Messrs. J. Wiley and Sons Ltd. for permission to reproduce as Fig. 223 the Penfield Axial Protractor from Dana's *Textbook of Mineralogy*, 4th Edition. Messrs. W. H. Freeman have been good enough to allow the use of the box device employed by Berry and Mason in their *Mineralogy* to illustrate monoclinic and triclinic crystals.

In writing this book I have been able to draw freely on the help and advice of others. Professor J. F. Kirkaldy has helped in very many ways and thanks are particularly due to him for his advice and critical reading of the manuscript. I should like to thank Dr. W. J. French for the time he has given in discussion and for his helpful and constructive criticism. Professor K. W. Sykes and Dr. E. H. Andrews have also been good enough to read the manuscript, the one from a chemist's and the other from the physicist's point of view. To all these colleagues and to my friend Dr. A. E. Mourant, who has made many most helpful suggestions, I am most grateful. Miss Margaret Knight deserves thanks for her care in preparing the typescript.

A.C.B.

QUEEN MARY COLLEGE,
University of London

PART 1

The Principles of Crystallography

CHAPTER 1

GENERAL INTRODUCTION
TO CRYSTALLOGRAPHY

History of crystallography

Compared with other sciences, crystallography is a new discipline, but the form and beauty of crystals have attracted attention since very early times. Every civilisation of note has used crystals as personal ornaments and the lapidary has flourished for thousands of years. Gemstones are frequently mentioned in the Old Testament; twelve different stones were used to decorate the breastplate of the high priest.[1]

Theophrastus[2] (372–287 B.C.) and Pliny[3] (A.D. 23–79) of the classical writers recorded the minerals then mined for use as gemstones, pigments or for smelting to metals. Nevertheless, although Pliny records that quartz crystals always have six angles, he left unexplained the regular arrangement of crystal faces. Yet it is the ancient Greek word *krustallos* from which our word crystal is derived. *Krustallos* was used to describe the transparent crystals of silicon dioxide (quartz, so commonly found in mineral collections) which was believed to be water frozen by intense cold, a belief that persisted into the Middle Ages.

The passing of Roman civilisation in the fifth century saw also the end of even the most rudimentary lines of scientific inquiry. The next thousand years contributed very little to the concepts of nature handed down from classical times. Medieval writers culled their material from classical sources, largely from Pliny, but it was embellished by magic and mysticism derived from Arabia and the Orient. In the Middle Ages minerals and gemstones were prized not only for their beauty but also because of the magical powers they were believed to possess. Minerals were grouped according to their colour and many legends were woven around them and seriously believed by learned men.

The growth of modern crystallography and mineralogy from this welter of superstition was, initially at least, a slow process and dates in

1. Exodus *28*, 17–20.
2. Theophrastus, *Concerning Stones*.
3. Pliny, *Natural History*.

essence from the publication in 1546 of Agricola's *De Natura Fossilium*, which, although containing no direct references to crystals, attempted for the first time a classification of minerals on modern lines and paved the way for the work of Haüy and others.

The first real contribution to crystallography was made by Steno[4] in 1669. Steno (the italianised form of the Danish name Niels Stensen) noticed that quartz formed hexagonal crystals whose external shape varied, but when outlines of sections cut in the same direction from different crystals were traced on paper, the angles between corresponding pairs of faces were constant (Fig. 1). The work he began was ex-

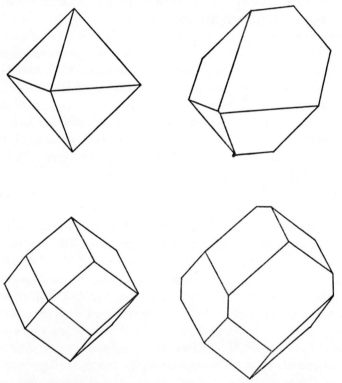

Fig. 1 Perfect and unequally developed octahedra (above) and rhombdodecahedra (below).

4. Steno, N., *De Solido intra Solidum naturaliter contento Dissertationis Prodromus*, Florena, 1669.

tended and confirmed by Guglielmini (1655–1710) and principally by Romé de l'Isle,[5] who in 1772 formulated what is now known as the *Law of Constancy of Angle*. The law states: '*In all crystals of the same substance the angles between corresponding faces have the same value when measured at the same temperature.*' This is true regardless of the size or shape of the faces and it follows that a similar constancy of angle must exist between corresponding crystal edges.

Crystallography was now beginning to take shape on a sound footing and in 1784[6] and 1801[7] Rene-Just Haüy formulated his theory of crystal structure. Haüy was the son of a poor weaver, but, through the interest and benevolence of the Prior of St. Just, his native town, he received a good education at Paris. He became a botanist and might have remained

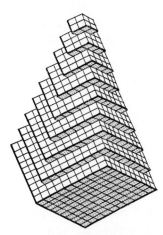

Fig. 2 Haüy's concept of the structure of calcite. A ditrigonal scalenohedron composed of small rhombohedral 'integrant molecules' (after Haüy).

one had it not been for a lecture on mineralogy which turned his attention to crystals. One day, after accidentally dropping a group of calcite crystals belonging to a friend, Haüy noticed that the cleavage fragments produced were bounded by smooth, rhomb-shaped faces. After breaking up many more calcite crystals of differing external shapes he concluded that all were composed of a repetition of a minute structural unit having the shape of the cleavage fragments (Fig. 2). Haüy called these small units *integrant molecules* and showed how cubic forms could be constructed by stacking together minute cubes. Modern work has shown that Haüy's concept of *solid* units of structure is unsatisfactory, but the validity of his theory of minute structural units has been amply confirmed. His discovery was fundamental to the science and Haüy is considered as being the 'Father of crystallography',

5. De l'Isle, R., *Essai de Cristallographie*, Paris, 1772.
6. Haüy, R. J., *Essai d'une théorie sur la structure des crystaux appliquée à plusieurs genres de substances crystallisées*, 1784.
7. Haüy, R. J., *Traité de mineralogie*, Paris, 1801.

notwithstanding the fact that Kepler and Guglielmini had previously suggested theories of crystal structure in terms of minute units, but in little-known works.

Haüy's work provided the impetus for the continued growth of crystallography through the nineteenth century when the development of the goniometer led to the systematic and more accurate description of the shape and symmetry of natural crystals.

The next milestone in the progress of the science came in 1912 when M. von Laue, together with W. Friedrich and P. Knipping, were investigating the nature of X-rays. They found that when X-rays, which are electromagnetic radiations similar to light but with a very small wavelength of the order of 10^{-8} cm, were passed through a crystal they were scattered in a regular manner as shown by the images produced on a photographic plate. These photographs, called Laue photographs or diffraction patterns, proved that crystals have a regular internal structure. Laue, Friedrich and Knipping in their studies used 'white' X-rays which cover a range of wavelengths.

This work was amplified by W. H. Bragg and his son W. L. Bragg, who were studying the properties of X-rays and investigating their wavelength. They learned of Laue's work and, using crystals as diffraction gratings, found that monochromatic X-rays were diffracted by the layers of atoms in the structure. In 1913 they published the results of their work: the determination of the structure of sodium chloride.

The discovery of X-ray diffraction made it possible to probe and elucidate the internal structural arrangement of crystals. The twentieth century has seen the development and refinement of this method of determining structures, so that now the science of crystallography has three major divisions:

(1) *Structural crystallography*—dealing with the symmetry and arrangement of the internal structure on which all other properties depend;

(2) *Morphological crystallography*—the study of the relationships between crystal faces which are the external expression of the fundamental structure and

(3) *Optical crystallography*—the study of the effects of crystalline matter on light, particularly polarized light.

Structural crystallography continues to grow as new techniques are discovered and applied to more and more branches of science. The study of the internal structure of crystals now no longer remains solely within the field of the solid-state physicist, although it is primarily to him that we owe refinements in technique and new lines of approach. X-ray diffraction methods are used by the chemist, metallurgist and geologist as an invaluable aid in the determination of the structure of crystalline materials. Some idea of the expansion of crystallography can be gained from the biennial report of crystallography in the *Chemical Society Annual Reports* for 1960 in which the authors state: 'The difficulty in writing such a report is to decide what to leave out.'[8] The growing use of high-speed computers and other calculating machines has widened the scope of structural analysis by speeding up the lengthy calculations that are sometimes involved. These techniques make possible the construction of projections of the electron density at a given plane in the crystal structure and show the spatial arrangement of the atoms in the crystal. An example of an electron density map is given in **Fig. 3**.

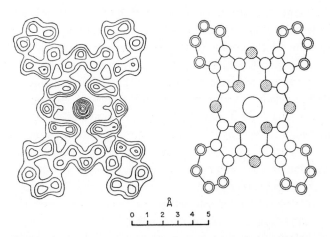

Å
0   1   2   3   4   5

Fig. 3   Left: An electron density map of nickel phthalocyanine, projected on to (010).
Right: A drawing of the molecule. Open circles — carbon; double circles — CH; stippled circles — nitrogen. Nickel is represented by the large circle at the centre.

8. *Chem. Soc. Annual Reports* 1960, *57*, 462.

The development of the nuclear reactor has provided a source of neutrons that are of value in crystallography.[9] It has been found that neutrons, electrons and other atomic particles are diffracted in the same general way as X-rays. Their behaviour is, however, sufficiently different to enable them to provide important information about crystal structures which X-ray diffraction fails to do.

Crystallography is making advances possible in fields of study in which only a few years ago it had no place as a working tool. We may cite an example from the biological field. That part of reproduction called *replication*,[10] by which new individuals are made and are essentially copies of their parents, has been a puzzle to biologists for many years. It was known that the solution of the problem lay in the understanding of the enzyme reactions causing gene replication in cell nuclei, and this, in turn, on the constitution and structure of the complex protein polymers of the enzymes. The search was narrowed down to a substance called deoxy ribosenucleic acid (DNA for short) which is present in the chromosomes bearing the genes of organisms as widely different as man, plants and bacteria. The replication of genes is linked with the properties of DNA. Although DNA was discovered in 1869, the spatial arrangement of the atoms in the molecule was unknown until 1953, when Watson and Crick,[11] using X-ray diffraction techniques, proposed a new structure which resolved the difficulties of earlier models of this complex molecule. Their work, and the theory of self-replication of DNA springing from it, have had a most dramatic effect on the whole field of genetics. Only slightly less fundamental, and even more complex, are studies now in progress on complex protein molecules, such as the haemoglobin of blood and myoglobin of muscle.

Such, then, is the range of modern crystallography. This book aims to concentrate attention on one particular part of the science, that of crystal morphology; the shape adopted by crystals when they are free to grow unimpeded and to develop natural faces. It is important at the very outset to appreciate that the subject cannot be divided into water-

9. Cockroft, Sir John, *Nuclear Reactors in Scientific Experiments*. Endeavour, 1950, *9*, 55–63.

10. For a concise discussion of the problem of replication see *New Biology*, No. *31*, Penguin Books, 1960.

11. Watson, J. D. & F. H. C. Crick, *A Structure for Deoxy Ribosenucleic acid*, Nature, 1953, *171*, 737–8.

tight compartments, and it will be necessary to refer constantly to the structural aspects of crystallography.

The definition of a crystal

We have seen that ideas as to the nature of crystals have changed with the times. At the outset it is as well to understand what is meant by the term *crystalline state*. For a substance to be classed as crystalline it must obviously be solid,[12] but much more is involved. There is very little difference externally between a piece of glass and a piece of quartz. Both are irregular in shape, colourless and frequently exhibit conchoidal fracture, yet quartz is crystalline and glass is not. The distinction is not one detectable by the naked eye, but depends upon the fact that crystalline material has a definite chemical composition and an ordered atomic arrangement, whereas gases, liquids and glasses (in reality, super-cooled liquids) in general vary widely in composition, and lack any regular arrangement of their constituent particles. It is this ordered atomic arrangement that is the criterion of the crystalline state and it may be detected by X-rays, by optical means or by such features as cleavage.

When a crystalline solid is allowed to grow unimpeded by external objects or constraints it is normally bounded by plane surfaces. These surfaces are called *crystal faces* and their regular disposition is an expression of the regular internal structure. The result is a *crystal* which may be defined as '*a homogeneous solid with a definite chemical composition and ordered atomic arrangement, bounded by naturally-formed plane faces*'.

A word or two of explanation is needed to elucidate two points in this definition. Care must be taken not to confuse a *definite* chemical composition with a *fixed* composition. The structure of many crystals is complicated and variations in composition may occur, as when one atom takes the place of another in the lattice. These variations are not random, however, but conform to a definite scheme. The second point concerns the words *naturally-formed* crystal faces. Cut and polished gemstones are familiar to everyone and are bounded by plane faces which are regularly disposed. They do not, however, conform to the

12. There is a possible exception in certain 'liquid crystals' but they need not concern us here.

B

definition of a crystal because the position and size of the faces is determined by the jeweller. In true crystals the faces are naturally produced and are the result of the processes of crystal growth.

Crystal symmetry

A novice examining a collection of crystals may be bewildered by the almost infinite variety of arrangement of faces he sees. Even the forms shown by a single mineral like calcite are sufficiently variable as to suggest capricious development. And yet a closer study, particularly of well-formed crystals, reveals that there is order in the facial arrangement

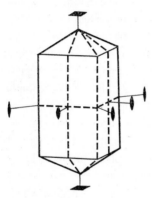

and that the crystals are *symmetrical*. Take for example a crystal of zircon like that shown in Fig. 4. It is evident that the faces have a regular, four-fold arrangement about the 'summit' of pyramid-shaped faces at either end. If the crystal is held between thumb and finger by these top and bottom corners (or *coigns* as they are sometimes called) and rotated, the same arrangement of faces is seen, when viewed from the side, four times during a complete revolution through 360°. Put another way, the shape of the zircon crystal in the starting position is that of a solid with faces that meet in definite measurable angles. If now the crystal is rotated through 90°, the arrangement of faces and angles is identical with that of the starting position. A further rotation through 90° gives another apparently identical position and so on, so that the crystal takes up this same position four times in a complete revolution. The crystal is thus symmetrical about the line joining the opposite corners; the symmetry is rotational symmetry and the line about which rotation takes place is called an *axis of symmetry*. The axis in this instance is a four-fold axis of symmetry because the same group of faces is repeated four times during a complete revolution. Other names are sometimes used, for example, axis of four-turn symmetry, or *tetrad* axis. The last is the terminology used throughout this book.

Fig. 4 Symmetry elements of a crystal of zircon.

If the crystal is held by the centres of the faces standing vertically in Fig. 4 and similarly rotated, it is again symmetrical but the repetition occurs now every 180°, i.e. its similar faces are seen only twice during a complete revolution. The axes joining the centres of the faces are *diad* axes or axes of two-fold symmetry. The same is true if the crystal is held by the mid-points of the edges in which the vertical faces meet and it hence has four such diad axes.

Further inspection of the crystal reveals symmetry of a different kind in that it would be possible to cut the crystal in half so that the two parts so produced are mirror images. There are five such directions in this particular crystal: four standing vertically and intersecting in the tetrad axis and the fifth perpendicular to the other four. The crystal is thus symmetrical about several *planes*. Lastly, it will be seen that every face of the crystal has a similar face lying parallel to it on the opposite side of the crystal, as though an image of itself was formed by a lens at the centre of the crystal. The crystal is thus said to have a *centre of symmetry*.

From the variation in shape of natural crystals it is obvious that all crystals will not show the same degree of symmetry, nor will they all be symmetrical about all the elements. It is clear, however, that crystals that are similarly shaped have allied symmetry and they may be grouped together on this basis. Fig. 5 shows two crystals that have slightly different symmetry and yet are broadly similar.

At this point it is well to realise the difference between *crystallographic symmetry* and *geometric symmetry*. A perfectly shaped, symmetrical crystal is both geometrically and crystallographically symmetrical in that corresponding faces are the same size and shape and the crystal is perfectly symmetrical as far as shape is concerned about its symmetry axes, planes and centre. A slightly misshapen crystal of the

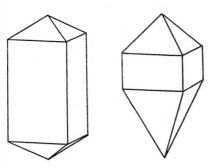

Fig. 5 Two tetragonal crystals belonging to different symmetry classes.

same substance is equally symmetrical crystallographically to the perfect one, but it is no longer symmetrical as a solid object. The difference arises from the fact that, for a crystal to be symmetrical crystallographically, the size and shape of the faces are of no importance; it is only their relative angular disposition that matters. This serves to emphasise the fact that external shape and symmetry are the expression of a more fundamental internal symmetry.

Haüy thought that tiny units of solid matter aggregated to form crystals. Modern knowledge of the crystalline state, gained principally from X-ray studies, shows that crystals are made of atoms that are arranged in a regular manner in three dimensions. Imagine it were

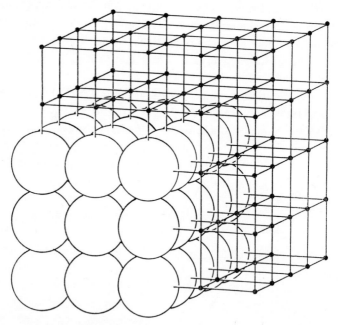

Fig. 6　The cubic P space lattice.

possible to join the centres of atoms by lines. The crystal would now look like a regular three-dimensional network of lines, or a *lattice* for short (Fig. 6).

The space lattice

The concept of a lattice is fundamental to the fabric of crystallography. The simplest of all patterns is that produced by a linear repetition of some simple unit as in Fig. 7A. The pattern can be extended indefinitely along the line by the repetition of the unit of pattern. This unit may be simple or complex according to the style of the pattern.

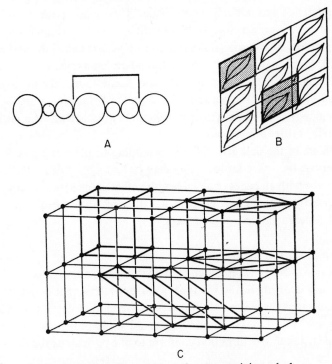

A

B

C

Fig. 7 A. A simple linear pattern. A pattern unit is marked.
B. A two-dimensional 'wallpaper' pattern. Two pattern units are shown.
C. A three-dimensional lattice, with three unit cells boldly outlined.

A more familiar example is that of the production of a two-dimensional pattern like wallpaper by the repetition of a small unit of pattern (Fig. 7B). Look at a wall covered with a patterned paper and find the unit of pattern. Notice that it is possible to outline the pattern unit by drawing lines that join identical points as in Fig. 6. If now the unit is moved parallel to these lines the pattern is reproduced indefinitely in two dimensions. Notice also that more than one unit of pattern may be chosen (Fig. 7B).

Imagine now that the corners of every unit in the wallpaper pattern are joined by lines so as to produce a regular network and that many such nets are stacked at regular intervals one above the other. The result is a three-dimensional network or lattice of points in space to which reference has already been made. This *space lattice* gives a picture of the way in which crystals are built and, just as wallpaper has a unit of pattern, so also a crystal has a unit of pattern called the *unit cell* (Fig. 7C). More than one unit cell can be chosen in any one space lattice and although they may differ in shape and size, all are alike in having the same symmetry. Translation of the unit cell (always a six-faced parallelepiped) parallel to its three principal edges extends the lattice indefinitely in three dimensions.

The shape of the unit cell will vary according to the arrangement of the points of the space lattice. They may be arranged so that the unit cell is a cube with all edges of equal length and all angles right angles; at the other extreme there may be three sets of edges all of unequal length and with different angles between them.

The fourteen Bravais lattices

A. Bravais and M. L. Frankenheim in the mid nineteenth century investigated mathematically the types of space lattice that could exist. They found that there are only fourteen possible different lattice types and they are known as the *Bravais lattices*. All crystalline substances are three-dimensional structures that conform to one or other of the Bravais lattices.

The crystal systems

It is possible to arrange the Bravais lattices according to shape into seven groups or systems as shown in Fig. 8. Study of this diagram shows that three lattices are alike in that they have edges that are of the same length and arranged at right angles. They have the shape of a cube and belong to the *cubic system*.

Two lattices differ from the cubic ones only in that one set of edges

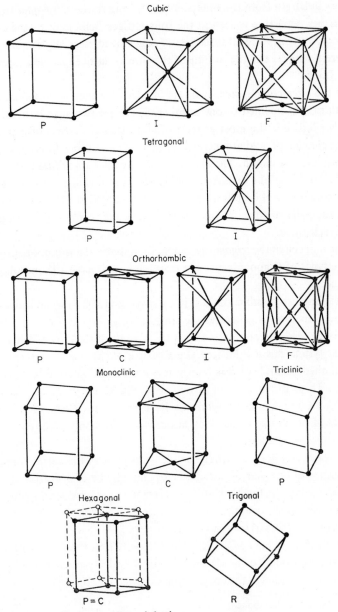

Fig. 8   The fourteen Bravais lattices.

differs in length from the others. These belong to the *tetragonal system*. A further departure is seen in the four lattices belonging to the *orthorhombic system*. Here all three sets of edges are at right angles but are of different lengths and the outline of the Bravais lattice has the shape of a matchbox.

In the *monoclinic system* two sets of edges are each at right angles to the third, but inclined to one another. There are two such lattices. The *triclinic* lattice is the most general of all in that all its sets of edges are unequal in length and are inclined to each other at three different angles.

Two lattices remain. The *hexagonal* lattice appears at first sight to be similar to that of the orthorhombic system, but it is distinctive in that it is a prism with a rhombus as its base with an angle of 120° between two opposite pairs of edges. If three such lattices are combined a hexagonal prism is formed.

The unit cell of the *trigonal* system has the shape of a rhombohedron.[13] Three types of trigonal lattice are possible but all have a rhombohedral outline.

The simplest possible unit cell in each system (Fig. 8) when translated in three dimensions generates the simplest or *primitive* (*P*) *lattice*. Such lattices have identical points only at the corners of the lattice. Thus each crystal system has a P lattice. The P lattice of the trigonal system is a rhombohedron and for this reason it is commonly referred to as the *R lattice*. Three other types of lattice exist. The *face-centred* or *F lattice*, besides having identical points at its corners, has them also at the centres of each of its faces. Such lattices are found only in the cubic and orthorhombic systems.

The *end-centred* or *C lattice* has identical points at its corners and at the centres of one pair of parallel faces and may be of orthorhombic or monoclinic type. A further distinction is made by some crystallographers in the case of the orthorhombic C lattices according to which of the three possible pairs of faces is centred.

Finally there is the *body-centred* or *I lattice* (from the German *Innenzentrierte*, internally centred) with identical lattice points at its corners and centre. It occurs in the cubic, tetragonal and orthorhombic systems.

13. The name rhombohedron is given to a six-faced solid figure, each face of which is a rhombus.

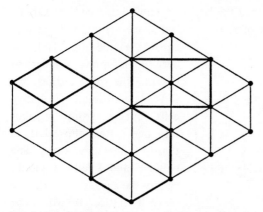

Fig. 9   Basal projection of part of a hexagonal space lattice showing the hexagonal P cell (left) and the hexagonal C cell (bottom). An orthogonal cell is also shown (right).

The primitive hexagonal lattice sometimes (and strictly correctly) is given the symbol C because it can also be considered as an end-centred type (see Fig. 9). There is a very close similarity between hexagonal and trigonal crystals that extends from their morphology to the details of their lattices. A full treatment of this topic lies beyond the scope of this account and belongs properly to the subject of structural crystallography.

The fourteen Bravais lattices, then, are:

Cubic	P, I, F
Tetragonal	P, I
Orthorhombic	P, C, I, F
Monoclinic	P, C
Triclinic	P
Hexagonal	P≡C
Trigonal	P≡R

It will be noticed that there is no F or C lattice in the tetragonal system. Such lattices can in fact be constructed (Fig. 10) but it is evident that the C lattice is equivalent to a P lattice with a smaller unit cell and that the F lattice is equivalent to a tetragonal I lattice, but with a different orientation. The same can be done for the other systems.

A further point emerges. The Bravais P lattices are co-extensive with the unit cell. In all other lattices it is possible to construct a unit cell that has points only at its corners. Movement of this unit cell parallel to its

edges will indefinitely extend the lattice. A cubic F lattice, for example
has a primitive unit cell of rhombohedral shape arranged diagonally
across the cube (Fig. 11). How-

Fig. 10 Tetragonal F (left) and C (right) lattices showing their equivalence to the I and P lattices that are heavily outlined.

ever, it is much simpler to
describe the space lattices, not
in terms of absolutely primitive
cells, but to group together
into one system those lattices
that have the same shape. The
cubic F and I lattices should
clearly be grouped with the
cubic P lattice. It would be
most inconvenient to describe
them in terms of unit cells
which differ in shape. Because
the F and I lattices contain more than one pattern unit they are sometimes called *compound unit cells*.

Crystallographic axes

The Bravais lattices, although only some of them are primitive and co-
extensive with the unit cell, will, if they are moved parallel to their edges,
extend the lattice indefinitely in space. The directions of the edges of the

Fig. 11 Cubic F lattice with a rhombohedral primitive cell heavily outlined.

Bravais lattices define the *crystallographic
axes* which may be formally considered as
vectors that define the lattice.

All the crystal systems other than the
hexagonal and trigonal have three crystallographic axes (Fig. 12). It is customary to
think of the axes as originating at a point at
the centre of a crystal and extending forwards
and back, up and down and sideways from
it in the manner shown in Fig. 12. The axis
running from front to back is called the *a*
axis, that running from side to side the *b*
axis and the vertical one is called the *c* axis. The positive ends of the
axes are those that lie forward, upward and to the right of the origin.

The negative ends are written $\bar{a}$, $\bar{b}$ and $\bar{c}$ and are referred to verbally as '*minus a*', '*minus b*' and '*minus c*'; never as '*bar a*', '*bar b*' and '*bar c*'.

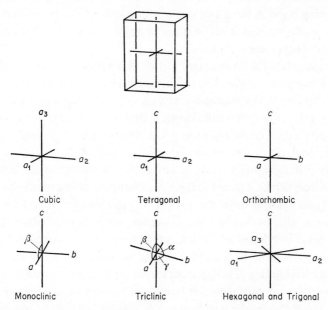

Fig. 12   Above: A simple crystal showing the crystallographic axes.
Below: The crystallographic axes.

The cubic system has its three axes arranged at right angles (orthogonal) and because identical lattice points are repeated at the same distance along the three vector lines the crystallographic axes are spoken of as being of equal length. To emphasise this they are labelled a_1 (front to back) a_2 (right to left) and a_3 (vertical).

The tetragonal and orthorhombic systems also have orthogonal axes but they differ in length. In the tetragonal system the two axes in the horizontal plane are of the same length and, as in the cubic system, are called a_1 and a_2, but the vertical axis, the c axis, differs in length from the other two. The a, b and c axes in the orthorhombic system differ in length. Many orthorhombic crystals are held so that the a axis is the shorter of the two in the horizontal plane, but this is not a general rule.

The axes of the monoclinic system are unequal in length. As in the orthorhombic system the a and b, and b and c axes are at right angles, but the a axis slopes upwards and away from the observer making an obtuse angle with the c axis. Because it is inclined in this way to the plane containing b and c, the a axis is sometimes called the *clino* axis and the obtuse angle between it and c is called angle β (Fig. 12). The b axis is sometimes called the *ortho* axis.

The irregularity is taken a stage further in the triclinic system in which, besides being of unequal length, the axes are all variously inclined to each other. As in the monoclinic system the angle between the positive ends of the a and c axes is called angle β, that between the positive ends of the b and c axes is called angle α and that between a and c is called angle γ.

The similarity between the hexagonal and trigonal systems has already been mentioned. This similarity is further shown in the fact that their lattices can be referred to the same arrangement of crystallographic axes. These systems differ from the others in that they have four axes that are parallel to the cell edges of the hexagonal Bravais lattice. Three are of equal length and are arranged symmetrically in a horizontal plane at an angle of $120°$ to each other. They are called a_1, a_2 and a_3. The vertical c axis differs in length from these and is at right angles to them. In this respect it resembles the tetragonal axial system, a feature that shows itself also in the development of crystal faces. It is possible to refer crystals with a trigonal R structure to three axes that are parallel to the edges of the Bravais lattice, but in morphological studies it is usual to use the hexagonal axial set.

The structural crystallographer uses a different nomenclature for the crystallographic axes. The letters x, y, z are used instead of a, b, c for crystals referred to three axes and x, y, u and z are used for the hexagonal and trigonal axes. Axes of equal length are not given the same letter in this nomenclature. Cubic crystals are referred to x, y and z axes; not to x_1, x_2 and x_3. This nomenclature is used because the letters a, b and c are used in structural crystallography to denote the lengths of the edges of the unit cell and it avoids confusion if different symbols are chosen for the crystallographic axes. Among geologists and mineralogists, however, it has long been the practice to use the older nomenclature and it is adopted here. The student should, of course, be familiar with both schemes.

Summarising, there are fourteen Bravais lattices that may be grouped (1) according to their shape giving seven crystal systems or (2) according to their crystallographic axes, in which case the hexagonal and trigonal become one (hexagonal) system, making six in all.

Whether the trigonal should have the status of a separate system or be regarded merely as a sub-system of the hexagonal system is a matter of opinion. The hexagonal and trigonal systems are regarded as being distinct in this book. It is felt that at an elementary level, there is much to be gained and less risk of confusion of thought if trigonal and hexagonal crystals which are, for the most part, morphologically distinctive, are considered separately. The more advanced student, however, will become increasingly aware of structural similarities between certain classes of these systems.

Suggestions for further reading
Adams, F. D., *The Birth and Development of the Geological Sciences* Dover Publications Inc. New York, 1954.
Bragg, W. L., *The Crystalline State*, Vol. 1, *A general survey* G. Bell & Sons Ltd., London, 1949
Buerger, M. J., *Elementary Crystallography*, John Wiley & Sons Inc., New York, 1956.
Phillips, F. C., *An Introduction to Crystallography*, Longmans, Green & Co. Ltd., London, 3rd Edition 1963.

CHAPTER 2

A CHEMICAL VIEW OF CRYSTALS

Crystals may, as we have seen, be considered as a three-dimensional array of points in space, called a space lattice, that can be extended indefinitely by translation of a unit cell.

This concept still falls short of the definition of a crystal given on p. 17. The definition, to be complete, links with an ordered structure a definite chemical composition. There is, therefore, a connection between the structure and the chemical composition of a crystal and it is necessary now to consider the material nature of the points in space that constitute the space lattice.

What, then, occupies the points of the space lattice? There is no simple answer to this question and in seeking a solution we must turn to the field of chemistry. It is necessary at the outset to examine the nature of the chemical bond.

Atomic structure

Solid chemical compounds, including crystals, are arrangements of atoms in space. An atom comprises a *nucleus* and *electrons*. The nucleus carries nearly all the mass of an atom and is composed of positively charged *protons* and neutral *neutrons*. The number of protons (the atomic number, Z) indirectly determines the chemical nature of the atom. An atom is rendered electrically neutral by a cloud of *electrons* each carrying a unit negative charge and, in a complete atom, equal in number to the number of protons. The nucleus takes no part in ordinary or non-nuclear reactions; only the electrons are involved.

The simplest atom is the hydrogen atom. It consists of a lone proton around which a single electron is in orbit (Fig. 13A). By 1913 E. Rutherford (later Lord Rutherford) and Niels Bohr had advanced a theory of atomic structure in which it was argued that electrons were restricted to definite orbits in much the same way that the planets revolve around the sun. It was considered that the electrons were free to move within these specified orbits without radiating energy. Only when an electron moved from one orbit to another was energy absorbed or emitted and then only in definite amounts or *quanta*.

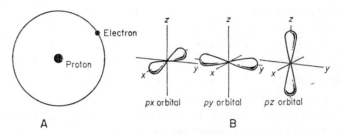

Fig. 13   A. Diagram of the Rutherford-Bohr hydrogen atom.
B. Diagram of the shape of the electron 'clouds' in the *px*, *py* and *pz* orbitals.

Orbitals

Further research has shown that this concept of electrons as particles moving in fixed orbits is too simple. In 1924 L. de Broglie showed that electrons behave not only as particles but also as waves. C. J. Davisson and L. H. Germer in the United States and G. P. Thomson in Britain demonstrated the reality of this concept by showing that electrons are diffracted by crystals in a similar way to X-rays.

W. Heisenberg proposed that it was impossible to define precisely and simultaneously both the position and velocity of an electron. In order to determine the position or velocity of an electron, some other particle must interact with it. This particle, e.g. a photon, has enough energy to displace the electron so much that its original position and velocity are unmeasurable. The related uncertainties in the two parameters were defined by the *Heisenberg uncertainty principle* which led to the replacement of the concept of a fixed orbit of an electron by a mathematical function giving the probability of electron distribution about the nucleus. This probability function is called an *orbital*. According to the orbital theory an electron may be found at any distance from its nucleus, but the locus of the places where it will most probably occur remains very close to the nucleus. In the case of the hydrogen atom, the fixed planar orbit of the Rutherford-Bohr atom is replaced by a spherical probability function. It is of interest to note that the electron will most probably be found at the surface of a sphere having the same radius as that of the Rutherford-Bohr orbit.

The quantum numbers

The orbitals are discrete energy states, or put another way, they are *quantised* with respect to energy. Each orbital may be described by four integers called the *quantum numbers*.

The *principal quantum number*, n, is an integer having the value 1, 2, 3, . . . n. All electrons having the same principal quantum number constitute a *shell*. The shells are called the K, L, M, N. . . . . shells when the principal quantum number has the value 1, 2, 3, 4. . . . A shell can contain no more than $2n^2$ electrons.

The electrons in any shell are distributed in sub-shells characterized by the subsidiary or *azimuthal quantum number*, l, where for each principal quantum number n, l has the value 0, 1, 2. . . . $(n - 1)$. When the azimuthal quantum number has the values 0, 1, 2, 3 the electrons in these sub-shells are called the s, p, d, and f electrons.

For a sub-shell l, there are a number $(2l + 1)$ atomic orbitals defined by the *magnetic quantum number*, m.

In 1927 it was discovered that an electron spins on its own axis rather like the earth and that any one atomic orbital can contain only two electrons and then only if they have opposite spins. This spin factor is called the *spin quantum number*. It has only two values; $+\frac{1}{2}$ and $-\frac{1}{2}$.

Every electron in an atom is uniquely defined by the four quantum numbers. No two electrons can have the same value for all quantum numbers. This is the *Pauli exclusion principle*.

The shapes of the orbitals

Hydrogen has an atomic number 1 and hence there is only one sub-shell ($l = 0$). There is therefore only one possible atomic orbital. The probability function is spherical and the orbital may be regarded as a sphere. This holds good for helium ($Z = 2$) in which two electrons can occupy the single orbital, but they must have opposite spins. In the case of lithium ($Z = 3$) the K shell is filled and the third electron enters the s sub-shell of the L shell. This orbital will be spherical because it is an s orbital.

Boron has the atomic number 5. The K shell and the s orbital of the L shell are filled, each containing two electrons with opposite spin. The fifth electron must hence enter the p sub-shell, since l, the azimuthal quantum number, is 1. Where $l = 1$, there are $(2l + 1) = 3$ atomic orbitals, each of which is capable of containing a pair of electrons. The probability of finding an electron is no longer the same in any direction in space; it is greater in some directions than in others. This means that the shape of the p orbital (and the d and f orbitals as well) is no longer spherical but is shaped rather like a dumb-bell. Moreover, the orbitals have a definite *orientation*; a most important feature in the theory of atomic bonding. The shape of the three p orbitals is illustrated in Fig. 13B and according to whether the dumb-bell-shaped electron cloud is aligned along the x, y or z axes, the orbitals are distinguished as the p_x p_y and p_z orbitals.

It is worth noting the electronic configuration of the elements succeeding boron (Table 1). Carbon, atomic number 6, clearly has two p electrons, but the second electron could either join the first to become a pair completing, say, the p_x orbital or it could enter the p_y orbital and so give two unpaired electrons in different orbitals. The latter course is adopted; electrons occupy as many orbitals as possible before they become paired. Thus nitrogen, atomic number 7, has a single electron in each of the p_x, p_y and p_z orbitals. The K shell and Ls sub-shell are, of course, filled.

In oxygen, pairing occurs in the p_x orbital and in neon, atomic number 10, there are paired electrons in each p orbital, thus completing the L shell.

The chemical properties of an element are determined very largely by its electron configuration. Elements having orbitals containing unpaired electrons enter more readily into reactions than those whose orbitals contain paired electrons. The inert gases neon, krypton, xenon and radon have in common an outer set of eight paired electrons ($s^2 p^6$) and to this they owe their great stability.

Crystals are aggregates of atoms that are bound together in a very stable manner and in definite proportions. It is the electronic configuration of the constituent atoms that is largely responsible for this. In particular, it is the outermost electrons through which links are made

c

TABLE 1

THE ELECTRONIC CONFIGURATION OF THE ELEMENTS OF LOW ATOMIC NUMBER

Element	Atomic Number Z	K shell	L shell				M shell					Period
		$1s$	$2s$	$2p_x$	$2p_y$	$2p_z$	$3s$	$3p_x$	$3p_y$	$3p_z$	$3d$	
Hydrogen H	1	↑										1st Period
Helium He	2	↑↓										
Lithium Li	3	↑↓	↑									2nd Period
Beryllium Be	4	↑↓	↑↓									
Boron B	5	↑↓	↑↓	↑								
Carbon C	6	↑↓	↑↓	↑	↑							
Nitrogen N	7	↑↓	↑↓	↑	↑	↑						
Oxygen O	8	↑↓	↑↓	↑↓	↑	↑						
Fluorine F	9	↑↓	↑↓	↑↓	↑↓	↑						
Neon Ne	10	↑↓	↑↓	↑↓	↑↓	↑↓						
Sodium Na	11	↑↓	↑↓	↑↓	↑↓	↑↓	↑					3rd Period
Magnesium Mg	12	↑↓	↑↓	↑↓	↑↓	↑↓	↑↓					
Aluminium Al	13	↑↓	↑↓	↑↓	↑↓	↑↓	↑↓	↑				
Silicon Si	14	↑↓	↑↓	↑↓	↑↓	↑↓	↑↓	↑	↑			
Phosphorus P	15	↑↓	↑↓	↑↓	↑↓	↑↓	↑↓	↑	↑	↑		
Sulphur S	16	↑↓	↑↓	↑↓	↑↓	↑↓	↑↓	↑↓	↑	↑		
Chlorine Cl	17	↑↓	↑↓	↑↓	↑↓	↑↓	↑↓	↑↓	↑↓	↑		
Argon A	18	↑↓	↑↓	↑↓	↑↓	↑↓	↑↓	↑↓	↑↓	↑↓		

Each arrow represents one electron, each orbital can accommodate two electrons, provided they have opposite spins, represented as ↑↓.

with other atoms. The outer electrons determine also the type of bond that is formed and the number of other atoms that are involved in the bond. An understanding of the crystalline state therefore must necessarily involve an examination of the bonds that hold atom to atom.

There are five main types of bond: ionic, hydrogen, covalent, metallic and van der Waals' bonds. A simple, non-mathematical treatment of each is given below.

The ionic bond

An *ion* can be regarded as an atom that has gained or lost electrons so that it is no longer electrically neutral but has a definite charge. If an atom gains one electron (and hence a unit negative charge) it becomes a negatively charged ion, called an *anion*. Similarly if an electron is lost from an atom then the resulting ion is positively charged and called a *cation*. It is rare for ions to have a charge greater than five.

We have seen that an outer group of eight electrons is a very stable configuration. Suppose that an element like sodium with an electronic configuration $1s^2 \, 2s^2 \, 2p^6 \, 3s^1$ could lose the single electron in its M shell, it would become a cation with a single positive charge and would at the same time acquire the stable eight electron pattern. Chlorine, on the other hand ($1s^2 \, 2s^2 \, 2p^6 \, 3s^2 \, 3p^5$), would achieve the same effect were it to gain an electron and become an anion. By transferring an electron from a sodium to a chlorine atom both substances acquire increased stability but in doing so they become oppositely charged. Oppositely charged particles attract each other and are bound together by non-directed electrostatic forces. Such bonds are called *ionic bonds* or electrovalent bonds and sodium chloride is an example of a substance with this type of bonding. Other elements may need to lose or gain two or more electrons in order to attain the stable eight electron configuration, but the principle of bond formation remains the same.

The hydrogen bond

Quite often a hydrogen atom acts as a link between two other electronegative atoms. At first this seems rather a puzzle because hydrogen has only one electron and might be expected to link with only one other atom. It can, however, lose its electron to either of the flanking atoms and it may be considered as losing it to them both at once so that the electron may be considered to oscillate rapidly between them. This oscillation, or *resonance* as it is called, draws the two flanking atoms together so that the hydrogen forms a bridge between them. This is the hydrogen bond. The formation of the hydrogen bond is strongest when the flanking atoms are oxygen, fluorine or nitrogen on account of their strong electronegativity.

The covalent bond

Hydrogen and chlorine both occur ordinarily as the molecules H_2 and Cl_2 and not as single atoms. Considerable energy is required to dissociate the molecules into the separate atoms and hence there are strong binding forces that hold atom to atom within the molecule. These forces cannot be ionic, because the two hydrogen or chlorine atoms have the same kind of charge and there is therefore no mutual electrostatic attraction.

In 1916 G. N. Lewis and, independently, W. Kossel suggested a mechanism to account for this *covalent* bonding. It was pointed out that if two chlorine atoms, each having seven outer electrons (Fig. 14A) were to get together and share these, each would in effect acquire the stable eight electron configuration. The two electrons between the chlorine atoms belong equal-

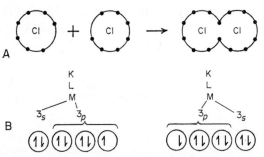

Fig. 14 A. Diagrammatic representation of covalent bond formation in chlorine.
B. A representation of the electronic configuration of two chlorine atoms. The filled *K* and *L* shells are indicated by their letters. The orbitals comprising the *M* shell are shown by circles and the arrows indicate the spin of electrons within the orbitals. A covalent bond forms by pairing of the unpaired electrons in the $3p$ orbitals.

ly to them both and the bond is produced by this sharing.

The later application of quantum mechanics to this theory made the picture of covalent bonding much clearer. The outer electrons of chlorine can be differentiated by their quantum numbers as shown diagrammatically in Fig. 14B, where each circle represents an atomic orbital (m) and the arrows indicate the spin (s) of the electrons within the orbitals. It is easy to see that the two unpaired p electrons can pair up and still maintain the Pauli exclusion principle. It is clear also that covalent bonding involves an overlap of orbitals so that the shared electrons belong equally to both atoms. We have seen already that all except the s orbitals are directional and this means that covalent bonds involving other than s orbitals can only occur in certain directions. This is an important difference between ionic and covalent bonds. Energetically it is more favourable for an electron to spread itself between two atoms and it explains why the H_2 and Cl_2 molecules are formed.

Not all covalent bonds are as simple as this. The eight electron configuration is not always formed, nor are the electrons always contributed equally from each atom. In some compounds one atom provides *both* shared electrons and this type of bonding is sometimes distinguished as *co-ordination* or *dative covalent bonding*.

Such bonding has a degree of ionic character in the sense that two electrons are 'given' by one atom to another, albeit they are shared between them. If this sharing is equal, then the atom donating the electrons becomes positively charged to some extent and the atom receiving them becomes negatively charged. The amount of this charge will vary according to whether the shared electrons are nearer to the donor or recipient atom. The nearer they are to the recipient, the more ionic the bond.

This emphasizes that the bond types are not absolute in themselves. There is a complete spectrum of bonds that vary in character between two extremes, the ionic and the covalent. It should be borne in mind that in relatively few crystals are the bonds wholly ionic or wholly covalent; most have a mixture of bond types.

The metallic bond

Although metals are not of prime importance to the mineralogist, a brief account of their structure is of interest. They are composed of atoms arranged like close-packed spheres except in metals with a body-centred cubic packing. An early theory regarded these spheres as cations that were surrounded by a cloud or gas of electrons that could move freely through the structure, making it electrically neutral and accounting for its high electrical and thermal conductivity. Quantum mechanics has shown that there is a similarity between the metallic and covalent bonds, in that in both electrons are shared between atoms. In metals there are many more atoms than there are free, unpaired electrons. These electrons are therefore spread between several atoms. An electron is free to move in the orbitals of six, eight or twelve atoms, but its movement is limited by the Pauli exclusion principle.

Van der Waals' bond

Some substances exist in the solid state as aggregations of molecules or atoms with filled shells, packed together as though they were spheres. Since atoms are electrically neutral there are only weak residual fields between them and such binding forces are called *van der Waals*' or residual forces. The inert gases, when cooled sufficiently, form solids of this kind.

The size of the particles: ionic and covalent radii

The concept of an open lattice of separated points in space is being filled as the abstract points are replaced by either single ions, or atoms, or groups of ions tightly bound by covalent bonds. Structural studies of crystals that are composed of one substance only (e.g. solid argon) show that in very many of them the atoms pack together as closely as possible in the way that a box of marbles or table tennis balls would do. This means that the dimensions of the unit cell are determined by the size of the particles occupying the lattice points and, moreover, that any departure from a spherical shape will also affect the way in which packing can take place. It is necessary, then, to examine the sizes and shapes of the constituent particles.

We have seen that modern atomic theory defines the size of an atom in terms of the most probable position of its furthest electron. Thus, although an electron can theoretically be found anywhere between the nucleus and infinity, its most probable position can be calculated to be close to the nucleus.

If two similar atoms are brought together they will take up an equilibrium position that is determined by the repulsion of two positive nuclei and the attraction to form a chemical bond, say, of covalent type. The interatomic distance or *bond length* can be calculated and is found to be of the order of a few Ångstrom Units (Å), i.e. 10^{-8}cm. The techniques used in measuring these very small interatomic distances are outlined in Chapter 3. The *atomic radius* is defined as half the bond length, or half the distance at which mutual repulsion balances attraction.

In covalent compounds with single bonds there is a simple relationship between bond lengths. The bond length between two atoms of a substance A can be calculated and is found to be $2x$ Å when x is the atomic radius of A (Fig. 15). The atomic radius of B can similarly be

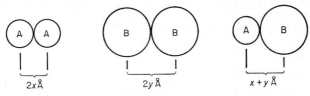

Fig. 15 Diagrammatic representation of bond lengths of covalent compounds with single bonds. For explanation see text.

shown to be y Å by halving the bond length $2y$ Å for B-B. The bond length for the compound AB is simply $x + y$ Å, provided AB is a covalent compound with single bonds. There is usually very good agreement between calculated and measured values.

If, however, the bond lengths of an ionic compound like sodium chloride are calculated in this way, there is a discrepancy between the calculated and observed values. A separate set of *ionic radii* must be compiled for use in ionic compounds. Table 2 gives the atomic and ionic radii of some common elements.

Notice that the radius of an anion is larger, and that of a cation is smaller than the atomic radius of the neutral atom. This is due in part to the fact that to acquire a positive charge an atom must lose one or more electrons. The result is that the remaining electrons become more tightly bound to the nucleus and effectively reduce the radius of the

TABLE 2

RADII OF SOME OF THE COMMONER ELEMENTS

Element		Atomic Radius (Å) *	Ionic Radius (Å) (Six fold co-ordination; after Ahrens)	Crystal radius of Pauling (Å)
Aluminium	Al	1·43	$0·51^{3+}$	$0·50^{3+}$
Barium	Ba	2·17	$1·34^{2+}$	$1·35^{2+}$
Beryllium	Be	1·14	$0·35^{2+}$	$0·31^{2+}$
Boron	B	1·00	$0·23^{3+}$	$0·20^{3+}$
Bromine	Br	1·14	$1·95^{1-}$	$1·95^{1-}$
Calcium	Ca	1·97	$0·99^{2+}$	$0·99^{2+}$
Chlorine	Cl	0·99	$1·81^{1-}$	$1·81^{1-}$
Copper	Cu	1·28	$0·96^{1+}$	$0·96^{1+}$
Fluorine	F	0·72	$1·36^{1-}$	$1·36^{1-}$
Iron	Fe	1·24	$0·74^{2+}$	$0·76^{2+}$
Lithium	Li	1·52	$0·68^{1+}$	$0·60^{1+}$
Magnesium	Mg	1·60	$0·66^{2+}$	$0·65^{2+}$
Oxygen	O	0·74	$1·40^{2-}$	$1·40^{2-}$
Potassium	K	2·31	$1·33^{1+}$	$1·33^{1+}$
Silicon	Si	1·17	$0·42^{4+}$	$0·41^{4+}$
Silver	Ag	1·44	$1·26^{1+}$	$1·26^{1+}$
Sodium	Na	1·85	$0·97^{1+}$	$0·95^{1+}$
Sulphur	S	1·04	$1·84^{2-}$	$1·84^{2-}$
Zinc	Zn	1·33—1·45	$0·74^{2+}$	$0·74^{2+}$

* For metals: half the metal-metal distance
For non-metals: half the single bond molecular distance

atom. In negatively charged ions which have gained electrons the opposite happens.

Since the degree of ionic or covalent character in a bond is variable it follows that the radius of an atom or ion can vary also. Further complications arise when actual crystals are considered, for bonds of several kinds can occur within the same crystal structure.

The type of bonding formed in any instance is controlled by the size and electron configuration of the atoms involved. According to *Fajans' Rules* a bond will tend to be covalent if the anions are large and cations small or if either the anion or cation is highly charged. On the other hand ionic bonding is favoured if the ions are comparable in size and have low charges.

Covalent bonds have a directional character, and form at definite angles that can be predicted by wave mechanics. This is because the directions in which bonds will most probably form are determined by the angular orientation of the bond-forming orbitals.

Stoichiometry

Suppose two elements A and B can combine to form a compound. The chemical formula of the compound may be AB, AB_2, AB_3, A_2B_3 and so on; it expresses the ratio of A atoms to B atoms in the substance. The study of such combining relationships is called *stoichiometry*. From our discussion of the structure of the atom and the nature of chemical bonds, it will be clear that the outermost, or *valence* electrons play an important part in determining whether one atom of A will combine with one, two, or more atoms of B. But there are other factors. For example, the relative sizes of the constituent atoms and the way in which atoms or molecules can pack together can also have an effect on the stoichiometry. For additional information on this most important topic the student is referred to the works listed at the end of the chapter.

Co-ordination number

A molecule AB_2 can only be planar, but it can be either linear like solid carbon dioxide or non-linear like water in which the bond angle is 105° (Fig. 16A & B). More complex molecules with formulae like AB_3 and AB_4, can form more complex groupings. Ions, although they may be of

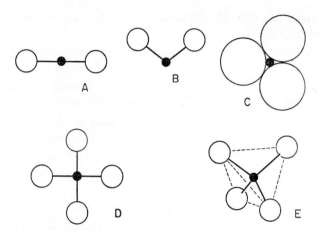

Fig. 16 Some possible arrangements of atoms in molecules.
A. Linear AB_2 molecule.
B. Asymmetric AB_2 molecule.
C. AB_3 molecule.
D. Planar AB_4 molecule.
E. Tetrahedral AB_4 molecule.
Bonds are shown formally in all except C, in which atoms are shown in
contact in order to illustrate the radius ratio. Atom sizes are arbitrary.

different sizes, generally pack together as closely as possible. In Fig. 16C
three B ions pack round each A ion so that they touch one another. If
the size of A with respect to B increases beyond a certain limiting value,
it is impossible for three B ions to remain in contact with A and with
each other and the structure becomes unstable. The smallest number of
ions that can pack around a central ion and remain in contact with each
other is called its *co-ordination number*. The co-ordination number is
controlled by the ratio of the radius of the cation to the radius of the
anion, or the *radius ratio*. Thus the ion A in Fig. 16D & E has a co-
ordination number of four but the orientation of the bonds may be
planar as in Fig. 16D or directed symmetrically towards the corners of a
tetrahedron (Fig. 16E). The limiting radius ratios for tetrahedral co-
ordination can easily be calculated; only ions with ratios between 0·225
and 0·414 can form this type of structure.

As the size of the cation, and hence the radius ratio, increases more
anions can pack around it and the co-ordination number increases also.
The effect of radius ratio on structure is illustrated by the compounds

CsCl, NaCl and ZnS, all of which have a 1:1 stoichiometric ratio. In zinc sulphide the radius ratio is 0·25 and the co-ordination number is four; each Zn^{2+} ion is surrounded by four S^{2-} ions disposed at the corners of a tetrahedron. The radius ratio for sodium chloride is 0·52 and each sodium ion is surrounded by six chloride ions in octahedral co-ordination. The limiting radius ratio for six-fold co-ordination is 0·732 and caesium chloride, with a radius ratio of 0·93, has a co-ordination number of eight. In six-fold co-ordination the bonds are often, but not always, directed at right angles towards the corners of an octahedron (Fig. 17A) and in eight-fold co-ordination towards the corners of a cube (Fig. 17B).

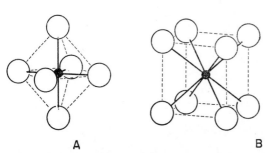

A

B

Fig. 17 A. Six-fold co-ordination (octahedral type).
B. Eight-fold co-ordination.

Relation between co-ordination number and ionic size

The relationship between co-ordination number and ionic size is reminiscent of the problem of the prior origin of the chicken and the egg. If ions were spheres of fixed radius, then the co-ordination number would depend directly on the radius ratio, but they have no such fixed property. The structure of many crystals is to a large extent controlled by the packing pattern of the larger ions, the small ions fitting into the spaces between them. These spaces may vary in size, shape and in the co-ordination number that an ion would adopt if it were to fill them.

This can be illustrated by considering the close packing of spheres. The closest packing that can be achieved by a single layer of uniform spheres has a hexagonal pattern and is shown in Fig. 18A. A second layer can fit on top of this most snugly by filling the 'holes' in the first layer as in Fig. 18B. The interstices between the spheres of these two layers are all tetrahedral sites, which, although not in fact tetrahedral in shape, are so called because lines joining the centres of the four bounding

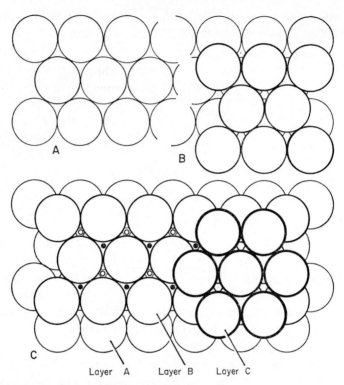

Fig. 18 Close packing of equal spheres.
A. First layer showing hexagonal arrangement.
B. A second layer resting in the 'hollows' of the first layer.
C. Two superimposed layers A and B showing octahedral sites (small open circles) and tetrahedral sites (small solid circles). At right, part of a third layer, C, is shown occupying the 'hollows' above the octahedral sites.

spheres define a tetrahedron. When a third layer of spheres is placed on top of the others, two kinds of site are produced (Fig. 18C). There are the tetrahedral sites marked ●, but, in addition, there are the sites marked ○, the centres of which are equidistant from six large spheres. These are octahedral sites and they are larger than the tetrahedral ones. Ions occupying octahedral sites would have six-fold co-ordination. Some ions can occupy either type of site. Aluminium, for example, can occur in four-fold, tetrahedral co-ordination with oxygen, or in six-fold octahedral co-ordination and its ionic size varies accordingly. Ionic size is thus related to co-ordination number. This interdependence means that the co-ordination number needs to be stated when quoting ionic

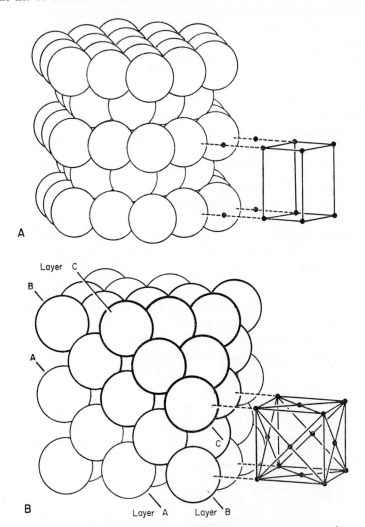

Fig. 19 Three-dimensional representations of (A) the hexagonal close packed and (B) the cubic close packed structures with their unit cells outlined to the right.

In Fig. 19B the top right-hand corner atom is omitted in order to show more clearly the close packing of spheres in layers. The layers A, B, and C correspond to those marked similarly in Fig. 18C.

size. For many years now, chemists have adopted six-fold co-ordination as the standard when quoting ionic radii. This practice is rarely followed by geologists who usually quote Pauling's *crystal radii* in which account is taken of the valency of the ion. A full treatment of this topic lies beyond the scope of this book and the reader is referred to the references quoted at the end of the chapter.

Cubic and hexagonal close packing

Returning to the close packing of spheres shown in Fig. 18C, and calling the lowest layer A and the second B, the structure built up by stacking successive layers in this fashion is of the ABABAB type (Fig. 19A). This structure has hexagonal symmetry and a unit cell can be outlined, showing that it has an end-centred or C type hexagonal lattice. This is the hexagonal close packing structure.

There is, however, an alternative way of packing the spheres equally closely. If, instead of placing the third layer of spheres directly over those of layer A, it is placed so that the spheres rest in the hollows marked o in Fig. 18C; it then has a structural position different from layers A and B. Calling this third layer C, the structure has the form ABCABCABC and is illustrated in Fig. 19B. The cubic symmetry of this structure is apparent if one looks down at a corner. The unit cell is of the face-centred cubic type and the structure shows cubic close-packing.

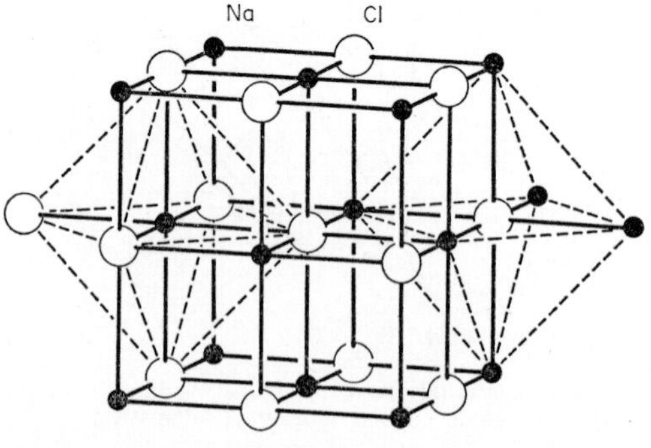

Fig. 20   The structure of sodium chloride. The octahedral co-ordination of both sodium and chloride ions is shown by broken lines.

Some simple structures

(1) *Sodium chloride*

These principles can be illustrated with reference to some simple structures. Among the best-known and most frequently quoted is the structure of sodium chloride illustrated in Fig. 20. All the bonds in sodium chloride are ionic. Each sodium ion with a single positive charge is surrounded by six negatively charged chloride ions in octahedral co-ordination. Similarly, to maintain the electrical neutrality of the structure, each chloride ion is surrounded by six sodium ions, again in octahedral co-ordination. The Bravais lattice has identical points at its corners and at the centres of its faces. The lattice points are occupied by sodium or chloride ions according to whether the unit cell is chosen to originate at a sodium or a chloride ion.

(2) *Sphalerite*

Not all compounds with a 1:1 stoichiometric ratio have the sodium chloride structure. Zinc sulphide crystal-lizes as the mineral sphalerite ZnS, and is cubic. The co-ordination number for zinc and sulphur in this structure is four and these ions occupy the tetrahedral sites in the cubic close-packed lattice and not the octahedral sites as in sodium chloride (see Fig. 21). The zinc ions have a cubic face-centred spatial arrangement and the sulphur ions occupy only half the available tetrahedral sites in a symmetrical and regular manner. Notice that the shaded zinc atom has four nearest neighbours and that similarly the dotted sulphur atom is in tetrahedral co-ordination.

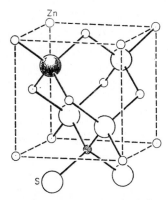

Fig. 21   The structure of sphalerite ZnS. Both zinc (shaded) and sulphur (dotted) atoms are in tetrahedral co-ordination.

(3) *Fluorite*

The structure formed when all the tetrahedral sites are filled is shown in Fig. 22. Fluorite CaF_2 crystallizes in this way. Notice that the structure is still a cubic close-packed arrangement and that the fluorine atoms have a co-ordination number of four and are surrounded tetrahedrally by calcium. Consider now the shaded calcium atom. Since all the tetrahedral sites are occupied it is surrounded by eight fluorine atoms disposed as though at the corners of a cube of which calcium is the centre.

There are twice as many fluorine as calcium atoms in the structure and the formula is hence CaF_2.

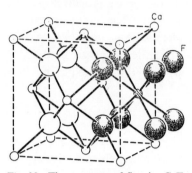

Fig. 22 The structure of fluorite CaF_2. The Ca atom (shaded) has eight F nearest neighbours; each F atom has four Ca nearest neighbours arranged tetrahedrally about it.

The ratio of the various atoms in a structure is frequently hard to see in a structural diagram. The numbers of the various atoms in a structure can be determined by first outlining the unit cell. Any atoms whose centres lie wholly within this polygon belong to this unit cell only. An atom lying on the face of a cell belongs equally to two unit cells and is reckoned as $\frac{1}{2}$ atom towards each. Similarly atoms lying on an edge are common to four cells and count $\frac{1}{4}$ to each whilst those at a corner count $\frac{1}{8}$ to each (or $\frac{1}{6}$ to each in the case of hexagonal cells).

There are very many ways in which atoms can be arranged to form structures and reference should be made to texts on structural chemistry for a fuller treatment of them.

Complex ions

In all the structures mentioned above the lattice points are occupied by single ions or atoms and treated as though they are perfect spheres. Some ionic crystals, however, are composed of both simple and *complex ions*. Complex ions are tightly bound groups of atoms that behave structurally as though they were single ions in that the forces binding them are stronger than those trying to separate them. Complex ions are usually bound by covalent bonds and the factors governing their orientation have been discussed earlier (p. 33). The larger a complex ion the more complex and irregular its shape. Some examples are illustrated in Fig. 23. Generally speaking complex ions remain constant in size although they may occur in crystals of differing structure. The size and shape of a complex ion can have a great effect on the crystal structure. Only if a complex ion is spherical, or behaves as though it were spherical

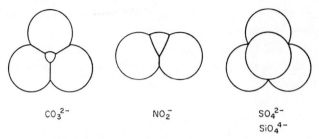

CO_3^{2-} NO_2^- SO_4^{2-}
                                          SiO_4^{4-}

Fig. 23 Some complex ions (after Bragg).

as a result of free rotation, is there a direct comparison with the simple structures considered earlier. Thus complex ions can occupy lattice points and their irregular shape may well affect the packing of other ions and with them the symmetry of the structure as a whole.

The planar CO_3^{2-} groups in calcite are a good example. There is a strong resemblance between the structure of calcite $CaCO_3$, and that of sodium chloride (Fig. 24) but the planar triangular shape of the CO_3^{2-}

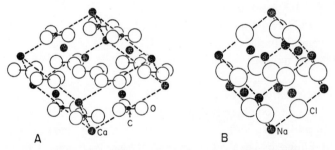

A   O   C   Ca   B   Cl   Na

Fig. 24 The calcite (A) and sodium chloride (B) structures drawn so as to show their similarity. Compare Fig. 24B with Fig. 20. The calcite cell drawn here is the morphological cell; the structural unit cell is a more elongated rhombohedron with Ca atoms at its corners only.

groups result in the structure having trigonal symmetry and not the higher symmetry of the cubic system.

Classification of crystal structures
It is now possible to combine the concepts of the shape of a complex ion and the close packing of atoms and to use them to help understand the

structure of the more complex silicates. In the crystals of these the commonest anions are oxygen or others of comparable radius like F^{1-} and OH^{1-}, and they pack together as closely as possible leaving the smaller cations to occupy the interspaces. There may very well be several kinds of bond within the structure and some of them may not be of pure bond type anyway.

Crystals may be classified according to bond type, but ionic, covalent, metallic and molecular crystals named on this basis have so many exceptions as to make the classification unsatisfactory. It gives to pure bond types an unwarranted importance. A bond that is intermediate between covalent and ionic is as much a normal one as the pure ionic bond itself.

The basis of classification used here is that of A. F. Wells who, in his *Structural Inorganic Chemistry*, classifies crystals according to the type of complex they contain. Crystals are grouped according to whether they contain:

   (1) Finite complexes
   (2) Infinite one-dimensional complexes
   (3) Infinite two-dimensional complexes
   (4) Infinite three-dimensional complexes.

These are now briefly examined in turn.

1. *Crystals containing finite complexes*

The term finite complex is applied to molecules and complex, though discrete and finite ions. The atoms comprising a finite complex are usually bound by covalent forces and the finite complexes themselves pack closely together and are bound to each other by undirected forces like van der Waals' forces. The type of lattice produced is determined by the close packing of the complexes and thus depends on the shape of the complexes.

Among the silicates, olivine is a good example of this type of crystal. The general formula of olivine is X_2SiO_4, where X is Mg^{2+}, Fe^{2+} or Mn^{2+} and the crystal consists of Mg^{2+}, Fe^{2+} or Mn^{2+} ions linked with SiO_4^{4-} finite complexes. Each SiO_4 group is a discrete and separate entity in the structure and occupies a point of the Bravais lattice. The structure is determined by the oxygens in the SiO_4^{4-} complexes. The oxygens pack together like spheres so as to form a hexagonal close-packed structure with silicon occupying tetrahedral and the Mg^{2+}, Fe^{2+} or Mn^{2+} ions the octahedral sites. There are very many tetrahedral sites between the spheres of a hexagonal close-packed structure but, in olivine, because of the presence of SiO_4^{4-} complexes, many of the tetrahedral sites do not contain silicon. In fact, only one in every eight tetrahedral sites is so occupied. The structure of olivine is shown diagrammatically in Fig. 25.

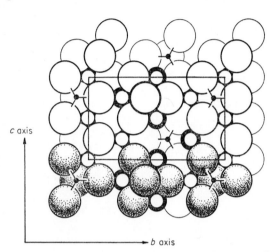

c axis

b axis

Fig. 25 Diagrammatic representation of the structure of olivine projected on to the plane (100) (after Bragg). One row of SiO_4 tetrahedra is shaded and the unit cell is outlined. The atoms are not drawn to scale. Oxygen — large circles; silicon — small solid black circles; magnesium — heavily outlined circles. Si-O bonds are shown formally.

matically in Fig. 25. Notice how the SiO_4^{4-} complexes are arranged in rows and also how the oxygens group in sixes around the cations. The unit cell is outlined.

2. *Crystals with infinite one-dimensional complexes*

An infinite one-dimensional complex is a linear arrangement of tightly bound atoms that extends throughout the crystal so as to form an easily recognised band- or chain-like structural unit. The chains may be simple and composed of a single type of atom, or they may be complex structures having their own unit of pattern that, when repeated, extends the chain. The pyroxenes and amphiboles are among the best known examples of this type of chain. A portion of a pyroxene chain is illustrated in Fig. 26A. The unit of pattern within the chain is outlined and contains Si_2O_6. The pyroxene structure as a whole is formed by these chains, which extend from end to end of the crystal parallel to the *c* axis

and are linked to one another by metallic cations as shown diagrammatically in Fig. 26B.

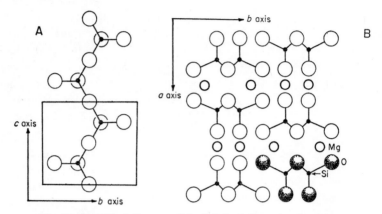

Fig. 26 Simplified diagram of the infinite 1-dimensional structure
of pyroxene. A. The Si-O chain projected on (100). The unit of
pattern of the chain is outlined.
B. A simplified pyroxene structure projected on (001). The shaded
group of atoms is a single chain viewed end on.

The unit of pattern within the chain must not be confused with the
unit cell of the structure as a whole. The Si_2O_6 pattern merely produces
the *chain* by translation in one direction; the unit cell necessarily includes
the linking metallic cations and by translation in three dimensions
produces the full crystal structure.

3. *Crystals with infinite two-dimensional complexes*

In these crystals the tightly bound atom complexes extend in two
dimensions to form sheets. Just as wallpaper is a two-dimensional
repetition of a unit of pattern, so the repetition of the unit of pattern of
the sheet extends it infinitely in two dimensions. The sheets may vary
widely in composition and may be bound together by van der Waals',
hydrogen or ionic bonds. Cations frequently link sheet to sheet. Among
the rock forming minerals there is an important series of layer silicates,
of which the micas are perhaps the best known. The structure of mica in
plan and section is shown in Fig. 27. The extended sheets of linked SiO_4
tetrahedra and OH's are joined together by cations to form double

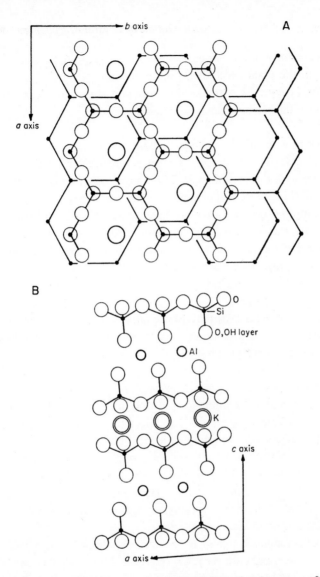

Fig. 27 Simplified diagram of the infinite 2-dimensional structure of mica (muscovite).
A. The Si-O sheet structure projected on (001); the single upper sheet with atoms shown in full has hexagonal symmetry. A second, lower sheet is also outlined showing the consequent loss of hexagonal symmetry. OH ions are shown as large open circles.
B. The mica structure projected on (010). Two double sheets each corresponding to Fig. 27A are shown linked by K atoms. The monoclinic symmetry is evident (After Bragg).

sheets and each double sheet is joined to the next double sheet by weak bonds in the planes containing the potassium cations. It is this weak bonding in contrast with the tightly-bound sheet complexes, that accounts for the perfect cleavage of mica.

4. *Crystals with infinite three-dimensional complexes*
In these crystals the complexes form a three-dimensional pattern co-extensive with the crystal itself. The simple ionic and covalent crystals belong to this group. Sodium chloride crystals consist of a regular array of sodium and chloride ions arranged in space so as to form a cubic lattice. In the silicates, the feldspars and quartz consist of SiO_4 tetrahedra linked together to form a three-dimensional framework. The metals and alloys belong here too.

5. *Intermediate structures*
Inevitably structures exist that do not fall easily into one or other of the above patterns. To attempt to accommodate them all would expand each group to an extent that it would lose its usefulness.

The effect of bond type on physical properties
Although it is an over-simplification to think in terms of specific bond types, it is useful to see how they affect the more tractable physical properties of crystals. In doing so it must be realized that few crystals have bonds of only one type. Within a single crystal it is possible for wholly ionic bonds and bonds with a part ionic, part covalent character to occur. However, the ideal bond types give rise to certain physical characteristics and, understandably, crystals with mixed bond types will have mixed or intermediate properties.

Metals are opaque except in the thinnest slices and are good conductors of heat and electricity. Crystals bound by weak Van der Waals' forces require little energy to break the bonds and hence have low melting and boiling points and are generally soft.

Ionic crystals are usually transparent and when coloured have the colour that the ion has in solution. Because of the electrostatic forces binding them they have fairly high melting points and are fairly hard in the sense that the undirected bonds extend equally through the crystal so that no part is weaker than any other. They frequently possess a distinct cleavage.

Covalent crystals are more difficult to describe because few crystals are entirely covalent. Diamond and some metallic sulphides are among the best known. They tend to be hard, with poor cleavage and high melting points.

It is the weakest bonds that in large measure determine the physical properties of a substance. Van der Waals' bonds for example, are easily broken and result in many organic 'covalent' compounds having low melting points. Similarly, the sheet silicates have infinite two-dimensional Si-O complexes strongly bound by covalent bonds but they also have an extremely good cleavage that is determined by the weak bonds that link sheet to sheet.

Crystals with mixed bond types depart markedly from this general pattern, but it must be emphasized that the physical and optical properties of crystals depend on their atomic arrangement and on the nature of the bonds that bind atom to atom whether or not these fall into convenient classificatory groups.

Suggestions for further reading
Addison, W. E., *Structural Principles in Inorganic Compounds*, Longmans, London, 1961.
Azaroff, L. V., *Introduction to Solids*, McGraw-Hill Book Company, New York, Toronto and London, 1960.
Bunn, C. W., *Chemical Crystallography*, University Press Oxford, 2nd Edition, 1961.
Evans, R. C., *An Introduction to Crystal Chemistry*, Cambridge University Press, 2nd Edition, 1964.
Fyfe, W. S., *Geochemistry of Solids*, McGraw-Hill Book Company Inc., New York, San Francisco, Toronto, London, 1964.
Hartshorne, N. H. and A. Stuart, *Practical Optical Crystallography*, Edward Arnold (Publishers) Ltd., London 1964.
Pauling, L., *The Nature of the Chemical Bond*, Cornell University Press, Ithaca, N.Y., 3rd Edition, 1960.
Wells, A. F., *Structural Inorganic Chemistry*, University Press, Oxford, 3rd Edition, 1962.

CHAPTER 3

METHODS OF STUDY

From the foregoing chapters it is apparent that crystals have a regular internal structure that finds expression in a regular external shape. The study of crystals is directly concerned with this regularity and has two main aspects. One is concerned with the internal structure pattern and, since X-rays are principally used in this study, it is sometimes called *X-ray crystallography* or *structural crystallography*. This has grown since the early days of Laue and Bragg into the modern discipline of solid-state physics. The other aspect of the study of crystals has to do with their external shapes. The science of crystallography began in this way and even now, when X-ray methods are readily available, much can be learned from a proper study of the arrangement of crystal faces. *Morphological* or *classical crystallography*, as it is called, commonly serves to introduce the student to the study of crystals. A grasp of the essentials of the subject can be obtained by this means with a minimum of apparatus and expense. The details of crystal morphology form the subject matter of Part 2 of this book.

INTERNAL STRUCTURE

The use of X-rays

X-rays are high-frequency electromagnetic waves that are produced when high-speed electrons collide with the atoms of a metal target. X-rays have short wavelengths, of the order of 1 or 2 Å. Their wavelength depends largely on the rate at which the electrons travel (and hence on the voltage used to accelerate them) and the atomic number of the material of which the target is made. Even if the voltage is fixed and target is made of pure metal, the X-rays produced cover a range of wavelengths (Fig. 28). Notice, however, that there are sharp peaks of great intensity occurring at a fixed wavelength. Two such peaks are shown for a copper target. They are known as the *K* series of copper because they are produced by energy changes within the *K* shell of electrons and are

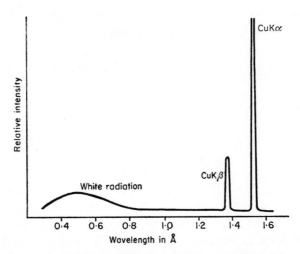

Fig. 28 The intensity distribution of X-rays produced from a copper target. The intensity of the $K\alpha$ peak is about six times that of $K\beta$.

distinguished as $K\alpha$ and $K\beta$ peaks. It is possible to filter the radiation so that, say, only the $K\alpha$ radiation passes the filter. The X-ray crystallographer uses these monochromatic X-rays in much the same way that a microscopist uses monochromatic light to obtain accuracy in his work.

Laue photographs
The discovery in 1912 by M. von Laue that crystals diffracted and scattered X-rays was one of major importance. At Laue's suggestion, Friedrich and Knipping passed unfiltered X-rays through a stationary crystal on to a photographic plate. On development, the plate showed a regular arrangement of spots (Fig. 29) indicating a scattering of the X-ray beam.

The Bragg equation
It is now known that the scattering of X-rays is caused by the electrons that surround the nuclei of atoms in a crystal. Although it is not strictly correct to do so, a crystal may be regarded as an array of points that lie in planes and the planes may as an approximation be regarded as reflecting surfaces for the X-rays. Using this model, W. L. Bragg in 1913

expressed the relationships that exist between crystal structures and diffracted X-ray beams. The equation governing this relationship, or *Bragg's law*, is simple and has the form:

$$n\lambda = 2d.\sin\theta$$

where n is a whole number, λ the wavelength of the X-rays, d the distance between identical planes of atoms in the crystal and θ the angle between the planes of atoms and the X-ray beam.

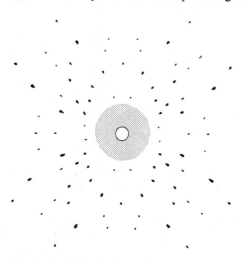

Fig. 29 A sketch of a Laue photograph. The stippled area is the part of the film that is intensively fogged by the direct beam. The mineral represented is pyrite.

In Fig. 30 A-A′, B-B′, C-C′ represent identical planes of atoms separated by distance d. P, Q and R are parallel beams of X-rays that meet the planes of atoms at angle θ. They are reflected by the planes and P′, Q′, R′ represent the reflected beams. The angle of reflection, like the angle of incidence is θ. For a diffracted beam to be produced, the waves comprising beams P′, Q′ and R′ must be in phase. Although the path length of Q-Q′ is longer than P-P′, the waves in both beams must be in phase if there is to be an intense resultant beam and the path length of Q-Q′ is longer than that of P-P′ by a whole number of wavelengths. This will only happen at a particular angle θ for a given plane spacing d. If θ were changed then the ratio of the path lengths of the beams would also change so as to throw the resultant wave out of phase. The same would happen if d were changed and angle θ remained the same. It is important to realise that a series of planes imposes restrictions not implicit in reflection from a single surface. In Fig. 30 the path length of Q-Q′ is longer than that of P-P′ by the distance SY + YT, since XS and XT are wave-fronts. Now this distance is a whole number of wavelengths. In triangles XYS and XYT, XY is the plane spacing d, and $\widehat{SXY} = \widehat{TXY} = \theta$.

Thus SY and YT each equal $d.\sin \theta$ and $n\lambda = 2d.\sin \theta$, which is the Bragg equation.

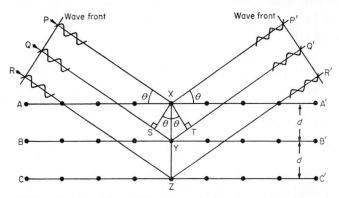

Fig. 30   The derivation of the Bragg equation. For explanation see text.

In spite of the fact that a crystal is not an array of points, this equation has enabled the plane spacings of many substances to be calculated and structural patterns deduced. Some of the applications are discussed below.

Powder photographs

Unlike light rays, X-ray beams cannot be focused so as to produce an image that permits the direct observation of the internal structure of a crystal. Diffracted X-rays do, however, form characteristic scatter-patterns and to obtain a picture of the structure, these indirect images need to be analysed mathematically in terms, basically, of the Bragg equation.

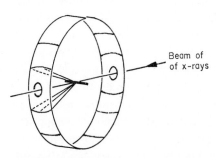

Fig. 31   A powder camera. The X-ray beam is diffracted by the planes of atoms in the powdered specimen to produce cones of diffracted X-rays that are recorded on the film.

P. Debye and P. Scherrer (1916) and A. W. Hull (1917) independently found that if a beam of monochromatic X-rays passed through a finely powdered crystalline solid, several distinct cones of diffracted beams were produced. These were recorded either as circles on flat photographic film or as arcs on a strip of film arranged so as to encircle the powdered specimen as in Fig. 31.

That a random aggregate of crystal fragments should produce a series of diffracted cones instead of a random scatter of the X-rays is due to the conditions for diffraction implicit in Bragg's law. There are very many sets of planes within a crystal and each set can reflect X-rays. From Fig. 32 it is apparent that the distance d between the layers of each

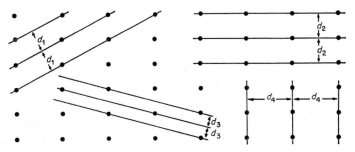

Fig. 32 A two-dimensional representation of a space lattice to illustrate different spacings (d) between different planes of atoms.

set differs with the orientation of the planes. Those planes that contain the greatest number of points are widest apart whereas those with relatively few points are set closer together. In order that diffraction can take place from a set of planes, the Bragg equation must be satisfied in that all the diffracted beams must be in phase and reinforce one another. Thus the diffracted beam can only flash out with high intensity at a given value of θ (actually, over a very limited range of arc) and this will vary with the value of d. For a single crystal a single diffracted beam would be produced but a powder that contains crystalline particles in random orientation produces reflections from those planes that happen to be at the correct angle θ to the incident X-ray beam. The aggregate effect of the individual beams is that cones of diffracted X-rays are produced.

The interpretation of powder photographs
The interpretation of powder photographs can be a difficult task and

details are given in the works referred to at the end of the chapter. It is sufficient here to say that since each crystalline substance has its own unique plane spacings determined by the dimensions of the unit cell, it has also a unique powder photograph in the same way that a person has his own specific fingerprint.

With powder photographs, as with fingerprints, the skill lies in their correct interpretation. It is not difficult to appreciate that the *position* of the arc on a powder photograph depends on the reflecting angle θ and thus on the spacing of the set of planes producing the reflection. In general the calculation of plane spacings from measurements taken from the film is the first task of the X-ray crystallographer and using these, the dimensions of the unit cell of the substance can often be calculated. This becomes increasingly difficult the lower the symmetry of the substance being investigated. The powder photographs of very many substances are known and catalogued according to the spacing of the planes producing the three strongest reflections. The A.S.T.M. index (American Society for Testing and Materials) is perhaps the best known of these.

The powder photograph can yield still further information. The various cones of reflected X-rays vary in *intensity* and this depends to a large extent on the position of the atoms in the unit cell. Under favourable circumstances it is possible to derive not only the cell dimensions of the crystal but also its Bravais lattice type.

Other X-ray methods
Although much information can be obtained from powder photographs, the determination of the unit cell dimensions of crystals with low symmetry involves the use of other techniques. Most of these methods involve the passage of a beam of monochromatic X-rays through a single rotating crystal and recording the reflections on cylindrical films. The Weissenberg camera incorporates a further refinement in that the reflections are recorded on a cylindrical film that moves in sympathy with the rotating crystal and hence further separates the reflections. These and other devices are used in structural determinations, but the student can go a long way, without using X-rays and with only the simplest of equipment, towards verifying for himself the symmetrical nature of crystals. Let us turn to this immediately.

EXTERNAL CRYSTAL SHAPE

The investigation of the external shape of crystals was the way that the science of crystallography began and it is still important to a proper understanding of the subject. The study of the inner structure of crystals has given the reason why crystal faces are arranged as they are and accounts for Steno's law of constancy of angle. The study of the shape of crystals, now as in Steno's day, depends on the measurement of the *interfacial angles* of crystals.

Interfacial angle

It is important to understand what is meant by interfacial angle. Fig. 33A represents a section through a crystal normal to a pair of faces. The interfacial angle is always that subtended by the normals to the crystal faces, i.e. angle ϕ in Fig. 33A, never the external angle θ, nor the angle

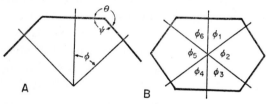

between the two plane faces ψ. Thus the sum of the interfacial angles between a complete circlet of faces that meet in parallel edges (shown in cross section in Fig. 33B), is always 360°. Steno measured interfacial angles by tracing the outline of crystals on paper, but later more sophisticated methods were devised.

Fig. 33   Interfacial angles (see text).

The instruments for measuring interfacial angles are called *goniometers*. The simplest of these is the *contact goniometer* (Fig. 34). Several designs are available but all are essentially a 180° protractor made of metal or plastic to which a straight-edge is pivoted. The instrument is manipulated so that it stands at right angles to the planes of the faces whose interfacial angle is required and so that the straight-edge of the scale fits snugly against one face and the movable straight-edge against the other. The angle between the normals of the faces is then read directly on the graduated scale. With a little practice, this simple instrument can be surprisingly accurate and with good crystals interfacial angles can be measured to within a degree. Accuracy in measurement is aided by holding the crystal and instrument against a light so that a close fit between the straight-edges and the crystal faces is more readily obtained. Care must be taken to ensure that the straight-edges do not ride on the corners and give an inaccurate reading.

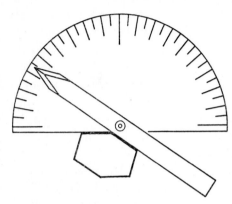

Fig. 34 A contact goniometer.

Goniometers capable of measuring angles with greater accuracy employ an optical principle rather than measuring directly the interfacial angle. The crystal is mounted with a spot of wax or Plasticine to the goniometer head which can be rotated through 360° and the amount of rotation measured against a vernier scale. Adjustments are made so that a set of crystal faces with parallel edges, called a *zone* of faces,[14] is arranged with the edges parallel to the axis of rotation of the goniometer head. A luminous image such as a rectangle or narrow line is projected on to a crystal face from which it is reflected and observed with the aid of a telescope. A reading is taken when the image is central to cross wires in the telescope. The goniometer head is then rotated until the reflected image from the next face is centred at the cross wires and

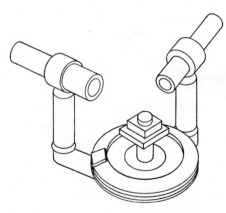

Fig. 35 A single circle optical goniometer.

14. A strict definition of a zone is a set of three or more faces whose normals lie in a plane. The normal to this plane is the *zone axis*.

another reading is made. The interfacial angle is obtained by subtraction. An example of a single circle reflecting goniometer is illustrated in Fig. 35. In this instrument the graduated circle revolves in a horizontal plane; in others the graduated circle is mounted vertically. Wollaston's original goniometer (Fig. 36) was of this type but used a slightly different means of determining the interfacial angle in that the signal reflected from the crystal face is made to

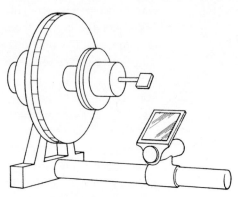

Fig. 36 A Wollaston goniometer.

coincide with a fixed image reflected by a mirror. The crystal was then rotated until the signal from the next face coincided with the fixed signal, and the readings taken in the usual way.

When a second zone of faces is to be measured it is necessary with a single circle goniometer to remount the crystal on the goniometer head so that the new zone is parallel to the axis of rotation. This difficulty is overcome in the *two circle* goniometer (Fig. 37) which permits rotation of the crystal about two mutually perpendicular axes. Goniometers with three circles have been made but they are rarities and are little used. Optical goniometers are capable of reading to minutes of arc.

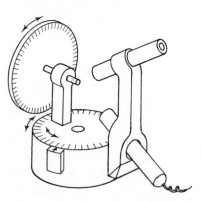

Fig. 37 A two circle optical goniometer.

Use of the goniometer

Although different techniques are required in handling contact and optical goniometers, the same general principles apply to both. The emphasis is placed here on the contact goniometer since this is the instrument that the student will handle most. Optical goniometers require a little more experience in handling and adjusting and details of their use are given in several texts listed at the end of the chapter.

At the outset the student should draw a sketch of the crystal to be studied, preferably in perspective, plan and elevation, and letter or number each face on the crystal (Fig. 38). A prominent reference face is

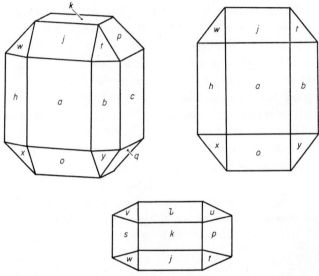

Fig. 38   An orthorhombic crystal with faces lettered to facilitate goniometric study.

chosen so that it is easy to return the crystal to its starting position. Next a prominent zone of faces is chosen and the interfacial angles taken for the entire zone. These are set down as follows:

$$
\begin{array}{ll}
a & e \\
\quad > 25° & \quad > 25° \\
b & f \\
\quad > 65° & \quad > 65° \\
c & g \\
\quad > 65° & \quad > 65° \\
d & h \\
\quad > 25° & \quad > 25° \\
e & a
\end{array}
$$

E

If an optical goniometer is used, the reading of the instrument is taken when each face is in the reflecting position and the interfacial angles obtained by subtraction. Clearly, when all the angles in the zone have been measured their sum should be 360°. If there is a serious discrepancy, measure the angles again taking special care to get a flat bed of the goniometer straight-edges against the crystal faces. Some faces may be difficult to measure because they are small, curved or badly etched. In these cases it may be necessary to omit them and measure the angle between the better faces on either side. The same problem is met in optical goniometry when the quality of the image varies. It is a good plan to indicate by a number code the degree of perfection of each face. Never attempt to guess or otherwise cook a reading; apart from being dishonest, such readings are valueless and a waste of time.

This procedure is repeated for each zone of faces. It is very likely that after this has been done, some interfacial angles will still remain unmeasured because some faces do not lie in zone with others. This is the case with face *t* of Fig. 38. The procedure now is to measure the interfacial angles between face *t* (and of course any other face so far unmeasured) and at least two other faces that have previously been recorded and that are not parallel, e.g. angles *at*, *bt* and *ct* (Fig. 38). The measurements are complete when the interfacial angles necessary to fix the position of all the faces on the crystal have been recorded.

Presentation of results

Crystals are three-dimensional objects and the crystallographer has to attempt to represent them accurately and conveniently in a two-dimensional form. There are many ways of doing this. An accurate drawing can be made in the way that engineers or architects set out their blueprints, but the shape, size and complexity of crystals make this a laborious and unrewarding task. Besides, we have seen that, although the shape and size of crystals may vary between different individuals belonging to one species, the interfacial angles between corresponding faces remain constant. It is the angular truth between crystal faces that is used in representing them and the angles between them are depicted on a projection of some kind.

Spherical projection

Imagine that the crystal of Fig. 38 is arranged so that its centre lies at the centre of a sphere (Fig. 39). From the centre of the sphere, imagine a

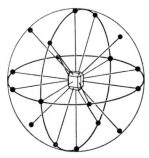

series of lines radiating outwards, each one being at right angles to one of the faces of the crystal. These normals to the faces are projected so that they intersect the surface of the sphere where the points of inter-section are represented by dots. These dots have neither size nor shape but are distri-buted relative to one another on the sur-face of the sphere in a way that reflects the angular distribution of the faces they re-

Fig. 39 Spherical projection of faces of the crystal drawn in Fig. 38.

present. The relationship of one point to any other can be described in angular terms in the same way that on the globe of the earth London can be described as being 74° from New York or 38° from Moscow. Each dot on the surface of the sphere is called the *pole* of the face it represents. Although the spherical projection takes no account of the shape or size of the crystal but emphasises only its inter-facial angles, it suffers from the disadvantage that it is still a three-dimensional model.

Stereographic projection

The stereographic projection is a device by which the essentials of the spherical projection can be represented in two dimensions. The plane of the projection, i.e. the plane of the paper on which the projection is made, is that of the equator of the sphere (Fig. 40). Pole P of any face of the spherical projection is projected on to the equatorial plane by join-ing it by a line to the south pole or nadir (S) of the sphere and marking with a dot (●) the point at which this line intersects the equatorial plane. A limit to the projection is provided by the circle formed by the inter-section of the sphere and the plane of the projection. This is the *primi-tive circle*. It will be appreciated that there is a need to distinguish on the stereographic projection between faces whose poles lie in the upper hemisphere and those whose poles fall in the lower hemisphere. All poles falling in the latter category would project beyond the primitive circle if they were projected from S. For convenience, therefore, the projection point is made the north pole or zenith, N, and they are distinguished by marking their intersection at the projection plane with a small ring, like a small letter o. It is possible to represent two faces, one in the upper and one in the lower hemisphere whose projected poles fall in the same place on the plane of the stereographic projection by a dot surrounded by a circle. In America it is common to use a cross instead of a small dot for the projection of upper hemisphere poles.

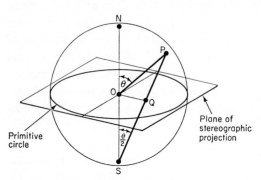

Fig. 40 Spherical projection showing the principle of stereographic projection.

Crystallography is approached in this book by way of the stereographic projection. The construction and interpretation of projections is described in some detail, using actual examples, for a clear understanding of stereograms is essential to a proper understanding of the subject.

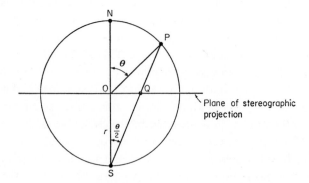

Fig. 41 Angular relationships in stereographic projection.

Properties of the stereographic projection

The primitive circle has no set radius; it can be made as large or as small as is convenient but whatever its size its radius represents an angle of 90°. This is the angle between the north or south pole and the equatorial plane of the projection.

(1) *The relationship between interfacial angles and linear distance on the stereographic projection.* Fig. 41 is a section taken vertically through the sphere of Fig. 40 such that it includes points P and Q. Let the interfacial angle between faces represented by poles N and P be θ. Q is the stereographic projection of the pole P and the distance OQ represents the angle θ. Consider the right angled triangle QOS. OS is the radius r of the sphere and QSO is $\frac{\theta}{2}$ since the angle at the centre is twice that at the circumference. By simple trigonometry, therefore, $OQ = r.\tan\frac{\theta}{2}$.

(2) *The stereographic projection of planes.* A plane passing through the centre of the sphere like that shown in Fig. 42A can be projected by

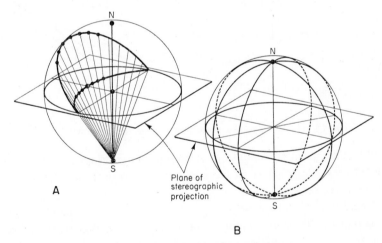

A

Plane of
stereographic
projection

B

Fig. 42 The stereographic projection of great circles.

joining an infinite number of points along it to the nadir (S) and taking their projected position on the stereographic plane. The locus of these points is a *great circle*. All great circles are subtended by a diameter of the primitive circle which is itself the great circle that lies in the plane of the projection. Those planes having NS as their diameter (Fig. 42B) are also great circles and are like the lines of longitude on a globe. They plot on the stereographic projection as diameters of the primitive circle and appear as straight lines radiating from the centre as lines of longitude appear on polar projections of the earth.

Now relate the stereographic projection to the actual crystal. The poles to a zone of faces that stand vertically will all plot on the primitive circle of the stereographic projection (Fig. 43A). Suppose now that the zone axis is tilted from the vertical, as in Fig. 43B. The poles to the faces

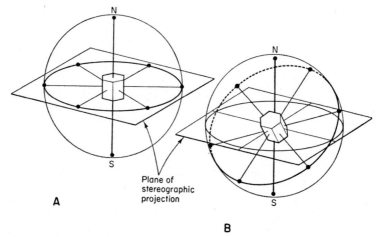

Fig. 43   The stereographic projection of poles to tautozonal faces.

still lie on a great circle, but this is no longer the primitive but an inclined great circle. Thus all faces in zone, when projected, lie on the same great circle.

There is an infinite number of planes that intersect a sphere without bisecting it. The stereographic projections of these planes are called *small circles*. Two limiting cases are illustrated in Fig. 44. Planes that are horizontal and lie parallel to the equatorial plane project as circles concentric with the primitive. Planes that stand vertically project as arcs that are not subtended by a diameter and are concave towards the primitive. Clearly, planes can intersect the sphere at any angle between the horizontal and vertical limiting cases. It is a property of the stereographic projection that such planes project as circles whose centre lies within the primitive. This can readily be seen from Fig. 45. AB in Fig. 45B is the plane cutting the sphere shown in three dimensions in Fig. 45A.

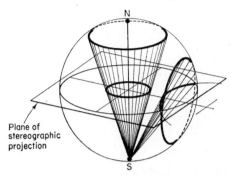

Fig. 44 The stereographic projection of small circles.

A stereographic projection of this plane is produced by projecting it from the south pole S of the sphere. The plane thus subtends a cone whose apex is S and with SQ as its axis. AD is a section of the cone at right angles to its axis and is elliptical. There are two circular sections through an elliptical cone. AB is one; the other, DE, is inclined to the axis QS at the same angle as AB.

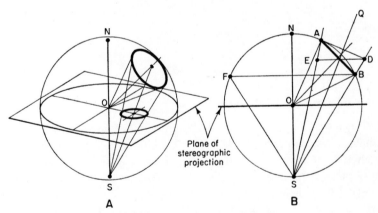

Fig. 45 The stereographic projection of small circles.

BF is drawn parallel to the equator. FS and BS are thus equal arcs of the circle and angles subtended by them at the circle are equal. Thus $\widehat{FBS} = \widehat{SAB}$. Because AB and DE are both similar circular cross-sections, $\widehat{EDS} = \widehat{FBS} = \widehat{SAB}$. ED is thus parallel to FB and hence to the equator. Because all parallel sections of a cone are similar, the small circle AB projects as a circle on the stereographic projection.

Each of these small and great circles can be constructed geometrically and details are given in Chapter 12. Time can be saved in constructing a stereographic projection by using a Wulff stereographic net (Fig. 46A).

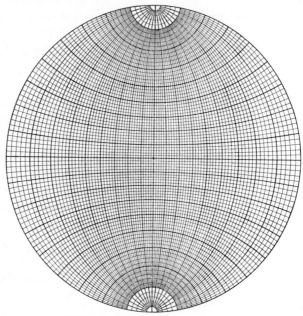

*Fig. 46*A.   A Wulff stereographic net.

This is a net, usually of 20 cm diameter, on which are drawn great and small circles centred on the primitive. The circles are drawn every 2° and each 10° line is thickened. By rotating a sheet of tracing paper placed over the net, the poles to crystal faces can be rapidly and accurately plotted. Some nets are in circulation that are graduated only at 10° intervals but they include also small circles about the centre and radii representing vertical great circles. They are sometimes called Federov nets and are used in the same way as the Wulff net (Fig. 46B).

Gnomonic projection

The plane of the gnomonic projection is a tangent to the sphere at its

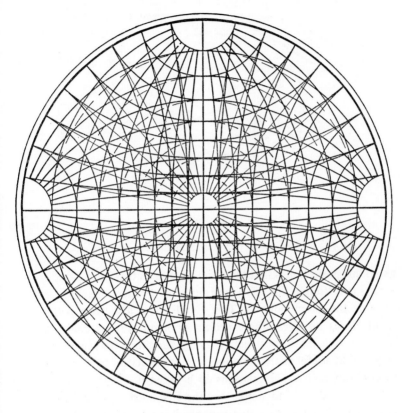

*Fig. 46*B.   A Federov stereographic net.

north pole and the point of projection is the centre of the sphere (Fig. 47A). The projection is not as useful to the student as the stereographic projection because poles to vertical faces that project on the equator of the sphere cannot be drawn gnomonically and the poles to faces inclined slightly from the vertical are projected at inconveniently large distances from the centre of the gnomonic projection.

Properties of gnomonic projection

The essential relationship between distance on the gnomonic projection and interfacial angle is shown in Fig. 47B. The interfacial angle θ is projected as NA, and NA is $r.\tan \theta$. A most useful property of the

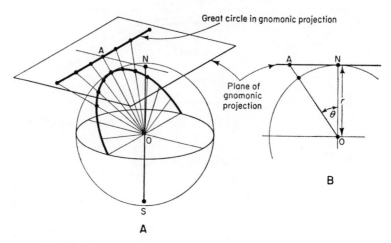

Fig. 47   The principle of gnomonic projection.

gnomonic projection is that the normals to faces that lie in zone, project always in a straight line. The zone circles of the stereogram are straight lines on the gnomonogram. This simplicity is lost when considering small circles however; these project gnomonically as conic sections which are difficult to construct. Although the gnomonic projection is not so generally useful as the stereographic, it has its contribution to make to crystallography. The relationship between it and the stereographic projection is direct and simple and there is much to be said for on occasion combining the two. For example, it is often much easier to assign indices to faces by using the gnomonic rather than the stereographic projection. The interested student is referred to T. V. Barker's *Graphical and Tabular Methods in Crystallography*.

The only other projection that is likely to be met is the *orthogonal projection* and that but very rarely. The projection point is at infinity on the N.S. line through the sphere and the plane of the projection is at right angles to this. It resembles the stereographic projection in all but the point of projection.

Identification of faces

We have now reached the point at which a stereographic projection of a crystal can be constructed in order to show its symmetry. The next requirement is to identify the faces in some way. This is done either by naming them or giving them an index that describes their orientation in space with respect to the crystallographic axes. Crystal faces need not always be described separately; they can often be grouped together as *forms*. We have seen in Chapter 2 that crystals possess symmetry elements. The particular combination of planes and axes of symmetry possessed by a crystal has the effect of repeating a given face at other

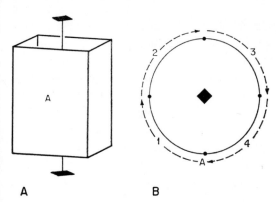

A   B

Fig. 48   Generation of prism by a rotation tetrad symmetry axis.

congruent positions in space. The total number of faces produced in this way by the symmetry elements, when one face is given, constitutes a *form* and a name given to the form covers also the individual faces that comprise it. In Fig. 48, for example, the face A is repeated by the tetrad axis of symmetry to produce a tetragonal prism. The stereographic projection of this symmetry operation is shown in Fig. 48B. The prism

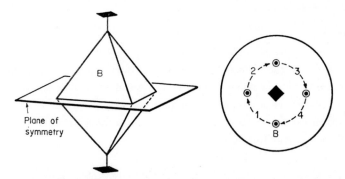

Fig. 49   Generation of bipyramid by rotation tetrad symmetry axis and a plane of symmetry perpendicular to it. The plane of symmetry is shown in projection by the thickened primitive circle.

form so produced is open at each end and is called an *open form*. Consider now the effect of a tetrad axis and a plane of symmetry normal to it on the inclined face B of Fig. 49. The face is repeated by the tetrad axis to produce a pyramid with its apex uppermost and then the plane of symmetry can be thought of as repeating the entire pyramid by reflection so that the form is a bipyramid, and totally encloses space. Such forms are *closed forms*. Note that whereas closed forms can by themselves form crystals, open forms can only occur naturally in *combination* with other forms and, logically, crystals composed of more than one form are called *combinations*. The outward appearance of crystals that are composed of several forms depends on the relative development of the forms. This variation in appearance is known as *habit* and is illustrated in Fig. 50 in which each of the crystals of orthoclase drawn is composed of the same forms.

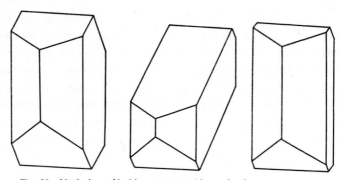

Fig. 50   Variation of habit as expressed by orthoclase.

Names are given to the many forms that can exist and, although for the most part the nomenclature is straightforward and unambiguous, there are occasions when several names are used to describe the same form and then personal preference, national usage or some other factor, is used in making a choice. The subject of nomenclature is treated in the second part of this book.

Indices

A more convenient and unambiguous way of identifying crystal faces is to assign to them an index. We have already said that crystals are referred to crystallographic axes. These are imaginary lines usually chosen so as to be parallel to the edges of the Bravais lattices that define the crystal systems. In fact, they can be chosen parallel to any possible edge of a crystal, but it simplifies matters considerably if a standard scheme is adopted. In drawings of crystals the axes are often represented as lines extending outwards from an origin at the centre of the crystal. Remember that this is only a useful way of showing them.

The length of the edges of the Bravais lattice of any particular substance depends on the shape and size of the atoms, ions or ion complexes present and the cell edges are hence specific to it. In the same way, the crystallographic axes are spoken of as having lengths, but they remain a convenient form of reference and not directly measurable properties of a crystal. The lengths of the edges of the unit cell, however, can be calculated from X-ray data. For example, the measured cell dimensions for the orthorhombic mineral forsterite, a member of the olivine group, are $a = 4\cdot756$ Å, $b = 10\cdot195$ Å and $c = 5\cdot981$ Å. The three edges are mutually at right angles. These lengths may be expressed as ratios, taking b as unity and these ratios are called the axial ratios. They are usually expressed as $\dfrac{a}{b} : \dfrac{b}{b} : \dfrac{c}{b}$. For forsterite the axial ratios are $0\cdot467 : 1 : 0\cdot586$.

Because the orientation of the planes in a crystal lattice is strictly controlled by the disposition of the points of the lattice and since crystal faces can only develop parallel to such planes, the axial ratio of a crystal can be derived quite simply from a stereographic projection of its faces. In fact axial ratios were accurately quoted many years before X-rays were used to determine cell dimensions, giving a further indication of the control of external shape by internal structure.

Cubic crystals are referred to three orthogonal axes of equal length and hence the ratios $\dfrac{a_1}{a_2} : \dfrac{a_2}{a_2} : \dfrac{a_3}{a_2}$ are unity. Similarly, tetragonal, hexagonal and trigonal crystals have horizontal axes that are equal in length and the axial ratio for these systems is given by $\dfrac{c}{a}$.

Haüy, from his study of crystals (and he did not have the help of X-rays) appreciated that the orientation in space of crystal faces was such that, if they were referred to the crystallographic axes, they made rational intercepts upon them. This led to the formulation of the *law of rational indices* which simply states that the relationship of a face to the crystallographic axes is given by three small whole numbers (four in the case of the hexagonal and trigonal systems).

Parameters

Consider the case of an orthorhombic crystal whose axes are shown in Fig. 51. Notice that the positive end of the *a* axis always points towards

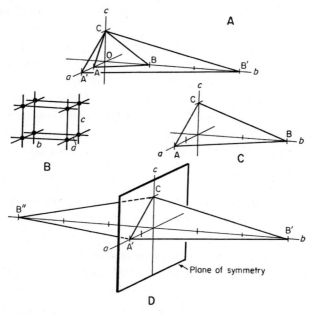

Fig. 51   Parameters and indices; for explanation see text.

the observer, the positive end of *b* is to his right and the positive end of the *c* axis points upwards. A plane parallel to a crystal face which intersects all three crystallographic axes is now chosen so as to define the unit lengths or *parameters* of the crystal. The form, of which this face is a member, is called the *unit form*.

The selection of a unit face may seem to be arbitrary and in a sense it is. A plane like that shown in Fig. 51C also makes an intercept on all three crystallographic axes and could equally well be chosen as the parametral plane.

The unit plane ABC in Fig. 51A defines the axial lengths so that OA is the unit length of the *a* axis, OB the unit length of *b* and OC the unit length of *c*. Since the unit plane defines the unit lengths of the axes, it must make with them intercepts having the ratios 1:1:1. It is a matter of observation that any other plane inclined to two or more crystallographic axes intercepts them at a distance that is a whole number multiple of the unit length of the axes. Thus the plane A′ B′ C makes intercepts $2a:3b:c$ on the three axes, and it is the ratios of the intercepts that is of great use in identifying crystal faces.

Weiss notation

The ratios of the intercepts can be used directly and this is the basis of the scheme devised by C. S. Weiss. The intercept on each axis is expressed in terms of its unit length. Thus the plane A′ B′ C has an index given by $\dfrac{OA'}{OA}:\dfrac{OB'}{OB}:\dfrac{OC}{OC}$ and it is written as 231.

Miller indices

The system in most general use however is that used extensively by W. H. Miller although not entirely devised by him. In this scheme it is the reciprocal of the Weiss symbol that is used and the index of the face A′ B′ C may be written

$$\frac{OA}{OA'}:\frac{OB}{OB'}:\frac{OC}{OC}\quad \text{or}$$

$$\frac{1}{2}:\frac{1}{3}:\frac{1}{1}$$

The index is simplified by clearing the fractions by multiplication. The Miller index is thus written as (326). The arrangement of the numbers is significant; they give, in order, the inverse of the ratio of the intercepts on the *a*, *b* and *c* axes respectively. Similarly, each digit in the index is significant in itself and the index is read as '*three, two, six*'; never as '*three hundred and twenty-six*'.

The presence of symmetry elements means that there are other faces like A′ B′ C of Fig. 51A which, although in other positions, still have similar intercept ratios on the crystallographic axes. Imagine a plane of symmetry containing the a and c axes. (Fig. 51D). This repeats the face A′ B′ C′ and A′ B″ C, which makes an intercept at the negative end of the b axis. The ratios of the intercepts of face A′ B″ C is exactly the same as A′ B′ C and hence its index is unchanged. However, in order to indicate that an intercept is made at the negative end of the b axis, a negative sign is placed over the appropriate digit. The index is written $(3\bar{2}6)$ and it is read as '*three, minus two, six*' and not as '*three, bar two, six.*' In this way every face present on a crystal can be separately identified by its index.

Some planes lie parallel to either one or two of the crystallographic axes and they can be thought of as intercepting these axes at infinity. A face having the intercepts $2a : 1b : \infty c$, can be written as $\frac{1}{2} : \frac{1}{1} : \frac{1}{\infty}$, and its Miller index is (120) which is read as '*one, two, nought*'.

The Miller index (326) has been assigned to the face A′B′C of Fig. 51A on the choice of ABC as the parametral form. Suppose, however, that face ABC of Fig. 51C had been chosen as the unit form instead. It has intercepts that are $2a : 2b : 1c$ if the unit form of Fig. 51A is taken as the standard of reference. Now face A′B′C according to our new standard of reference has intercepts that have the ratios $1a : 1\frac{1}{2}b : 1c$. To obtain the Miller index the ratios of the intercepts are inverted to give $\frac{1}{1} : \frac{2}{3} : \frac{1}{1}$ and the fractions cleared to give the index (323).

Notice that although the face makes a fractional intercept on the b axis, the ratios of the intercepts as expressed in the Miller index are rational.

If it is possible to select as the parametral form virtually any face that intersects all three axes, does it not follow that there is also a very large number of different ways of indexing a crystal? The short answer is 'yes', but it is not the complete answer. Each of the different schemes of indices that may be chosen has its own axial ratio and these different axial ratios are simply related to one another. Moreover, the indices assigned to faces become increasingly complex the more complex the axial ratios become.

Before the crystallographer had X-rays to help him, it was customary and logical to choose as the most appropriate parametral plane the one giving the simplest indices to commonly occurring faces. We have seen that X-rays can be used to determine the length of the cell edges of the structural units of crystals. When the axial ratios deduced from crystal morphology are compared with the ratios of the cell edges determined by X-rays, they are very often found to be identical and when they are not, there is always a simple relationship between them. Usually one of the dimensions of the structural unit is twice or half that of the morphological unit. X-rays, therefore, enable a correct choice of axial ratios to be made when the simplest morphological unit differs from the structural one.

The experimentally determined structural unit is shown diagrammatically in Fig. 51B and its dimensions agree with those of the parametral form ABC of Fig. 51A. This then is the usual case in which the parametral plane giving the simplest indices gives also an axial ratio that agrees with the cell dimensions determined by X-ray diffractometry.

It is possible to assign a Miller index to every face of a crystal and we have seen that all the faces of a given form are similarly related to the symmetry elements and therefore to the crystallographic axes. This means that the Miller indices of every face contain always the same integers. For example, the faces of the octahedron (Fig. 1) have the indices (111), ($\bar{1}$11), ($\bar{1}\bar{1}$1), (1$\bar{1}$1), (11$\bar{1}$), ($\bar{1}$1$\bar{1}$), ($\bar{1}\bar{1}\bar{1}$), (1$\bar{1}\bar{1}$). It is clearly very much more convenient to refer the form as a whole by a *symbol* which is the index of the face that intersects the positive ends of the axes, or the face that most nearly approaches this. It is essential that the form symbol and a face index should be clearly distinguished because numerically they can be identical.

The accepted practice is to use the index enclosed by round brackets e.g. (321) to denote an individual face and to enclose the index in braces e.g. {321} when the form symbol is intended. In the past the unbracketed index was used to denote the face index, but this is now used by X-ray crystallographers to denote a reflection from a set of planes; in this instance those parallel to the face (321). The significance of square brackets enclosing an index e.g. [321] is given on p. 89.

Some forms can have only one index. The octahedron, for example, can only have the index {111}. Other forms, however, can have several

F

intercept ratios on the crystallographic axes whilst having the same general attitude to the symmetry elements. The pentagonal dodecahedron, a commonly occurring form of many pyrite crystals, can have

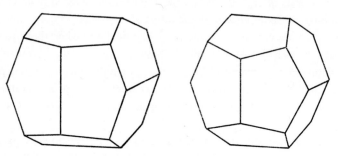

Fig. 52   Pentagonal dodecahedra {210} and {310}.

indices like {210}, {310}, {410} etc. (Fig. 52) and it is most convenient to be able to refer to such forms in a general way by substituting letters for numbers in the symbol. The pentagonal dodecahedron thus becomes the form {hk0}, where h and k represent different whole numbers.

Similarly a form that makes a different intercept on all three axes has a general symbol {hkl}, where h, k and l represent different whole numbers. Forms with a general index {hhl} would have actual indices like {221}, {331} etc. and {hll} forms would have indices like {211}, {322} and so on. General reference to forms in this way is used extensively in this book. In the case of hexagonal and trigonal crystals which have four axes the general symbol {hkil} is used.

Stereographic projection of a crystal to illustrate the foregoing principles
The foregoing principles will be more readily appreciated if an actual crystal is plotted stereographically and its faces indexed. Take for example the crystal drawn in Fig. 53. It *appears* to have tetragonal symmetry about an axis parallel to the length of the crystal; other axes at right angles to this *appear* to be diads. Accordingly it is reasonable to hold the crystal with its apparent tetrad axis vertically. Several zones of faces are at once apparent. These zones are marked on Fig. 53A and cross-sections through the crystal in the plane of the zones are shown in

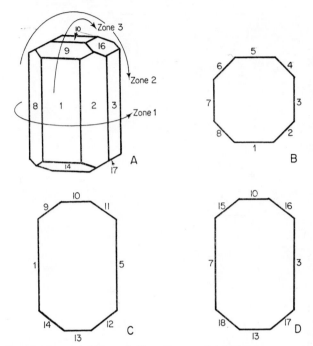

Fig. 53   Stereographic projection of a crystal; initial steps.

Fig. 53 B-D. Each face on the crystal is given a number and measurements taken are set out as in Table 3.

The measurements show that faces 10 and 13 are at right angles to the large faces that stand vertically and they must also be at right angles to the smaller faces 2, 4, 6 and 8. This can be checked with a goniometer. We can now plot the stereogram beginning with zone 1. Faces in this zone are vertical and their poles project on the primitive circle of the stereographic projection.

Push a drawing pin carefully through the centre of a Wulff net from the back. A small piece of 'Sellotape' placed at the centre of the net at the back will prevent the hole from enlarging with use. Place a sheet of tracing paper over the Wulff net so that it rotates about the pin and draw in the primitive circle. Mark on the primitive, anywhere, a small dot and let this represent the pole to face 1. Label it as such. Place this dot over a thickened 10° line on the net and then mark in the positions of the pole

TABLE 3

CONTACT GONIOMETER READINGS OF INTERFACIAL ANGLES OF THE CRYSTAL SHOWN IN FIG. 53

Zone 1

face 1		face 5	
1		5	
	>45°		>45°
2		6	
	>45°		>45°
3		7	
	>45°		>45°
4		8	
	>45°		>45°
5		1	
	360°		360°

Zone 2

face 7		face 3	
7		3	
	>53°		>53°
15		17	
	>37°		>37°
10		13	
	>37°		>37°
16		18	
	>53°		>53°
3		7	
	360°		360°

Zone 3

face 1		face 5	
1		5	
	>53°		>53°
9		12	
	>37°		>37°
10		13	
	>37°		>37°
11		14	
	>53°		>53°
5		1	
	360°		360°

to face 2 by counting 45° (the interfacial angle between faces 1 and 2) anticlockwise round the primitive and marking another dot (Fig. 54).

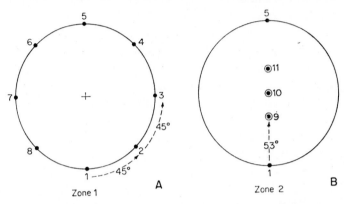

Fig. 54   Stereographic projection of a crystal; plotting technique.

Without moving the paper, continue plotting the interfacial angles $\widehat{2\ 3}$; $\widehat{3\ 4}$ etc. in an anticlockwise direction until all the faces in zone 1 have been plotted. If the faces had been measured by going from 1 to 8 to 7 and so on, the plotting would have been done in a clockwise direction. Remember that one looks down as it were on to the top of the crystal when plotting a stereographic projection.

Face 1 is the starting point for zone 2 and the faces in this zone have poles which lie in a vertical plane since $\widehat{1\ 10}$ and $\widehat{3\ 10}$ are both 90°. The poles lie on a great circle that stands vertically and therefore passes through the centre point of the projection (see Fig. 42, p. 69). Such great circles plot as diameters of the primitive circle and two are drawn on the Wulff net at right angles to one another. Rotate the tracing over the net until pole 1 lies at the point at which one of the diameters meets the primitive. The position of the pole to face 9 is plotted by counting 53° along the diameter from the primitive and marking the pole with a dot and labelling the point (Fig. 54B). The pole to face 10 lies another 37° further on and is marked with a dot at the centre of the projection. The plotting is continued in this way to pole 5.

The position of face 12 is found by counting inwards 53° along the great circle from the primitive as before and this is the same position as that occupied by face 11. The pole to face 12, however, intersects the sphere in the lower hemisphere and is hence plotted as a small ring enclosing the dot marking the pole to face 11. The remainder of the zone is plotted in this way.

Zone 3 is plotted in exactly the same way as zone 2, but face 7 is the starting point and not face 1. The stereogram is now completed but it requires to be orientated with respect to the crystallographic axes and appropriate indices assigned to the various faces. The symmetry of the crystal must also be deduced. The first step is the selection of the parametral plane. This, it will be remembered, is a plane that intersects the three crystallographic axes and is used to define their unit lengths. The Miller index of the parametral plane is thus (111).

In the crystal under consideration there is only one form that can be chosen as the parametral one; the bipyramid composed of faces 9, 16, 11, 15 and 14, 17, 13, 18. This becomes the form {111} and hence the horizontal crystallographic axes must emerge from the centres of the smaller vertical prism comprising faces 2, 4, 6, 8. Fig. 55 shows the stereogram in the correct reading position with the crystallographic axes inserted and the faces of the parametral form indexed. The upper index refers to the face in the upper hemisphere; The lower index refers to the face that cuts the c axis at its negative end and hence the third digit is always $\bar{1}$.

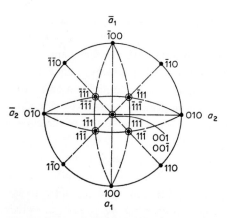

Fig. 55 Stereographic projection of a crystal; the completed stereogram with zones, Miller indices and crystallographic axes inserted.

The selection of the parametral plane is easy enough in this instance, but what of crystals where there is more than one face that can be taken as the parametral form? Can any form be selected at the whim of the crystallographer? We have already mentioned that the professional will have X-ray data to guide him, but there is a simple general rule that the student may follow with some confidence. When more than one form satisfies the requirements of the parametral plane, then select the one that is better developed, i.e. choose the one with the largest faces. This is not as arbitrary as it seems. As a crystal grows the faces of lowest index tend to grow at the expense of the others (Chapter 11) and hence usually the best developed faces will tend to be those of lowest index.

Returning now to the stereogram, the crystallographic axes may now be marked, having first rotated the projection so that the parametral form will lie in its correct position between them. In this instance, because the crystal has tetragonal symmetry the parametral form will bisect the angle made by the two horizontal axes but this is not necessarily always so. The axis running from front to back is the a_1 axis and the one running from right to left the a_2 axis. In crystals of lower symmetry these axes would be called the a and b axes respectively. The vertical or c axis is represented by the centre point of the projection.

With the stereogram in its reading position it is apparent that it has a definite regularity or symmetry. For instance if the face (111) be taken as a starting point then it is clear that there are three more faces with the same orientation in the upper hemisphere. This is true also of the vertical faces and the c axis is thus an axis of four-fold symmetry or, better, a *tetrad* axis. It is at once obvious that if the projection were to be cut in two with scissors along the line of the a_1 axis, the left hand and right hand halves would be mirror images. The vertical plane containing the a_1 and c axes is hence a plane of symmetry. The plane that passes vertically through a_2 is the same and so are the two planes that pass vertically through the projected poles of {111}. The crystal hence has four vertical planes of symmetry, two that contain the crystallographic axes, or *axial* planes, and two diagonal. Notice too that every upper hemisphere face that plots inside the primitive as a dot has a face corresponding to it in the lower hemisphere that plots as a circle round the dot. This means that the horizontal plane, i.e. the plane of the paper is also a plane of symmetry. If it were not, then the dots and circles would not coincide. The same result is obtained if the crystal is rotated through 180° about the a_1 and a_2 axes and about axes bisecting the angle between these two. Each of these axes is hence a *diad axis*. There is also a centre. The symmetry elements are drawn and represented stereo-graphically in Fig. 56.

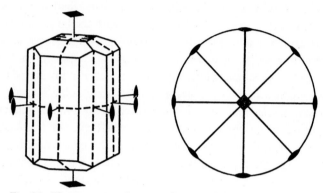

Fig. 56   The symmetry elements of a crystal shown in block form and in stereographic projection.

The indices of the remaining faces may be fixed with reference to the crystallographic axes. Face 8 is vertical and is thus parallel to the c axis. It is parallel also to the b axis but makes an intercept on a. Its Miller index will thus be (100). It will not be (200) or (300) because an intercept of more than a unit distance only becomes significant in relation to an intercept on another axis. Put another way, changing the first digit in the index does not alter the attitude of the plane in space when the plane is parallel to two other axes and hence an index (300) is no more signifi-cant in classical crystallography than (100). The concept is of value however to the X-ray crystallographer.

Similarly, face 2 is parallel to the a_1 and c axes but cuts a_2. Its index is therefore (010). Now these two faces, with those parallel to them ($\bar{1}00$) and ($0\bar{1}0$), together constitute the form {100} because they are generated by the symmetry elements when one face is given.

Face 1 is parallel to c but makes an equal intercept on a_1 and a_2 because it lies in zone with the parametral form {111}. Its index is, hence (110). There are three other faces beside (110) in the form {110}; they are ($\bar{1}10$), ($\bar{1}\bar{1}0$) and ($1\bar{1}0$).

The faces that form the 'top' and 'bottom' of the crystal clearly cut the c axis and lie parallel to the horizontal axes and hence have indices (001) and ($00\bar{1}$) respectively.

From the initial measurements taken on the crystal it was obvious that certain faces were in zone. Those plotting on the primitive circle and those lying in vertical zones are good examples. By rotating the tracing over the Wulff net, however, it will be seen that several faces lie on the same inclined great circle and are hence equally in zone, e.g. faces 8, 9 16, 4. These zones are drawn with broken lines in Fig. 55.

The Weiss zone law and the zone symbol

Faces that are in zone meet in parallel edges that are parallel to an axis called the *zone axis*. This is a line that has its origin at the centre of the sphere in the same way as the normal to a face and it can thus be given a Miller index according to where it plots on the stereographic projection. These *zone symbols* are distinguished from other indices and symbols by enclosing them in square brackets [001].

The zone symbol is expressed in general terms as [uvw], where u, v and w represent small whole numbers.

The indices of faces that lie in the same zone have a relationship to one another that is of great value in crystallography. This was appreciated by C. S. Weiss (1780–1836), a German crystallographer after whom the *Weiss zone law* is named. In Fig. 55 it is clear that there is a simple numerical relationship between the indices of faces in the same zone. The index of any truncating face may be found by the addition of the indices of the faces on either side of it in the same zone. Thus in Fig. 54, if the indices of faces 1 and 3 are known, then the index of face 2 which truncates the edge between them is found by addition. In this case $(100) + (010) = (110)$. The same holds true for (111) that lies in zone between (001) and (110). Put another way, if the indices of two faces lying in the same zone are added, their sum is the index of the face that truncates the edges between them.

The zone symbol can be calculated empirically from the Miller indices of any two faces in the zone. If two faces have indices (hkl) and (pqr) respectively, then it is possible to prove that $u = (kr\text{-}lq)$, $v = (lp\text{-}hr)$ and $w = (hq\text{-}kp)$. The values of u, v and w may very easily be obtained by a scheme of cross-multiplication and subtraction that uses the principle of determinants. It works as follows. Write down twice, in succession, the index of one of the faces (hkl) and beneath it write twice the index of the other face (*pqr*) and cross off the first and last number in each line thus:

$$h \mid k\,l\,h\,k \mid l$$
$$p \mid q\,r\,p\,q \mid r$$

Working from left to right, take the numbers in pairs and multiply top left with bottom right (solid arrow) and from it subtract the product of top right and bottom left (open arrow) giving $(kr) - (lq)$.

This gives the figure *u*.

$$\begin{vmatrix} k\,l\,h\,k \\ \times \\ q\,r\,p\,q \end{vmatrix}$$

The next pair of numbers is *lh* and *rp* and their products give
$$v = (lp) - (hr)$$

$$\begin{vmatrix} k\,l\,h\,k \\ \times \\ q\,r\,p\,q \end{vmatrix}$$

For the last pair $w = (hq - kp)$.

$$\begin{vmatrix} k\,l\,h\,k \\ \times \\ q\,r\,p\,q \end{vmatrix}$$

Let us now take an example and determine the zone symbol of the zone containing faces 1 and 2 of Fig. 53. Their indices are (100) and (110) respectively and the zone index is hence

$$1 \mid 0\;0\;1\;0 \mid 0$$
$$\times\times\times$$
$$1 \mid 1\;0\;1\;1 \mid 0$$

$u = (0 - 0) = 0$; $v = (0 - 0) = 0$; $w = (1 - 0) = 1$.

The zone symbol is hence [001].

The order in which the indices of the two faces are written is immaterial as the following example shows.

$$1 \mid 1\;0\;1\;1 \mid 0$$
$$\times\times\times$$
$$1 \mid 0\;0\;1\;0 \mid 0$$

$u = (0 - 0)$; $v = (0 - 0)$; $w = (0 - 1)$

giving the zone symbol [00$\bar{1}$].

Remember that the zone axis is a line which therefore intersects the sphere at two points 180° apart. The zone symbol can thus be equally

[001] and [00$\bar{1}$], the indices corresponding to the two intersection points.

The indices of any face within a zone must bear a definite relationship to the zone symbol since the latter may be derived from the indices of any two faces in the zone. This relationship, called the *zonal equation*, is

$$uh + vk + wl = 0.$$

Where *uvw* is the zone symbol and *hkl* the index of a face in the zone whose zone symbol is [*uvw*].

Some faces, for example face 3 of Fig. 54, are common to two or more zones, which may be thought of as intersecting in the face.

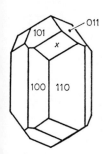

Fig. 57 For explanation see text.

The index of such a face must thus satisfy the zonal equation for both zones. If both zone symbols are known, then the index of the face is fixed and may be determined by combining both zonal equations or by using the 'cross multiplication' device on the two zone symbols.

As an example consider the crystal in Fig. 57. Face *x* lies in zone between faces (100) and (01$\underline{1}$) and also faces (101) and (110). The zone symbols for these zones are thus [0$\bar{1}$1] and [1$\bar{1}\bar{1}$] respectively. By 'cross multiplying' these the index of face *x* is obtained.

$$0 \ \left| \ \bar{1} \ 1 \ 0 \ \bar{1} \ \right| \ 1$$
$$1 \ \left| \ \bar{1} \ \bar{1} \ 1 \ \bar{1} \ \right| \ \bar{1}$$

$$u = (1 - \bar{1}); \ v = (1 - 0); \ w = (0 - \bar{1})$$

The index is hence (211)

These calculations may be used to determine whether a face whose index is known can belong to a given zone, or to determine the index of a face that occurs at the intersection of two zones.

Suggestions for further reading
Barker, T. V., *Graphical and Tabular Methods in Crystallography*, Murby, London, 1922.
Bragg, W. L., *The Crystalline State*, Vol. 1, *A general survey* G. Bell & Sons Ltd., London, 1949.
Buerger, M. J., *Elementary Crystallography*, John Wiley & Sons Inc., New York, 1956.
Bunn, C. W., *Chemical Crystallography*, University Press Oxford, 2nd Edition, 1961.
Henry, N. F. M., H. Lipson and W. A. Wooster, *The Interpretation of X-ray Diffraction Photographs*, Macmillan and Co. Ltd., London, 1961.

PART 2

Systematic
Crystallography

CHAPTER 4

THE THIRTY-TWO CLASSES
OF SYMMETRY

Space groups and point groups

Any crystalline substance can be allocated to one or other of the seven crystal systems on the basis of the shape of its Bravais lattice. If the substance also shows crystal faces, then as we have seen, such crystals reflect this regularity of internal structure in outward symmetry about planes, axes or a centre.

As early as 1830, long before the discovery of X-rays, J. F. C. Hessel correctly predicted that these symmetry elements could be combined in thirty-two different ways. The thirty-two combinations of symmetry elements give rise to the *thirty-two classes of crystal symmetry*.

Because there are more crystal classes than crystal systems it follows that the *shape* of the space lattice cannot account for the observed or mathematically predictable variation of the shape of crystals; there must be a more fundamental principle.

The space lattice is a regular three-dimensional array of points and each Bravais lattice has a definite symmetry of its own. If each point of the space lattice is the centre of a spherical atom, as in NaCl (Fig. 20), then the symmetry of the three-dimensional array of *atoms* is the same as the three-dimensional array of *points* or the space lattice.

In Chapter 2 we saw that this simple arrangement is only relatively rarely found in nature and that commonly the lattice points are the centres of groups of atoms arranged round them. Such groups of atoms have definite shapes and hence a symmetry of their own. For example the CO_3^{2-} complex is like a flat triangle (Fig. 24). This means that different arrangements of atoms are possible within, say, a tetragonal space lattice and it is this that accounts for the observed variability of crystal symmetry. There are, in fact, 230 possible kinds of internal arrangement. This was discovered quite independently and at about the same time (between 1890 and 1895) by the Russian L. S. Federov, A. M. Schoenflies in Germany and the British scientist W. Barlow. To the structural crystallographer these 230 kinds of internal arrangement are known as the 230 *space groups*, because the arrangement of the symmetry elements of the internal structural units is three-dimensional and extends through space. By contrast, the planes and axes of symmetry that can combine to give the thirty-two classes all pass through an imaginary point at the centre of the crystal that is also the imaginary intersection point of the crystallographic axes. This point is not repeated by the symmetry elements and the structural crystallographer calls the thirty-two classes *point groups*. For further details of space and point groups the reader is referred to the references at the end of the chapter; its further treatment lies beyond the scope of this book.

Nomenclature of the thirty-two classes; Hermann-Mauguin symbols
A system of nomenclature of the various crystal classes is now required. The structural crystallographer has a rigorous notation for the 230 space groups, but for the student a simpler notation of the thirty-two crystal classes is needed. The one commonly used is based on the combination of the elements of symmetry that define the point group. They are expressed as a *symmetry symbol*. This is supplemented by giving to each class the name of its general crystal form (see Chapter 5) and, for the eleven most commonly occurring classes, the name of a mineral chosen as representative of that class.

In deriving the *International Symmetry Symbol* or *Hermann-Mauguin*[15] *Symbol*, the concept of a centre of symmetry is discarded although symmetry about a plane and an axis is retained.

The kind of symmetry produced by mirror reflection across a plane is denoted by *m*.

Axial symmetry is of two kinds:

(a) *Rotation axis*. The rotation axis is the elementary axis of symmetry with which the student is already familiar. Rotation about this axis through $\dfrac{360°}{n}$ restores congruence and the axis is called an *n-fold axis of symmetry*. It is denoted by arabic numerals according to whether $n = 1$, 2, 3, 4 or 6. The axes are referred to verbally as *identity*, *diad*, *triad*,

15. The Hermann-Mauguin notation was devised by Ch. Mauguin and C. Hermann in 1935. The present standard work on structure notation is the *International Tables for X-ray Crystallography*, Vol. 1 (1952) which uses the same point group notation.

tetrad and *hexad axes* respectively and they are represented graphically by the following symbols:

identity axis	•
diad axis	◗
triad axis	▼
tetrad axis	◆
hexad axis	⬢

(b) *Inversion axis.* This is the symmetry element that obviates the need for a centre of symmetry. It is a compound symmetry element in that in addition to rotation through $\frac{360°}{n}$ it involves an inversion through 180° about the centre. Inversion axes are written $\bar{1}$, $\bar{2}$, $\bar{3}$, $\bar{4}$ or $\bar{6}$ and pronounced '*bar one*', '*bar two*' etc. There is no general agreement as to how they should be symbolised; some schemes are given below:

	Phillips	International	de Jong
		Tables	
$\bar{1}$	○		•
$\bar{2}$	◑	*m*	*m*
$\bar{3}$	▽	▼	▽
$\bar{4}$	◇	◈	◇
$\bar{6}$	⬡	⬣	⬡

Of these schemes the one used by Phillips is the simplest and clearest. De Jong uses for rotation axes the symbols used by Phillips for inversion axes, so the student needs to be on his guard. The symbols used in the *International Tables* for $\bar{4}$ and $\bar{6}$ have the advantage of indicating that crystals with these elements possess a superficial 'diad' and 'triad' appearance. The simple scheme of Phillips is adopted in this book, but the *International Tables* symbol is used for $\bar{4}$ and $\bar{6}$.

The operation of an inversion axis is most clearly seen from Fig. 58, which shows the operation of an inversion tetrad axis. The inversion tetrad stands normal to the plane of the paper and the pole of a given face A is indicated conventionally. The inversion tetrad causes it to be rotated through 90° and then inverted through 180° about the centre so that the next face appears in the lower hemisphere at B (Fig. 58A). The pole next moves 90° from B in the lower hemisphere and in the same anticlockwise direction as the initial movement. It then inverts 180°

G

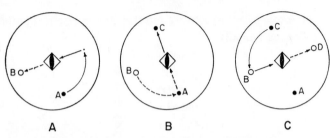

Fig. 58 The operation of an inversion tetrad axis. Solid arrow shows movement of a pole in the upper hemisphere; dotted arrow in the lower hemisphere.

from directly below A to give the position of the next face at C (Fig. 58B). Two more such movements (Fig. 58C) produce face D and then reproduce face A again; this completing the symmetry operation. The resulting form is an elongated, wedge-shaped form called a sphenoid

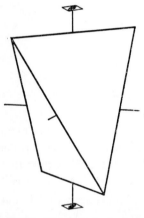

(Fig. 59). The form could be regarded as having a diad axis of symmetry in so far as its shape is concerned. The *structure* of the form produced by an inversion tetrad, however, has a higher order of symmetry.

Stereograms of the other inversion axes are given in Fig. 60 and it should be noticed that some are equivalent to a combination of other symmetry elements. Thus $\bar{6}$ is equivalent to a rotation triad axis normal to a plane of symmetry, and $\bar{2}$ is equivalent to a single plane of symmetry.

The International Symmetry Symbol for any crystal class is derived by writing down the symmetry elements it possesses according to the following plan:

Fig. 59 The tetragonal sphenoid {111}.

1. The character of the principal axis; n or $\bar{n}$.
2. A plane of symmetry normal to the principal axis; written n/m and pronounced 'n over m'. The principal axis in every case is a rotation axis. An inversion axis normal to a plane cannot retain its character and $\bar{2}$ and $\bar{6}$ may be regarded as having a planar element of symmetry implicit in them. A plane normal to $\bar{1}$, $\bar{3}$ and $\bar{4}$ immediately

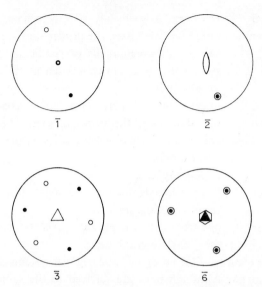

Fig. 60   Stereograms illustrating forms generated by the operation of inversion axes.

converts them to the higher classes $2/m$, $6/m$ and $4/m$ respectively.

3. A plane of symmetry containing the principal axis, written nm or $\bar{n}m$.
4. A diad axis or axes normal to the principal axis, written $n2$. Again $\bar{n}2$ is an impossible combination.

Thus the symbol n/mm refers to a crystal class having an n-fold rotation axis as its principal axis and with planes of symmetry both normal to it and containing it. Special conventions are needed for the cubic system and they are described in Chapter 9.

Symmetry characteristics of the crystal systems

We know that crystal systems can be referred to crystallographic axes. The symmetry elements discussed above give the axes a deeper significance; each crystal system has certain symmetry elements peculiar to itself. Thus although the principal (crystallographic) axes of cubic crystals may be either tetrads or diads, *all* cubic crystals possess *four triad axes* regardless of the symmetry class to which they belong and this distinguishes them from crystals of all other systems. The elements of symmetry that are characteristic of the other systems are:

Tetragonal	one tetrad axis which is the principal axis.
Orthorhombic	*either* one diad axis, the principal axis, at the intersection of two mutually perpendicular planes. The principal axis is always chosen as the *c* crystallographic axis. *or* three mutually perpendicular diad axes.
Monoclinic	one diad axis, the principal axis. This is always chosen in morphological studies as the *b* crystallographic axis.
Triclinic	an identity axis.
Hexagonal	one hexad axis, the principal axis: always chosen as the *c* crystallographic axis.
Trigonal	one triad axis, the principal axis: always chosen as the *c* crystallographic axis.

The separate identity of the hexagonal and trigonal systems is demanded by the symmetry. Although both are referred to the same crystallographic axes, to group them together is to obscure to some extent the fact that they are structurally different and for this reason they are treated as separate and distinct systems in this book.

The arrangement of the faces of a crystal is not always a faithful reflection of its internal symmetry. Some crystals have a low internal symmetry and yet form such simple crystals that they appear to be more symmetrical than in fact they are. But internal symmetry can find expression in other ways than facial arrangement. Forces within the crystal structure bind the atoms together, and we know that they frequently differ in strength in different directions in the crystal. This means that the crystal will break more readily in some directions than others and gives rise to *cleavage*. In those crystals that have a good, well-defined cleavage the very close dependence on the atomic arrangement is often apparent. This is particularly so in the micas, the pyroxenes and amphiboles and in such minerals as calcite and galena, which break most easily along the planes across which the attractive forces are weakest.

The hardness of different crystal faces varies also according to the underlying atomic arrangement, as does their resistance to attack by solutions. It is not unusual to find crystals with faces that are etched differently by natural or laboratory solutions. If the small depressions or *etch-figures* are magnified, they are seen to have a definite shape that is

often a reflection of the symmetry of the underlying structure. Crystals of corundum (Al_2O_3) for example are often hexagonal in form and yet etch-figures on their basal surface have a triangular form (Fig. 61), showing that the crystal belongs to the trigonal and not to the hexagonal system as the faces alone would suggest.

Fig. 61 Etch figures on the basal plane of corundum.

Occasionally some physical property may emphasize the crystallography. Tourmaline, for example, is a representative of a crystal class that has a polar principal axis. The structure at opposite ends of this axis is different and there is hence no plane of symmetry normal to it. This is shown, not only by

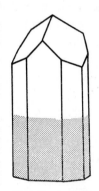

a difference in the way the crystal is terminated but also, in some crystals, by a difference in colour along its length. Most mineral collections contain tourmalines that are pink at one end and pale green at the other (Fig. 62). Although optical crystallography is beyond the scope of this book, there is a wealth of symmetry information to be obtained by this means.

Fig. 62 A parti-coloured crystal of tourmaline.

Scheme of systematic crystallography

The following chapters are concerned with the systematic description of the thirty-two classes of symmetry from a morphological standpoint.

The systematic study in this book commences with the tetragonal system, followed by the orthorhombic, monoclinic, triclinic and cubic in that order, leaving the hexagonal and trigonal systems until last. The cubic system, although the most regular, has a complexity of symmetry elements and a special nomenclature and is best left until the general principles are mastered. The student can grasp most easily the concept of orthogonal crystallographic axes and from the relatively simple forms of the tetragonal system can progress logically to the inclined axial plan of the triclinic.

The cubic system then completes the list of systems that are referred to three axes and by now the student has sufficient familiarity with principles to appreciate its complexity. Finally the hexagonal and trigonal systems are considered. They are referred to four axes and in consequence necessitate changes in index notation. The similarity between the tetragonal, hexagonal and trigonal systems is emphasized by a comparative table.

In each system the class with the highest order of symmetry is described first. In these *holosymmetric classes*, as they are called, the crystal has the same symmetry as the lattice. The lower symmetry classes, sometimes called *merosymmetric classes*, are described in the following order showing a general decrease in symmetry:

holoaxial classes (those classes having no planes of symmetry, but only axes of symmetry) $n2, \bar{n}m, nm, n/m, \bar{n}, n$.

This order is not followed in the cubic and trigonal systems, in which the two commonly occurring classes of lower symmetry are treated immediately following the holosymmetric class. This is done so that the book may be used with greater facility by the student who does not wish to go beyond the eleven most common crystal classes. These are further distinguished by an asterisk and by bearing the name of the associated common mineral.

Suggestions for further reading
de Jong, W. F., *General Crystallography*, W. H. Freeman & Company, San Francisco, 1959.
Phillips, F. C., *An Introduction to Crystallography*, Longmans Green & Co. Ltd., London, 3rd Edition, 1963.

CHAPTER 5

THE TETRAGONAL SYSTEM

The Bravais lattices of tetragonal crystals have mutually perpendicular edges. Two sets of edges are of the same length and the third is either longer or shorter than the other two. The lattice may thus be referred to three orthogonal axes, called a_1, a_2 and c such that $a_1 = a_2 \neq c$. The c axis is always held vertically and is always a rotation or inversion tetrad.

Class 4/mmm, Tetragonal holosymmetric, ditetragonal bipyramidal, zircon type

The symmetry elements of this class are a rotation tetrad (the principal axis) normal to a plane of symmetry, with two additional *sets* of planes that intersect along the principal axis. Each set of planes comprises two planes that are mutually perpendicular; one set is coincident with the a_1 and a_2 crystallographic axes, the other set bisects the angle between them. Fig. 63 illustrates these elements in block form and as a stereogram.

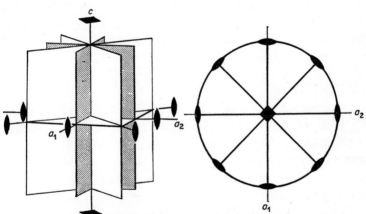

Fig. 63   The symmetry elements and crystallographic axes of class 4/mmm. There are two sets of vertical planes of symmetry; one set of planes is stippled. There are two sets of diad axes; one set is coincident with the crystallographic axes, the other bisects the angle between them.

Crystal faces can develop parallel to the planes of atoms in the crystal lattice and these are disposed in space in accordance with the symmetry elements. Thus if the stereographic projection of a pole to one crystal face is given, the symmetry elements demand its repetition in congruent positions.

SPECIAL FORMS

{100} *Tetragonal prism*

The symmetry elements cause the face (100) to be repeated in three other positions to produce a four-faced open form arranged parallel to the principal or *c* axis. The name *prism* is given to a form that consists of three or more faces that meet in edges that are parallel. The form {100} is therefore a *tetragonal prism* and its constituent faces have the indices (100), (010), ($\bar{1}$00) and (0$\bar{1}$0).

{110} *Tetragonal prism*

Midway between (100) and (010) there is the face whose index is (110). The symmetry elements repeat this face so as to produce another *tetragonal prism* {110} that has the same shape as {100} but which is differently orientated with respect to the crystallographic axes. These two prisms are sometimes called the *first order prism* {110} and the *second order prism* {100}, but since they are accurately and precisely defined by the Miller indices, the names first and second order are superfluous.

{*hk*0} *Ditetragonal prisms*

Between (100) and (110) there is a series of faces with indices like (210), (310), (320) etc. All are alike in that their indices have the form (*hk*0) where *h* and *k* represent different small whole numbers. The symmetry elements cause repetition of the faces, but because the pole to the face (*hk*0) projects between and not directly on the vertical planes of symmetry, there are seven more faces occupying congruent positions. Thus an eight-faced prism is produced. The prism is not a regular octagonal prism; the angles between pairs of faces are alternately more obtuse and acute. This form is the *ditetragonal prism* {*hk*0}. Its relationship to the other prisms is shown in Fig. 64.

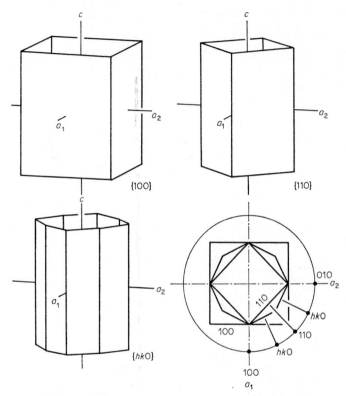

Fig. 64 Prism forms of class 4/*mmm* drawn in the solid and in stereographic projection.

{001} *Pinacoid*

A face at right angles to the prism faces plots at the centre of the stereogram and has the index (001). Since the principal axis is perpendicular to the face (001), the tetrad cannot repeat it. The horizontal plane of symmetry or the horizontal diad axes, however, repeat the face at the opposite end of the crystal. The resulting form is a pair of parallel faces to which the name *pinacoid* is given. This pinacoid has the index {001}.

The faces so far described lie either at the centre of the stereographic projection or on the primitive circle. Clearly, there are inclined faces lying in zone between the pinacoid and the various prisms and they may be grouped according to the prism with which they are in zone.

{h0l} Tetragonal bipyramids

The suite of faces in zone with (001) and (100) will have indices that may be written generally as (*h0l*). Actual indices of faces will be (101), (102), (203) etc. The principal tetrad axis repeats the given face (*h0l*) so as to produce a four-sided, square-based pyramid but the plane of symmetry normal to the principal axis causes the repetition of these four faces in the lower hemisphere and the form is thus an eight-faced closed form called the *tetragonal bipyramid {h0l}*. (Fig. 65A).

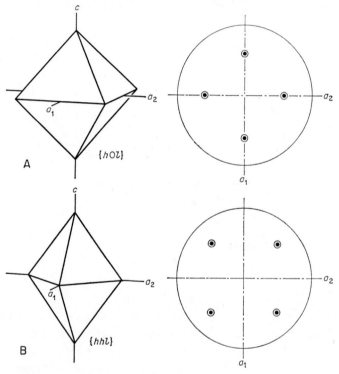

Fig. 65   The tetragonal bipyramids {*h0l*} and {*hhl*}.

In general the prefix '*bi-*' implies the repetition of faces by a *plane* of symmetry, whereas '*di-*' is used to denote the operation of an *axis* of symmetry.

{hhl}   Tetragonal bipyramids

Faces in zone with (001) and (110) will have the index (*hhl*). The effect of the symmetry elements on them is the same as for *{h0l}* and a similar eight-faced closed form, the tetragonal bipyramid *{hhl}*, is produced (Fig. 65B). Like the prisms with which they are in zone, these bipyramids have been described as second and first order respectively. They are accurately distinguished by their Miller indices and the names are superfluous.

Notice that all the forms so far described bear a special relationship to the elements of symmetry, in that they lie either parallel or normal to planes or axes of symmetry. Such forms are therefore called *special forms*.

GENERAL FORMS

{hkl}   Ditetragonal bipyramids

Faces that are in zone with (001) and (*hk*0) will have indices (*hkl*). The symmetry elements cause repetition of the face (*hkl*) to give a sixteen-faced closed form which is in zone with the ditetragonal prism and the pinacoid {001}. It is called the *ditetragonal bipyramid* {*hkl*}. It is clear from Fig. 66 that the faces of the form {*hkl*} bear a *general* and not a

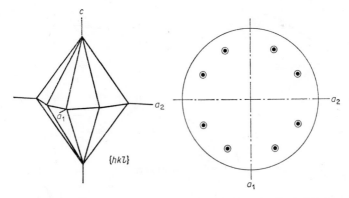

Fig. 66   The general form {*hkl*} of class 4/*mmm;* the ditetragonal bipyramid.

special relationship to the symmetry elements. Each of the thirty-two classes of symmetry has one such *general form* which may thus be used to identify it. It will be seen that special forms commonly occur in several symmetry classes of the same crystal system.

EXAMPLES

There are very many minerals that crystallize with tetragonal holosymmetric symmetry. Besides zircon $ZrSiO_4$, which gives its name to the class, there are the minerals anatase TiO_2, rutile TiO_2, apophyllite K, $Ca_4(Si_4O_{10})_2$ F. $8H_2O$, cassiterite SnO_2, and pyrolusite MnO_2. Some typical crystals are shown in Fig. 67.

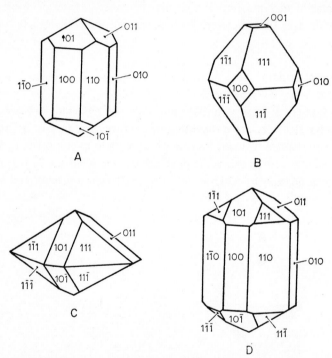

Fig. 67 Some crystals belonging to class 4/*mmm*. A. zircon; B. apophyllite; C. cassiterite; D. rutile.

Class 422, Tetragonal holoaxial, tetragonal trapezohedral

This symmetry class has a rotation tetrad axis with a set of two diad axes normal to it (Fig. 68). The face A (Fig. 68) is repeated by the tetrad at B, C and D and the horizontal diads produce faces A′, B′, C′ and D′.

Inspection of the stereogram shows that a further pair of diad axes are immediately introduced such that they bisect the angle between the first set. The International Symmetry Symbol is 422 but since 42 is sufficient to describe fully the symmetry, the second 2 is often omitted or is sometimes bracketed as 42(2).

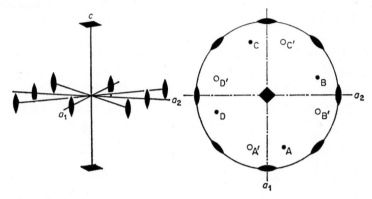

Fig. 68   Symmetry elements, crystallographic axes and projection of the general form of class 422.

The symmetry of this class could be expressed in less formal terms as a vertical tetrad, four horizontal diads, no planes and no centre. Less formally still, it could be described as the holosymmetric class minus the planes and centre of symmetry.

SPECIAL FORMS

$\left.\begin{array}{l}\{100\} \\ \{110\}\end{array}\right\}$ *Tetragonal prisms*

$\{hk0\}$ *Ditetragonal prisms*

$\{001\}$ *Pinacoid*

$\left.\begin{array}{l}\{h0l\} \\ \{hhl\}\end{array}\right\}$ *Tetragonal bipyramids*

These forms are the same as the special forms of the holosymmetric class. The lattice planes parallel to which these special forms develop are independent of planes of symmetry and hence the same special forms are present in both classes. It is therefore possible to have crystals that are morphologically identical and yet structurally distinct. The structural differences may be revealed by a study of etch-marks or by X-ray investigation.

GENERAL FORMS

{hkl} Tetragonal trapezohedra

Only in the general form does the holoaxial class differ morphologically from the holosymmetric class of the tetragonal system. A stereogram of the general form is given in Fig. 68. It is an eight-faced closed form with each face an irregular quadrilateral, or trapezium. The form is thus named the *tetragonal trapezohedron*. The form differs from the tetragonal bipyramids in that it has neither planes nor centre of symmetry. The form illustrated in Fig. 69A is the form *{hkl}*. It has a mirror image (Fig. 69B) with an index *{h̄kl}*. The term *enantiomorphism*[16] is used to describe

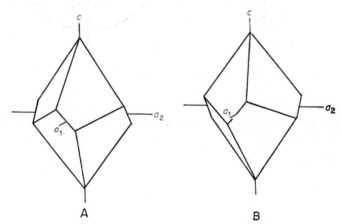

A   B

Fig. 69   Drawings of tetragonal trapezohedra *{hkl}* (A) and *{h̄kl}* (B), the general form of class 422.

16. Crystals of substances belonging to classes having rotation axes as their only symmetry elements can exhibit two distinct though related morphological styles which can never, by rotation, be made to occupy the same position in space just as a right hand cannot be superposed exactly on a left hand. The two morphological styles are developed because there are two distinct crystal lattices which cannot be superposed by rotation. These left- and right-handed crystals, as they are called, are mirror images of each other, and what is more important, the underlying lattices are in mirror image relationship as well. The term *enantiomorphism* is used to describe this feature which is shown only by crystals belonging to classes that have two equivalent lattices of opposite hand. These classes are: class 1 (triclinic); 2 (monoclinic); 222 (orthorhombic); 3, 32 (trigonal); 4, 422 (tetragonal); 6, 622 (hexagonal); 23 and 43 (cubic).

this feature. According to whether the {*hkl*} or {*h̄kl*} form is developed, the crystals have a right- or left-handed appearance.

A crystal belonging to this class can be distinguished morphologically from the holosymmetric only if the general form is developed. Unfortunately it rarely appears in natural crystals and most of the substances are placed in this class for structural reasons.

EXAMPLES

Phosgenite $PbCO_3.PbCl_2$ is the best known mineralogical example, but even so the student is unlikely to meet it practically. Some examples of crystals belonging to this class are illustrated in Fig. 70.

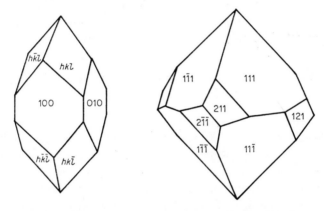

Fig. 70 Possible forms of crystals belonging to class 422. Forms present are (left) prism {100} and tetragonal trapezohedron {*hkl*}; (right) tetragonal bipyramid {111} and tetragonal trapezohedron {211}.

Class $\bar{4}2m$, Ditetragonal scalenohedral, ditetragonal bisphenoidal

In this class the principal axis is an inversion tetrad and the a_1 and a_2 axes are rotation diads. There is one pair of planes of symmetry intersecting in the principal axis and bisecting the angle between the a_1 and a_2 axes (Fig. 71). Crystals belonging to this class cannot be described fully in terms of elementary symmetry elements. Morphologically, the principal axis appears to be a diad, but the symmetry of the lattice and the arrangement of the faces are such that the symmetry is of a higher

order. There is no centre of symmetry, a fact readily appreciated from
the shape of the crystals.

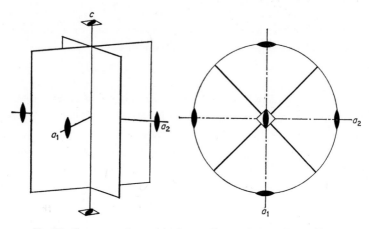

Fig. 71 Symmetry elements and crystallographic axes of class $\bar{4}2m$.

The symmetry symbol given in the *International Tables* is not always
the simplest combination of symmetry elements needed to account for
the morphological symmetry of a particular symmetry class. In this
class, for example, the symbol $\bar{4}m$ contains all the elements needed to
account for the morphology, although it introduces also a set of horizontal diads. The figure 2 is introduced into the symbol for structural
reasons that are explained in the section comparing the symmetry of
tetragonal, hexagonal and trigonal systems on p. 250.

SPECIAL FORMS

$\left.\begin{array}{l} \{100\} \\ \{110\} \end{array}\right\}$ *Tetragonal prisms*

An inversion tetrad axis causes a face (100) or (110) to be repeated so
as to produce a prism.

{*hk*0} *Ditetragonal prisms*
The planes of symmetry cause the face (*hk*0) to be repeated so as to
produce the eight-faced ditetragonal prism.

{001} *Pinacoid*

The inversion axis or horizontal diads repeat (001) in the lower hemisphere to produce a pinacoid.

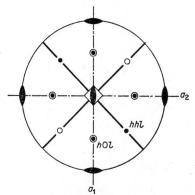

Fig. 72 Stereographic projection of forms {*h0l*} and {*hhl*} in class $\bar{4}2m$.

{h0l} *Tetragonal bipyramids*

The effects of the symmetry elements on the inclined faces should be carefully studied (see Fig. 72). The face (*h0l*), being in zone with (100) and (001) is specially related to the a_1 axis and the symmetry elements cause its repetition to form a tetragonal bipyramid. Notice that all the forms so far described occur also in the classes of higher symmetry.

{hhl}, {h̄hl} *Tetragonal sphenoids*

The pole to the face (*hhl*) projects on a vertical plane of symmetry. The operation of the inversion tetrad produces a four-faced, double wedge-shaped form called the *tetragonal sphenoid* whose faces are isosceles triangles. The four triangular faces of this form meet at the top and bottom of the crystal in two shorter edges that are set mutually at right angles (Fig. 59). The crystallographic axes emerge from the centres of the long edges of the form which may be regarded as being derived from a tetragonal bipyramid by developing alternate faces. The sphenoid therefore has half the number of faces of the bipyramid; this feature was termed *hemihedrism* by early crystallographers. The sphenoid {*hhl*} has a corresponding form {*h̄hl*}.

GENERAL FORMS
{hkl}, {h̄k̄l} *Ditetragonal scalenohedra, ditetragonal bisphenoids*

The face (*hkl*) is generally related to the symmetry elements and is repeated by them to give an eight-faced closed form consisting of four pairs of faces resulting from the reflection of the face (*hkl*) across the plane of symmetry. The form has half the number of faces of the

H

ditetragonal bipyramid and may be regarded as derived from it by developing alternate pairs of faces (Fig. 73). Alternatively it may be regarded as developed by raising two faces symmetrically on each face of the sphenoid.

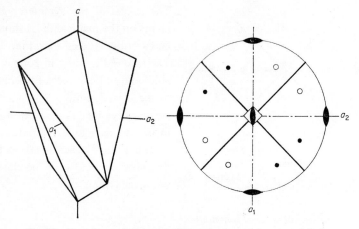

Fig. 73   Drawing and stereographic projection of the general form, the ditetragonal scalenohedron, of class $\bar{4}2m$.

Several names are applied to this form. The term *tetragonal bisphenoid* is perhaps the commonest and is in accordance with the use of the prefix *bi-* to denote a plane of symmetry. The form, however, is related to the ditetragonal bipyramid in the same way that the sphenoid is related to the tetragonal bipyramid. It is suggested therefore that this affinity can be shown by calling it the *ditetragonal bisphenoid*. The term *bisphenoid* is sometimes used for the form {*hhl*} in this class which is here called the sphenoid. The reason for this is so as to distinguish this form from the two-faced sphenoid of class 2 of the monoclinic system. The two forms are not related by the operation of a plane of symmetry as would be expected from the use of the prefix *bi-*.

There is another name, the *ditetragonal scalenohedron*, which is derived from the close relationship between the general form and the ditrigonal scalenohedron that is the general form of class $\bar{3}m$ of the trigonal system. The faces of each form are scalene triangles; the ditrigonal scalenohedron has three pairs of faces and the ditetragonal scalenohedron has two pairs.

The student may well ask 'which is correct?' There is, of course, no unequivocal answer. The choice of name is, in the ultimate, a matter of personal preference, other things being equal. The term ditetragonal scalenohedron emphasizes the close similarity between classes $\bar{4}2m$ and $\bar{3}m$ and for this reason it is here given rather more prominence than ditetragonal bisphenoid which is, however, a good alternative.

EXAMPLES

Chalcopyrite ($CuFeS_2$) and the melilites are the best known mineralogical examples of this class. Drawings of typical crystals are given in Fig. 74.

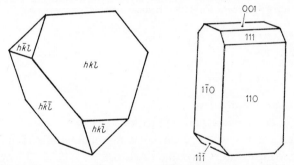

Fig. 74   Crystals belonging to class $\bar{4}2m$. Left: a crystal (chalcopyrite) comprising two sphenoids {*hkl*} and {*h̄kl*}; right: a sphenoid {111} in combination with a prism {110} and pinacoid {001}.

Class 4*mm*, Ditetragonal pyramidal

The symmetry elements of this class are a vertical rotation tetrad axis at the intersection of two sets of vertical planes of symmetry. One set contains the a_1 and a_2 axes and the other set bisects the angle between them (Fig. 75). There are neither horizontal diads nor a symmetry plane normal to the principal axis and therefore no elements that can cause repetition in the lower hemisphere of faces whose poles plot in the upper hemisphere. The upper and lower ends of crystals belonging to this class are dissimilar. The principal axis is thus *polar* or *uniterminal* in character and polar crystals are sometimes called *hemimorphic*.

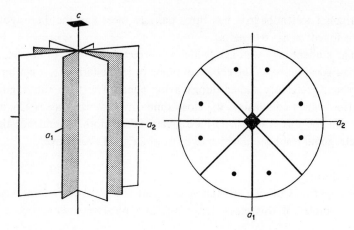

Fig. 75 The symmetry elements, crystallographic axes and stereogram of the general form (ditetragonal pyramid) of class 4*mm*.

SPECIAL FORMS

$\{100\}$ ⎫
$\{110\}$ ⎬ *Tetragonal prisms*

$\{hk0\}$ *Ditetragonal prisms*

The lack of horizontal symmetry elements has no effect on forms with a vertical zone axis which are therefore morphologically identical with those occurring in the holosymmetric class.

$\{001\}$, $\{00\bar{1}\}$ *Pedions*

The lack of horizontal symmetry elements precludes the repetition of (001) in the lower hemisphere and thus the form consists of a single face or *pedion*. The forms $\{001\}$ and $\{00\bar{1}\}$ are therefore independent; each can appear on a crystal independently of the other.

$\{h0l\}$, $\{h0\bar{l}\}$ ⎫
$\{hhl\}$, $\{hh\bar{l}\}$ ⎬ *Tetragonal pyramids*

These forms are four-faced open forms of pyramidal shape that, owing to the absence of horizontal symmetry elements, can be regarded as the upper half of a bipyramid. The forms $\{h0l\}$ and $\{hhl\}$ are independent of $\{h0\bar{l}\}$ and $\{hh\bar{l}\}$.

GENERAL FORMS

{hkl}, {hkĪ}   Ditetragonal pyramids

Comparison with the holosymmetric class shows that the hemimorphic form of the ditetragonal bipyramid is the eight-faced open form,

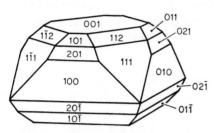

the ditetragonal pyramid. The general form, however, is rarely if ever present in natural crystals and they are therefore indistinguishable, morphologically, from those belonging to class 4.

Fig. 76   A crystal of diaboleite; class **4mm**. Forms present: prism {100}; tetragonal pyramids {111}, {112}, {101}, {201}, {10Ī}, {20Ī}; pedions {001} {00Ī}.

EXAMPLES

Diaboleite $2Pb(OH)_2.CuCl_2$ is placed in this class on the basis of its internal structure (Fig. 76).

Class 4/m, Tetragonal bipyramidal

This class has but two symmetry elements; a rotation tetrad which is always chosen as the *c* crystallographic axis, and a plane of symmetry normal to it (Fig. 77). There are neither vertical planes nor horizontal diads and therefore the ditetragonal forms are not developed.

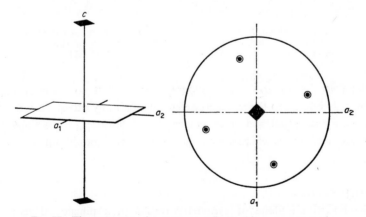

Fig. 77   The symmetry elements, crystallographic axes and stereogram of the general form (tetragonal bipyramid) of class 4/m.

SPECIAL FORMS

{100} ⎤
{110} ⎬ *Tetragonal prisms*
{hk0} ⎦

The rotation tetrad is the only symmetry element causing repetition of a vertical face. The resulting form is a tetragonal prism whatever its index. All such forms can be described by the general index {*hk*0}. The forms {100} and {110} are simply tetragonal prisms that are more specially

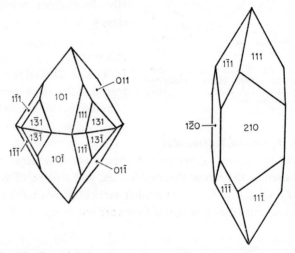

Fig. 78 Crystals belonging to class 4/*m*. Left: a crystal of scheelite of bipyramidal habit; right: a crystal of wulfenite, comprising the forms tetragonal prism {210} and tetragonal bipyramid {111}.

related to the horizontal crystallographic axes, but no prism is more generally related to the symmetry elements than any other. To attempt to distinguish {100} and {110} as second- or first-order prisms would be to erect differences where none exist and the terms should not therefore be used.

{001} *Pinacoid*
The horizontal plane of symmetry results in a pinacoidal pair of faces.

GENERAL FORMS

$\{h0l\}$
$\{hhl\}$ $\left.\right\}$ *Tetragonal bipyramids*
$\{hkl\}$

The ditetragonal bipyramid is not a possible form in this class owing to the absence of vertical planes or horizontal diads. As with the prisms, so with the bipyramids in zone with them, all are equally generally related to the symmetry elements. They can therefore be described by the general index $\{hkl\}$ although the forms $\{h0l\}$ and $\{hhl\}$ are more specially related to the horizontal crystallographic axes.

EXAMPLES

Scheelite $CaWO_4$, and wulfenite $PbMoO_4$, belong here, but both can crystallize as simple combinations of prism and bipyramid in zone and appear to be identical with crystals belonging to the holosymmetric class. The distinction therefore, would depend upon structural determinations or the study of etch-marks.

More complex crystals do occur and are illustrated in Fig. 78.

Class $\bar{4}$, Tetragonal sphenoidal

The only symmetry element in this class is an inversion tetrad axis and it is always chosen as the c crystallographic axis (Fig. 79). Crystals

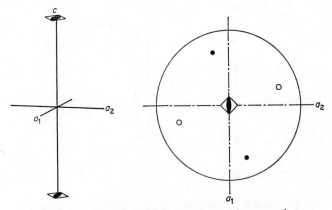

Fig. 79   The symmetry elements, crystallographic axes and stereogram of the general form (tetragonal sphenoid) of class $\bar{4}$.

belonging to this class possess neither planes nor a centre of symmetry and although superficially the principal axis might appear to be a diad, the symmetry is in fact tetragonal.

SPECIAL FORMS

{100}
{110} }Tetragonal prisms
{hk0}

As in class 4/m above, the absence of vertical planes of symmetry means that all forms parallel to the [001] zone axis are tetragonal prisms, and all can be described by the general index {hk0}. The forms {100} and {110} are forms that are more specially related to the crystallographic axes.

{001} *Pinacoid*

GENERAL FORMS

{h0l}
{hhl} }Tetragonal sphenoids
{hkl}

These closed forms, on their own, are similar in shape to those with the index {hhl} that occur in class $\bar{4}2m$. They are quite different structurally,

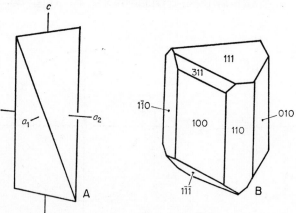

Fig. 80 Class $\bar{4}$; A. the sphenoid {hkl}; B. a possible habit of a crystal of cahnite. Forms present: tetragonal prisms {100} and {110}; tetragonal sphenoids {111} and {311}.

however, in that they possess no planes of symmetry (Fig. 80). Etch-marks and X-ray studies would emphasize this difference and combinations of two or more sphenoids show morphologically the lack of planes of symmetry. In this class any possible sphenoid is a general form and can be described by the index $\{hkl\}$. The sphenoids $\{h0l\}$ and $\{hhl\}$ are specially related to the crystallographic axes.

EXAMPLES
Cahnite $Ca_4B_2As_2O_{12}.4H_2O$, although rare, is the best mineralogical example (Fig. 80B).

Class 4, Tetragonal pyramidal
The only symmetry element in this class is a rotation tetrad, again chosen as the c crystallographic axis (Fig. 81). The shapes of the crystals

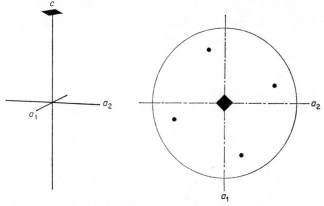

Fig. 81   The symmetry elements, crystallographic axes and stereo-gram of the general form (tetragonal pyramid) of class 4.

are therefore correspondingly simple and, since there is no element of symmetry present to cause repetition of upper hemisphere faces in the lower hemisphere, the crystals are hemimorphic.

SPECIAL FORMS
$\{100\}$ ⎫
$\{110\}$ ⎬ *Tetragonal prisms*
$\{hk0\}$ ⎭

The lack of vertical planes of symmetry makes all prisms of equal standing and the index {*hk*0} may be used to describe them all. The forms {100} and {110} are, however, more specially related to the crystallographic axes.

{001}, {00$\bar{1}$} *Pedions*

GENERAL FORMS

{*h*0*l*}, {*h*0$\bar{l}$} ⎫
{*hhl*}, {*hh$\bar{l}$*} ⎬ *Tetragonal pyramids*
{*hkl*}, {*hk$\bar{l}$*} ⎭

The rotation tetrad axis causes the face (*hkl*) to be repeated so as to produce a four-faced open form, the tetragonal pyramid. The index {*hkl*} may again be used to cover the more special forms {*h*0*l*} and {*hhl*}. These tetragonal pyramids are similar in shape to those occurring in class 4*mm* which also has polar symmetry, but they differ from them structurally in that they lack planes of symmetry. Notice also that the forms {*hk$\bar{l}$*} can occur independently of the forms {*hkl*}.

Simple crystals in this class appear to possess the higher symmetry appropriate to class 4*mm*. To be certain that they do, in fact, belong to class 4 it would be necessary to determine their structure, either directly by X-ray methods, or indirectly by using etch figures.

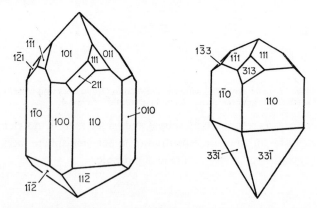

Fig. 82 Possible crystals belonging to class 4. Forms present: left, tetragonal prisms {100}, {110}; tetragonal pyramids {101}, {111}, {211}, {11$\bar{2}$}; right, tetragonal prism {110}; tetragonal pyramids {111}, {313}, {33$\bar{1}$}.

EXAMPLES

This class is without a mineralogical example. Some possible crystals are illustrated in Fig. 82.

Stereographic projection of a tetragonal crystal, using a Wulff net

The preparation of a stereographic projection of a tetragonal crystal should commence with the selection of the correct holding position. The crystal is held in the reading position with the tetrad axis vertical as in Fig. 83. It can, of course, be plotted in any other position but then the poles of the completed stereogram would later have to be moved so as to make the tetrad axis vertical.

Start the projection with the vertical faces which will plot on the primitive circle. First make a careful sketch of the crystal and number or letter the faces; then, with a contact goniometer, measure and record the interfacial angles between the vertical faces. Mark on the tracing paper placed over the Wulff net a point on the primitive circle to represent face 1 (Fig. 83). The faces 2, 3, etc., are plotted by counting round the

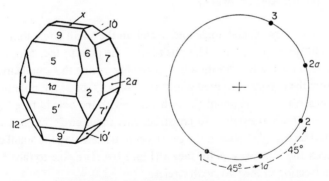

Fig. 83 A tetragonal crystal in the reading position. Right: the commencement of a stereographic projection. The position of face 1 on the primitive circle has been randomly selected.

primitive the measured interfacial angles and marking the positions of the poles with small dots.

Next plot the inclined faces. They are best plotted empirically, without making any symmetry assumptions, by using the small circle method. If, for example, the crystal were rotated about the pole to face 1, the pole to face 5 would describe a small circle about it as shown in Fig. 84A. This small circle can be sketched in on the stereographic projection as follows. Measure the interfacial angle between faces 1 and 5, taking care to get a flat bed of the contact goniometer on both faces. Now rotate the tracing paper over the Wulff net so that the pole to face 1 lies over the point of origin of the small circles and count along the primitive circle

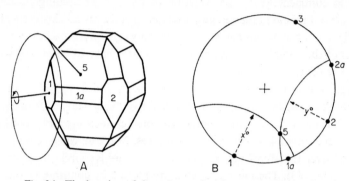

Fig. 84   The location of the pole to a face in stereographic projection by small circle plotting.

the measured interfacial angle and sketch in the small circle that meets the primitive at this point. The position of the pole to face 5 when the crystal is in the reading position lies somewhere along this small circle.

If now the crystal is rotated about the pole to face 2, the pole to face 5 will describe another small circle this time with the pole to face 2 as its centre and the next step is to construct this small circle by measuring the interfacial angle between the two faces and sketching the small circle in exactly the same way as for face 1 (Fig. 84B). The pole to face 5 is at the intersection of the two small circles.

The remainder of the inclined faces can be plotted in this way, by measuring the interfacial angles between them and two faces whose poles plot on the primitive circle and constructing the appropriate small circles.

If the inclined faces are small and separated from the prism faces by another form, the interfacial angle may be difficult to measure with a contact goniometer. It is then possible to construct a small circle about two adjacent inclined faces, but there are no guide lines on the Wulff net that can be followed and the small circles have to be constructed using the method described in Chapter 12.

Although the small circle method can be used with the optical goniometer, it is more usual when using this instrument to measure interfacial angles in as many zones as possible and to plot these by following great circles on the Wulff net. For example in Fig. 83 it is quickly checked that face x lies at 90° to the prism faces. The zones including faces 1a, 5, 9, x . . . and 2a, 7, 10, x . . . must lie along the diameters of the stereographic projection that have an origin in faces 1a and 2a respectively.

The student does not normally have access to the optical goniometer and it should be stressed that a projection of any crystal can be made by using only the small circle method. The method is of great value because, after choosing an initial orientation, no assumptions of symmetry or zonal relationships are necessary; the projection can be completed by plotting interfacial angles as small circles. It is not essential to have a Wulff net either. Small circles can be constructed about the pole to any face whether it is at the centre of the projection, on the primitive or between the two. Full details are given in Chapter 12 and the student should practise and be familiar with the construction of accurate projections by this means.

Zonal relationships

The completed stereographic projection is shown in Fig. 85A. The next step in its analysis is to determine which faces are in zone, or *tautozonal*. Tautozonal faces meet in edges that are parallel. The poles to such faces lie in a plane that is always a diameter of the sphere and hence they project always along great circles. The technique for locating these great circles is to rotate the projection so as to bring a pole on the primitive to the point of origin of the great circles on the Wulff net. Sketch in all the great circles along which the plotted poles lie and then rotate the projection until the next pole on the primitive lies at the origin of the great circles. Repeat the procedure until all such zones have been drawn (Fig. 85B). If the projection has been made without the aid of a Wulff net, the great circles will have to be constructed using the methods described in Chapter 12.

Determination of symmetry

After all the zones have been drawn the symmetry of the crystal is usually more apparent than from the plotted poles themselves. It is clear from Fig. 85B that the crystal has tetragonal symmetry because

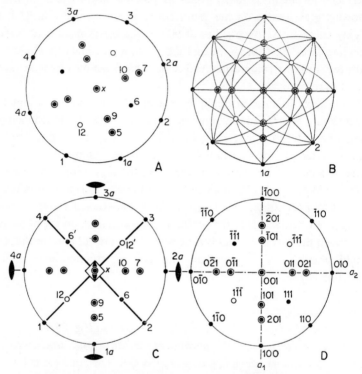

Fig. 85 Stereographic projections of the crystal shown in Fig. 83.
A. The completed projection drawn with the same orientation as Fig. 83 and 84B.
B. The completed projection with zones inserted and re-orientated so as to bring it into a conventional reading position.
C. The completed projection with symmetry elements inserted.
D. The projection with Miller indices and crystallographic axes shown.

of the distribution of vertical zones of faces at angles of 45° to each other. The symmetry elements may now be inserted.

A plane of symmetry passes through faces 2, 6, x, etc. and another plane of symmetry at right angles to the first also passes through x, because each of these planes divides the stereogram into two mirror image halves. Symmetry planes do not coincide with the zones that contain faces 1*a*, 5, 9, *x* or 2*a*, 7, 10, *x*, because face 6 is not repeated in the upper hemisphere in the appropriate position on the other side of the plane. The face in this position (face 12) lies in the *lower* hemisphere. The relative positions of faces 6 and 12 are consistent with a horizontal diad axis passing through pole 1*a*. Further inspection of the projection reveals another horizontal diad axis at right angles to the first. The fact that there is no pole that projects in the position of face 6 in the lower hemisphere means that the crystal has neither a horizontal plane of symmetry nor a diad axis passing through pole 2. Still concentrating on face 6, for it is most informative, notice that it has only one other counterpart in the upper hemisphere, the face 6′. The principal axis cannot therefore be a rotation tetrad axis. The presence of faces 12 and 12′, having the same angular relationships as 6 and 6′, but in the lower hemisphere, is consistent with an inversion tetrad as the principal axis. The International Symmetry Symbol may thus be written as $\bar{4}2m$. The forms present are two prisms (1*a*, 2*a*, . . . etc. and 1, 2, 3, 4), two bipyramids (5, 7, . . . etc. and 9, 10, etc.) a pinacoid (*x*) and a sphenoid (6, 6′, 12, 12′).

Selection of the parametral form

The next task is to select the parametral form and thus to determine the positions of the crystallographic axes. This seems to present unusual difficulty to some students, stemming largely from the conception that the choice of parametral form is entirely arbitrary and that any one face will do as well as any other.

In Chapter 3 it was seen that faces with high Miller indices grow forwards more rapidly than those of low index. In a three-dimensional object like a growing crystal, this means that the faces of high index will tend to be absent from a crystal or will be present as small faces, and that the faces of low index will be large. This is true in practice; newly formed, small crystals tend to show forms of high index but well-developed crystals are usually composed of forms with low indices.

The parametral form has always a simple relationship to all three crystallographic axes and it must therefore have a simple index. Inclined faces plotting very close either to the primitive or the centre of the projection will have high indices and may be ignored. In Fig. 85C, for example, a case could be argued for each of faces 6, 9 and 5, as the parametral form, although it is clearly a slender one in the case of face 5.

The choice of parametral form must be made only after a careful study of the stereogram showing all the zonal relationships of faces, the forms present and the symmetry. Account should also be taken of helpful physical features like cleavage. In Fig. 85 the form most generally related to all others is the tetragonal sphenoid (face 6) and this would accordingly be chosen as the parametral form. This form then is given the index {111} which thus determines the positions of the crystallographic axes as shown in Fig. 85D. The indices of the other faces may now be given either by zonal addition or by making use of the Weiss zone law. The fully indexed stereogram is shown in Fig. 85D.

Calculation of the axial ratio

Although there are very many tetragonal minerals, the actual cell dimensions are unique for a given mineral species because they depend on the type and shape of the atom or atom groups occupying the points of the space lattice and on the forces that bind them. We have seen that the actual cell dimensions can be measured and because, for a given crystal they are fixed and unique, it follows that the *ratio* between them must also be unique. Because the crystallographic axes are chosen parallel to the edges of the Bravais lattice it follows that the ratios of the lengths of the cell edges is the same as the axial ratio (see Chapter 3).

The angular disposition of the faces of a tetragonal (or any) crystal is a reflection of its atomic arrangement and hence may be used to determine the axial ratio of the crystal. For tetragonal crystals this is expressed as $\frac{a}{a}:\frac{a}{a}:\frac{c}{a}$, or simply as $1:1:\frac{c}{a}$.

Fig. 86A is the positive quadrant of the stereographic projection of the tetragonal crystal plotted in Fig. 85. The relationship between the *a* and *c* axes is most clearly seen if a projection is made of the plane that contains (001), (101) and (100) (Fig. 86B). This projection is part of the spherical projection of the crystal. The tangent to the sphere at point B is the trace of the face (101) and when produced it intercepts the *c* and a_1

axes at different but unit distances from their origin O. The ratio of these intercepts, marked c and a on Fig. 86B, and expressed relative to a as unity, is the axial ratio. The ratio may be determined graphically by

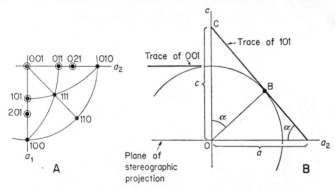

Fig. 86   Determination of the axial ratio of a tetragonal crystal.
A. Part of the stereogram of Fig. 85.
B. A vertical section through the spherical projection in the plane containing the a_2 and c crystallographic axes.

accurately constructing Fig. 86B from the measured interfacial angles and taking the ratio of the measured lengths a and c. Alternatively, the ratio may be determined using plane trigonometry.

It is clear from Fig. 86B that $\frac{c}{a} = \tan \alpha$. By similar triangles, $\widehat{COB}$ is also α and this is the interfacial angle between (001) and (101), which can be taken from the stereographic projection.

The importance of the selection of the parametral plane now becomes more apparent. In the example chosen, the face (101) is present on the crystal and is plotted directly on the stereogram, but its index is given only after the parametral form {111} has been chosen. If another face had been chosen as (111) then a possible position of (101) could be constructed by using great circles, but the axial ratio obtained therefrom would not agree with that determined by X-ray measurements, although there would, of course, be a simple relationship between them. Although, as a rule, it is obvious which face is the parametral form, the validity of the choice can be checked by comparing the chosen morphological axial ratio with that determined from the measured cell dimensions.

J

Graphical determination of the index of a face, given the axial ratio

If the axial ratio of a tetragonal crystal is known, the Miller index of any face may be determined graphically. Fig. 87A is part of a stereogram of a tetragonal crystal whose axial ratio is $1:1:0.537$, showing the pole to face x, whose index is required. First draw a line from O through x and

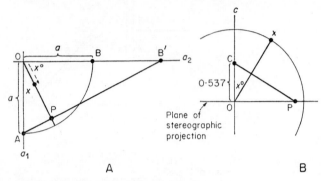

Fig. 87   Graphical determination of indices.

produce it to the primitive. Next construct a line perpendicular to Ox so that it meets the primitive at A. This line AB' is in effect the horizontal trace of face x. OA and OB are the unit lengths of the a axes. The line AB' intersects OB produced at B' and because OB' is 2OB, the face cuts the a_2 axis at twice the unit distance.

In order to determine the intercept on the c axis it is necessary to construct a section through the spherical projection in the plane OxP (Fig. 87B). First, the distance OP is transferred from Fig. 87A and marked as shown on Fig. 87B. The position of the pole to x is now marked by reading the angle Ox of Fig. 87A and marking this angle with a protractor on Fig. 87B. The slope of face x is now given by a line perpendicular to Ox through P. This line intersects the c axis at C, whence OC is the intercept of face x on the c axis. The distance OC relative to the unit length of a given by the radius of the sphere, is 0.537. The face x hence makes a unit intercept on c because the axial ratio is $1:1:0.537$. The ratio of the intercepts is thus $1:2:1$, from which the Miller index of the face is (212).

CHAPTER 6

THE ORTHORHOMBIC SYSTEM

The Bravais lattices of orthorhombic crystals have edges that are mutually perpendicular and of unequal length. Orthorhombic crystals are therefore referred to three orthogonal axes of unequal length, called a, b and c. By convention the c axis is held vertically and is the principal axis of the crystal. In all orthorhombic crystals the principal axis is a diad and in two of the three symmetry classes of the orthorhombic system the a and b axes are diads as well.

The simplest orthorhombic shape is that of a match-box, comprising three pairs of parallel faces meeting in edges at right angles. Diad axes of symmetry can be imagined as emerging from the centre of the three pairs of faces as in Fig. 88A.

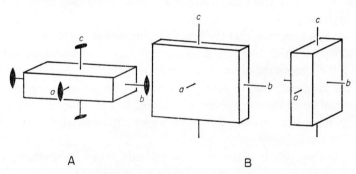

Fig. 88 A simple crystal of orthorhombic shape, showing three of the six possible orientations.

Choosing which of the axes are a, b and c is often a problem in orthorhombic crystals, because clearly the matchbox can be held in six different ways (Fig. 88B) without altering the relationship of the axes and, strictly, it doesn't really matter which is chosen as the principal axis; all are equally 'correct'. When the Bravais lattice dimensions of orthorhombic minerals are known, it is customary to orientate the lattice so that, in terms of edge length, $b > a > c$. It has long been the rule that an orthorhombic crystal is held so that its shortest axis is vertical (c) and the shorter of the two remaining axes runs from front to back and is hence the a axis. This, however, is simply convention and there are many exceptions to the general rule. Barytes is one of the commonest of orthorhombic minerals. The ratio of the length of the a cell dimension determined by X-ray methods is double the ratio of a deduced from the morphology and it is larger than b.

A nomenclature of the horizontal axes is in common use and is based on the general rule that the a axis is shorter than b. Accordingly, the a axis is sometimes called the *brachy* axis (Greek, *brachos*, short) and the b axis the *macro* axis (Greek, *macros*, long) and forms parallel to them have received the same prefixes. However, since a is not always shorter than b, the nomenclature can be misleading and it is not used here; the forms can be accurately and unambiguously identified by using Miller indices.

* **Class *mmm*, Orthorhombic holosymmetric, orthorhombic bipyramidal, barytes type**

We have already seen that the simple orthorhombic shape of a match-box possesses three diad axes of symmetry. Further examination shows that if the figure were cut in half in turn along the three planes containing the axes, each half so produced would be the mirror image of the other and hence the three planes containing the axes are planes of symmetry. Moreover, since each face has a counterpart parallel to it, there is a centre of symmetry also.

Expressing this in terms of the Hermann-Mauguin notation, the principal axis is always a diad and there is a plane of symmetry normal to this, therefore we can write $2/m$. In addition there is a plane of symmetry containing the principal axis and hence the symbol becomes $2/mm$. These symmetry elements are inserted on the stereogram in Fig. 89 together with the general form and it will be noticed that although the symbol $2/mm$ fully accounts for the observed symmetry it at once introduces more elements, viz. an additional vertical plane and two horizontal diads. The symbol could thus be written $2/mm(m)$ or, as some American authorities do, $2/m \ 2/m \ 2/m$. It is usual to use the International Symmetry Symbol *mmm* in referring to this class. Notice again that there are three possible orientations of a holosymmetric crystal, each fulfilling the symmetry. Some of the implications of this will be discussed as they arise.

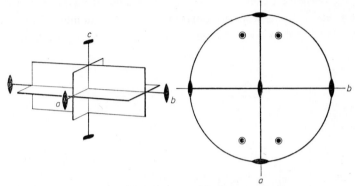

Fig. 89   Symmetry elements, crystallographic axes and stereogram of the general form (orthorhombic bipyramid) of class *mmm*.

SPECIAL FORMS

{100}
{010} $\Big\}$ *Pinacoids*
{001}

The symmetry elements cause the face (100) to be duplicated by another face lying parallel to it and, in keeping with the nomenclature already used in the tetragonal system, the name given to a parallel pair of faces is a *pinacoid*. The pinacoid {100} lies parallel to the *b* axis and has in consequence been called the macropinacoid but, for the reasons given above, identification by Miller index is to be preferred.

The faces with indices (001) and (010) are as similarly related to the symmetry elements as (100) and consequently they are also pinacoids. The names basal pinacoid {001} and brachy pinacoid {010} have been applied, but these terms are not used further.

{hk0} Orthorhombic prism

Because only axial planes of symmetry are present, every possible face lying in zone between (100) and (010) will be repeated so as to produce a four-faced open form parallel to the *c* axis. This form is a prism and its general Miller index is *{hk0}*. The prism {110} is simply more specially related to the horizontal crystallographic axes in that it makes a unit intercept on them. It is instructive to compare the prisms {110} in the tetragonal and orthorhombic systems. Both forms make unit intercepts on the horizontal axes but, whereas the tetragonal prism has a square cross-section, that of the orthorhombic prism is a rhombus. This difference is shown also in the stereographic projection in Fig. 90. Notice also

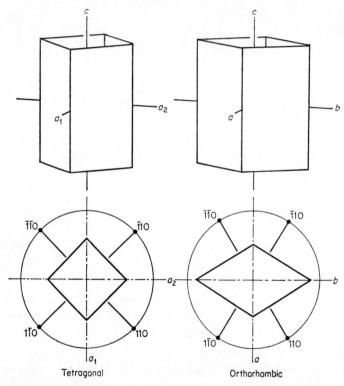

Fig. 90 Comparison of the prisms {110} in the tetragonal and orthorhombic systems.

that the interfacial angle between (110) and (1$\bar{1}$0) is in this instance less than 90° making $a < b$; remember that in some crystals it would be greater than 90° making $a > b$.

It is possible for there to be an orthorhombic prism with an interfacial angle of 90°, but its index cannot be {110}.

$\left.\begin{array}{l} \{h0l\} \\ \{0kl\} \end{array}\right\}$ *Orthorhombic prisms*

A series of faces whose general index is $\{h0l\}$ lie in zone with $\{001\}$ and $\{100\}$. Any one of these faces is repeated by the symmetry elements so as to produce a four-faced open form lying parallel to the *b* axis and whose zone axis is [010].

Similarly, between $\{001\}$ and $\{010\}$ there are faces with index $\{0kl\}$ that are repeated by the symmetry to produce a four-faced open form parallel to *a*.

These four-faced open forms have exactly the same relationship to the *a* and *b* axes that the prism $\{hk0\}$ has to the *c* axis and, for this reason, they are called *prisms* also. This is consistent with the interchangeability of the orientation of orthorhombic holosymmetric crystals; the orientation can change without changing the name of any of the forms. The forms $\{h0l\}$ and $\{0kl\}$ are sometimes called *domes*, and, in addition, the prefixes macro- and brachy- are used, according to the axis to which

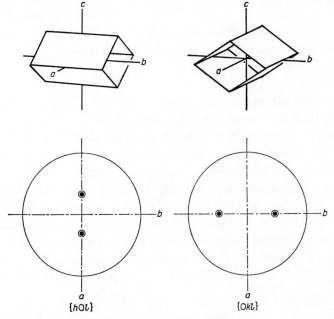

Fig. 91 The orthorhombic prisms $\{h0l\}$ and $\{0kl\}$.

they are parallel. The case against this has been presented already; there is no morphological difference between the forms; they are similarly related to the crystallographic axes and different names are not required (Fig. 91). Moreover, the term *dome* is used in its correct sense for forms in class *mm*. (q.v.).

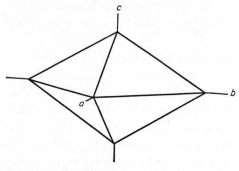

Fig. 92 The orthorhombic bipyramid {*hkl*}, the general form of class *mmm*.

GENERAL FORMS
{*hkl*} *Orthorhombic bipyramid*

Any face that is inclined to all three crystallographic axes is repeated by the symmetry elements so as to produce the eight-faced closed form shown in Fig. 92. The general index for this form is {*hkl*}; {111} is the parametral form that makes a unit intercept on all three axes. The form is called the *orthorhombic bipyramid* and gives its name to the class.

EXAMPLES

The crystals of many important minerals belong to this symmetry class, among them the olivines; the orthorhombic pyroxenes and amphiboles; the sulphates barytes $BaSO_4$, celestine $SrSO_4$, anglesite $PbSO_4$, anhydrite $CaSO_4$ and thenardite Na_2SO_4; the carbonates aragonite $CaCO_3$, strontianite $SrCO_3$, witherite $BaCO_3$ and cerussite $PbCO_3$. Other minerals include andalusite Al_2SiO_5, bournonite $PbCuSbS_3$, brookite TiO_2, carnallite $KMgCl_3.6H_2O$, cordierite $Al_3(Mg.Fe^{2+})_2Si_5AlO_{18}$, diaspore $AlO(OH)$, goethite $FeO(OH)$, lawsonite $CaAl_2(OH)_2Si_2O_7$. H_2O, marcasite FeS_2, monticellite $CaMgSiO_4$, mullite $Al_6Si_2O_{13}$, nitre KNO_3, sillimanite Al_2SiO_5, staurolite[17] $FeAl_4Si_2O_{10}(OH)_2$, stibnite Sb_2S_3, sulphur S, topaz $Al_2SiO_4(OH,F)_2$ and zoisite $Ca_2Al_3Si_3O_{12}(OH)$ (Fig. 93).

17. Staurolite is actually monoclinic, but angle β is very nearly 90°.

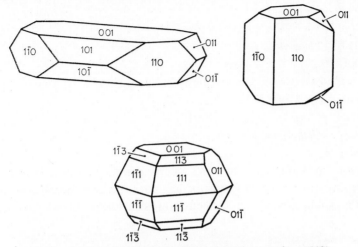

Fig. 93 Crystals of left; barytes (forms present are: prisms {110}, {101}, {011} pinacoid {001}); right; andalusite (forms present are: prisms {110} and {011}, pinacoid {001}) and below; sulphur (forms present are: prism {011} pinacoid {001}; orthorhombic bipyramids {111} and {113}). Class *mmm*. For other crystals, see Figs. 38 and 100.

Class 222 Orthorhombic holoaxial, orthorhombic sphenoidal

Planes of symmetry are absent in this class, the only symmetry elements are three mutually perpendicular rotation diad axes (Fig. 94). As with the holosymmetric class there are six possible orientations of any given crystal.

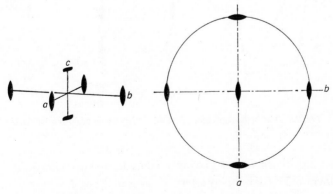

Fig. 94 Symmetry elements and crystallographic axes; class 222.

SPECIAL FORMS

{100} ⎫
{010} ⎬ *Pinacoids*
{001} ⎭

The diad axes cause the single faces (100), (010) and (001) to be repeated so as to give a pinacoid.

{hk0} ⎫
{h0l} ⎬ *Orthorhombic prisms*
{0kl} ⎭

These forms are similar to those occurring in the holosymmetric class; the absence of planes of symmetry does not affect them morphologically, although the symmetry of the underlying structure is somewhat reduced,

GENERAL FORMS

{hkl}, {h$\bar{k}$l} Orthorhombic sphenoids

The lower symmetry of this class is shown morphologically only by the general form. The symmetry elements and the general form are shown on the stereogram in Fig. 95. The general form is a four-faced, wedge-

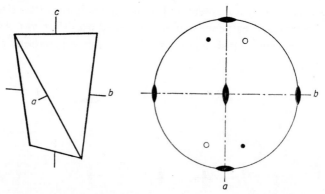

Fig. 95   The orthorhombic sphenoid {hkl}; the general form of class 222.

shaped closed form that can be regarded as derived from the orthorhombic bipyramid by developing alternate faces to the exclusion of others. It is similar in appearance to the tetragonal sphenoid and it is logically

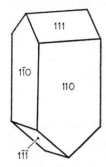

called the *orthorhombic sphenoid*. They can be told apart, however, for whereas the tetragonal sphenoid, when seen in plan, has upper and lower edges that cross at right angles, those of the orthorhombic sphenoid cross at an angle other than 90° (Fig. 95).

The sphenoids are *enantiomorphic*; the form $\{hkl\}$ has a related form $\{h\bar{k}l\}$ and crystals on which the general form is developed will be right- or left-handed.

Fig. 96 A crystal of epsomite; class 222. Forms present; prism $\{110\}$; orthorhombic sphenoid $\{111\}$.

EXAMPLES

Epsomite $MgSO_4.7H_2O$ is the best known example of a mineral crystallizing in this class (Fig. 96).

Class $mm2$ ($= 2m$) Orthorhombic pyramidal

This is the least symmetrical orthorhombic class. Only the principal axis is a diad axis of symmetry and thus there is only one possible orientation of the crystal; the diad axis is always chosen as the *c* axis. The diad axis is at the intersection of two perpendicular planes of symmetry and thus the symmetry may be written $2m(m)$. The symmetry elements $2m$, although fully accounting for this symmetry, introduce another plane, and the symbol given in the *International Tables* is $mm2$

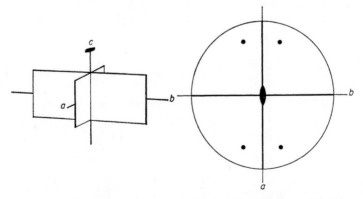

Fig. 97 Symmetry elements, crystallographic axes and stereogram of the general form (orthorhombic pyramid) of class $mm2$.

(Fig. 97). Since there is neither a horizontal plane nor axes, the principal axis is polar and the crystals are hemimorphic.

SPECIAL FORMS

{100}
{010} } *Pinacoids*

The faces (100) and (010), because they lie parallel to the planes and the axis of symmetry, are repeated so as to produce pinacoids.

{001}, {00$\bar{1}$} *Pedions*

The face (001) is in such a position that no symmetry element causes its repetition and it is therefore a pedion. {00$\bar{1}$} is another, independent pedion.

{hk0} *Orthorhombic prisms*

As in the two more symmetrical classes, this form is a four-faced open form parallel to the principal axis and is hence a prism.

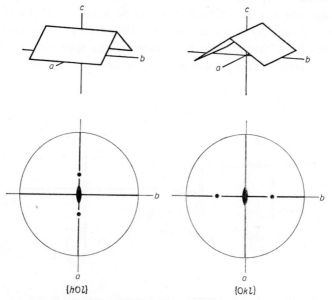

{h0l}   {0kl}

Fig. 98   The orthorhombic domes {h0l} and {0kl}.

$\{h0l\}, \{h0\bar{l}\}$
$\{0kl\}, \{0k\bar{l}\}$ $\Big\}$ *Domes*

From Fig. 98 it is clear that the symmetry elements repeat the face $(h0l)$ or $(0kl)$ once only, so as to produce a two-faced, roof-like form called a *dome*. The Greek word *doma*, a roof, is thus aptly used to describe the form. The forms $\{h0l\}$ and $\{0kl\}$ have corresponding forms $\{h0\bar{l}\}$ and $\{0k\bar{l}\}$ in the lower hemisphere.

GENERAL FORMS

$\{hkl\}, \{hk\bar{l}\}$ *Orthorhombic pyramids*

The absence of horizontal symmetry elements means that the face (hkl) is repeated to give a four-faced open form, the orthorhombic pyramid. There is the related, although independent form $\{hk\bar{l}\}$ in the lower hemisphere. Crystals belonging to this class therefore have different terminal development.

EXAMPLES

Mineral examples include childrenite $AlPO_4.Fe(OH)_2.H_2O$, enargite Cu_3AsS_4, hemimorphite $Zn_4Si_2O_7(OH)_2.H_2O$ (note the name), natrolite

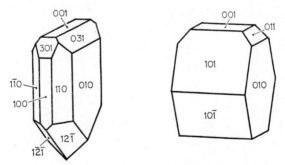

Fig. 99 Crystals of hemimorphite (forms present; prism {110}, pinacoids {100} and {010}; pedion {001}; domes {031} and {301}; orthorhombic pyramid {12$\bar{1}$}, and struvite (forms present; pinacoid {010}; pedions {001} and {00$\bar{1}$}; domes {011}, {101} and {10$\bar{1}$}. Class *mm2*.

$Na_2Al_2Si_3O_{10}.2H_2O$, prehnite $Ca_2Al_2Si_3O_{10}(OH)_2$, struvite $NH_4MgPO_4.6H_2O$, and thomsonite $NaCa_2[(Al,Si)_5O_{10}]_2.6H_2O$. (Fig. 99).

Stereographic projection of an orthorhombic crystal, using a Wulff net
The practical steps of plotting an orthorhombic crystal are precisely the
same as those involved in plotting the tetragonal crystal described above
and hence they are not repeated. The student is referred to pages 123–5.
One or two points are, however, worthy of further mention.

Except for class *mm2*, there are three possible orientations of an
orthorhombic crystal. It can therefore be plotted, the symmetry deduced
and the faces named and indexed, regardless of which orientation is
chosen. It is as well, however, when handling an unknown crystal to
follow the convention that, in general, the unit cell has $b > a > c$. In
addition, pay particular attention to any cleavages that may be present.
From the nature of crystal architecture we known that these will be
parallel to planes of low index. Pinacoidal cleavages intersect at right
angles, but prismatic cleavages intersect at obtuse angles and, if only one
prismatic cleavage is present, it is customary to make this the $\{hk0\}$
direction.

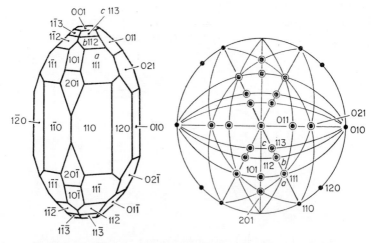

Fig. 100 **Drawing** and stereogram of a crystal of topaz; class *mmm*.

The choice of the parametral plane is again of importance, and is
often more difficult than in the tetragonal system. Generally, the
lattice planes that are spaced furthest apart and hence of lowest Miller
index, might be expected to form prominent crystal faces. In a crystal

like the topaz of Fig. 100, there may be several faces that could be taken as the parametral form; in this instance faces *a*, *b* or *c*. Face *a* is the largest and, as the stereogram shows, is in zone with more faces than either faces *b* or *c*. It may therefore be chosen as the form {111}. A strong case could be presented for choosing face *b* as the unit form. If however the axial ratio obtained on this basis is compared with that obtained from the cell dimensions it would be found to be in error by a factor of two. Before the determination of the cell dimensions, face *b* was invariably chosen as {111}.

Calculation of the axial ratios

The axial ratios of an orthorhombic crystal, in common with the other systems referable to three axes unequal in length, is: $\dfrac{a}{b} : \dfrac{b}{b} : \dfrac{c}{b}$.

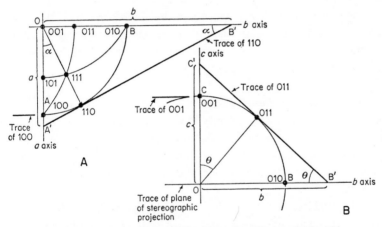

Fig. 101 Determination of the axial ratios of an orthorhombic crystal.
A. Part of a stereographic projection.
B. A vertical section of the spherical projection in the plane containing the *b* and *c* crystallographic axes.

Fig. 101A shows the positive quadrant of a stereographic projection of an orthorhombic crystal. To obtain the ratio *a/b* consider the face (110) which makes a unit intercept on the *a* and *b* axes. The trace of this face is drawn in as the tangent to the circle at (110) and it meets OA produced at A′ and OB produced at B′. The distances OA′ and OB′ are thus the unit lengths of the *a* and *b* axes and are shown as such in Fig. 101A. The ratio *a/b* is thus tan α and, from similar triangles, angle α is $\widehat{(100)\ (110)}$.

The axial ratios may be determined graphically by constructing accurately Fig. 101A and, taking the distance *b* (OB′) as unity, the distance *a* (OA′) is the relative length of the *a* axis.

The ratio *c/b* is obtained by considering (011) because this makes a unit intercept on the *b* and *c* axes. Fig. 101B is part of a spherical projection in the plane containing the *b* and *c* axes. The spherical projection of the pole to (011) is inserted and in this projection it plots on the primitive. The trace of (011) is inserted as the tangent to the circle at (011) and the axial ratio may be determined graphically by taking the intercept on *b* as unity and expressing the intercept on *c* as a proportion of this.

Trigonometrically, *c/b* is tan θ and, by similar triangles, this is tan $\widehat{(001)\ (011)}$. If faces (110) and (011) are not actually present on the crystal, their position may be constructed using zonal methods so that the axial ratios can be calculated.

Graphical determination of indices

Orthorhombic crystals frequently have many inclined faces and it may prove tedious to determine their Miller indices by constructing zones and using the zone symbol calculation. Their indices may, however, be determined graphically provided the axial ratios of the crystal are known.

In Fig. 102 let *p* be the stereographic projection of the face whose index (*hkl*) is required and let the axial ratios be 0·467 : 1 : 0·586 (forsterite). Draw a line from the centre of the projection through *p* and then construct the normal to this line such that it has an origin at the pole to (010). The line AQB is the trace of the face *p* on the horizontal plane of the projection. The distance *b* is taken as unity and the distance *a* will be a whole number multiple of the axial ratio of the *a* axis i.e. 0·467. In this instance it is 0·47, the unit intercept, and the index of the face is (*hhl*).

To determine the third integer, let Fig. 102B be part of the spherical projection in the plane containing the c axis and the face p. The position of the pole to face p is shown. From Fig. 102A it is clear that the *plane p* makes an intercept OQ on the horizontal line OQp. The distance OQ is then transferred to Fig. 102B which is, of course, drawn to the same

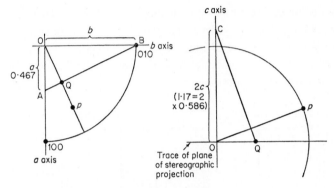

Fig. 102   Graphical determination of indices.

scale. Draw in Op, the normal to face p. The trace of face p is now given by the line normal to Op passing through Q. This makes the intercept OC on the c axis. This intercept is $1 \cdot 17$, that is, twice the unit intercept of $0 \cdot 586$ and thus the index of face c is (221). A similar procedure can be adopted for other faces and the same method can be used to determine the position on a stereographic projection of a face of given Miller index provided the axial ratios are known.

CHAPTER 7

THE MONOCLINIC SYSTEM

Many, but by no means all, monoclinic crystals have a distinctive 'out of square' look. This is a reflection of the fact that their Bravais lattices, besides having three sets of edges of unequal length, have two sets of edges which are not at right angles to one another; the third is, however, perpendicular to the plane containing the other two (Fig. 103). They can

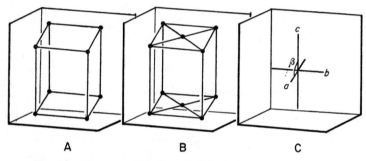

Fig. 103 The monoclinic P and C lattices (A and B) and the crystallographic axes (C).

thus be referred to three unequal crystallographic axes but, unlike the situation in the orthorhombic system, there are only two ways of orientating a monoclinic crystal if its Bravais lattice is known.

All monoclinic crystals possess a single diad symmetry axis and this is always chosen in morphological studies as the *b* crystallographic axis. A convincing case can be presented for making the *c* axis the principal axis, in common with the other crystal systems but the practice of making *b* the principal axis is so firmly established that there is no point in changing it. The *International Tables for X-ray Crystallography* mention both settings and, whilst recommending that the *b* setting be used for most morphological work, they recognize the value of the *c* setting in certain special circumstances. In this account, therefore, the principal axis is the *b* axis. Having identified the *b* axis, either of the other two axes may be chosen as the *c* axis which is, as usual, held vertically. The *a* axis is inclined to the plane containing the *b* and *c* axes. Apart from conventions as to relative length, the *a* and *c* axes are interchangeable; both are perpendicular to *b*. The axial cross is shown in the reading position in Fig. 103. Notice that it is the convention that the *a* axis slopes downwards and towards the observer and that in consequence the angle between the positive end of the *a* axis and the positive end of the *c* axis is an obtuse angle. This angle, angle β, is so called because it is normal to the *b* axis.

It is the practice of all modern crystallographers to quote angle β as an obtuse angle, but the student should be aware that in older works the acute angle between *c* and $\bar{a}$ was more often than not the one that was quoted, based presumably, on the conception that acute angles were more easily understood than obtuse ones. Thus whereas here angle β for orthoclase is given as 116°, in some texts it is quoted as 64°.

The name monoclinic is thus logically derived; however the axes are chosen one of them must be inclined. It is sometimes the custom to refer to the axes by name, the *a* axis being called the *clino* axis and the *b* axis the *ortho* axis. It is doubtful whether such names are necessary but in contrast to the names applied to orthorhombic axes, they at least have the virtue of being specific to the axis they describe; there is no possibility of muddling them. The longest axis may, in individual cases, be *a*, *b* or *c*.

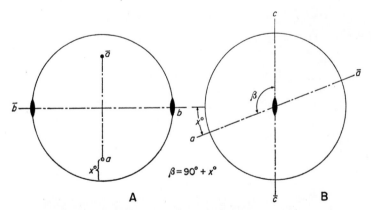

Fig. 104 Stereographic projections of monoclinic crystallographic axes.
A. With the *c* axis at the centre of the projection.
B. With the *b* axis at the centre of the projection.

In the tetragonal and orthorhombic systems the principal axis, the c axis, is always plotted at the centre of the stereographic projection. In monoclinic crystals, however, it is the b crystallographic axis that is the principal axis and consequently there are two ways of representing monoclinic crystals stereographically. Either the c axis is made the centre of the projection as in Fig. 104A or the b axis, as the principal axis, is made to occupy this position (Fig. 104B). Both projections have their merits and the student should know them both. The monoclinic symmetry is perhaps more easily seen in projection B of Fig. 104 because angle β is directly visible, but on the other hand projection A affords the closer comparison with stereographic projections of crystals belonging to other systems. In this projection, angle β is obtained by adding to 90° the angle $x°$, because the positive end of a projects as though it was a pole in the lower hemisphere. The plotting of stereographic projections of monoclinic crystals is described at the end of the chapter.

Quite a few monoclinic crystals exhibit *pseudosymmetry*, in that it requires the closest examination, often with X-rays, to be certain that they are not orthorhombic or even tetragonal. The angle β may be only a few minutes of arc from 90° and the lengths of the a and b cell dimensions may be so close that the crystals appear tetragonal. Some of the minerals belonging to the zeolite group are notorious in this respect.

* **Class 2/m, Monoclinic holosymmetric, monoclinic prismatic, gypsum type**
The simplest kind of monoclinic crystal is shown in Fig. 105 and looks

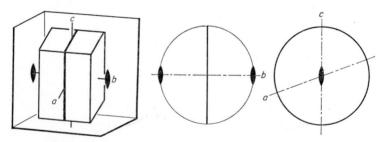

Fig. 105   Symmetry elements and crystallographic axes, class 2/m.

rather like a distorted matchbox held upright. An examination shows that it has but two symmetry elements, a rotation diad axis and a plane of symmetry normal to it. Its International Symmetry Symbol is thus $2/m$.

SPECIAL FORMS

{100} ⎫
{010} ⎬ *Pinacoids*
{001} ⎭

The symmetry elements cause the repetition of the faces (100), (010) and (001) so that in each instance one more parallel face results and the forms are pinacoids. Although the pinacoids can be distinguished by their Miller indices, the pinacoid {100} is sometimes called the *ortho-pinacoid* because it lies parallel to the ortho or *b* axis and the pinacoid {010} is sometimes called the *clinopinacoid*. By analogy with the

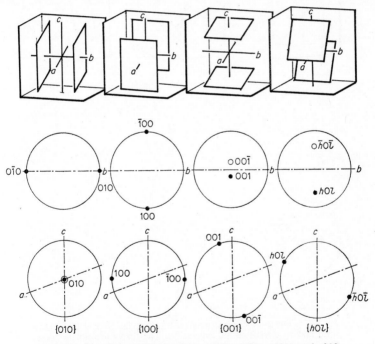

Fig. 106 The monoclinic pinacoids {010}, {100}, {001} and {h0l} drawn in the solid, and in stereographic projection with the *c* axis as the centre of the projection (middle row) and with the *b* axis at the centre of the projection (bottom row).

tetragonal and orthorhombic systems the pinacoid {001} is often termed the *basal* pinacoid. (Fig. 106).

{hk0} See below under general form.

{h0l}, {h̄0l} *Pinacoids*

The face (h0l), lying in zone with (001) and (100) is, like them, repeated by the symmetry elements so as to produce a parallel pair of faces, called a pinacoid. There is, however, a less exact nomenclature in use deriving from the alleged similarity of the forms {h0l} in the orthorhombic and monoclinic systems. Thus the monoclinic form {h0l} may be regarded as having only half the faces of the orthorhombic {h0l} form

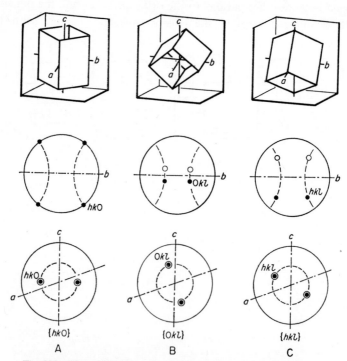

Fig. 107 The monoclinic prisms {hk0}, {0kl} and {hkl} drawn in the solid and in stereographic projection. The forms are not in zone; they represent the same prism in three orientations with respect to the crystallographic axes. The dashed lines are small circles followed by the poles to prism faces on rotation about the *b* axis. Zonal relationships between forms of simple index are shown in Fig. 108.

and is, in a sense, 'hemihedral.' The orthorhombic $\{h0l\}$ form is called a dome by some writers (unfortunately, for reasons given in Chapter 6) and thus the monoclinic form $\{h0l\}$, lying, as it does, parallel to the b or ortho-axis, becomes a *hemi-ortho-dome*. This nomenclature is rather cumbersome when compared with the term *pinacoid* $\{h0l\}$ which describes the form perfectly. This informal nomenclature reaches impossible lengths in the triclinic system with long, ugly, hyphenated names. There seems little to be gained by it and it is mentioned here merely to afford easy reference with other works on crystal morphology.

The form $\{\bar{h}0l\}$ is the counterpart of $\{h0l\}$ in the lower hemisphere. The two forms are sometimes distinguished informally by calling $\{h0l\}$ the *positive hemi-orthodome* and $\{\bar{h}0l\}$ the *negative hemi-orthodome*, but the Miller index serves quite simply and clearly as a means of distinction.

GENERAL FORMS

$\{hkl\}$, $\{\bar{h}kl\}$ *Prisms*

The face (hkl) is repeated by the symmetry elements to produce the four-faced open form shown in Fig. 107. The name previously applied to a four-faced open form is a *prism* and logically this is the term to describe this form. Two such prisms, although still generally related to the symmetry elements, are in special positions with respect to the crystallographic axes. These are the forms $\{0kl\}$ which is parallel to the a axis, and $\{hk0\}$, parallel to the c axis. All are equally prisms and the general index $\{hkl\}$ can be used to cover them all. There are complementary forms $\{\bar{h}kl\}$.

The informal nomenclature for these forms is most confusing. The form $\{hk0\}$ is correctly called a prism owing to its similarity with the orthorhombic form. The form $\{0kl\}$ is sometimes called a *clino-dome*. The form $\{hkl\}$ is, in the orthorhombic system, a bipyramid. Its 'hemihedral' monoclinic 'equivalent' thus becomes the *hemi-bipyramid* and most illustrations emphasize this relationship by drawing it as shown in Fig. 108. A careful comparison of Fig. 108 with Fig. 107B, however, will reveal that there is no difference between them. These *hemi-bipyramids* are further distinguished as positive- and negative- according to whether the index is $\{hkl\}$ or $\{\bar{h}kl\}$.

The general form is the monoclinic prism and the class is thus called the monoclinic prismatic class.

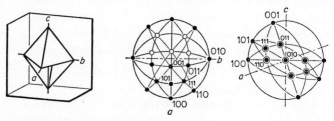

Fig. 108 Left: the monoclinic prism {*hkl*} drawn to emphasise its apparent 'hemibipyramid' form.
Right: stereograms to illustrate the zonal relationships of forms of simple Miller indices in class 2/*m*.

EXAMPLES

Very many minerals crystallize in this class, among them the monoclinic members of the pyroxene, amphibole and epidote groups; the potash feldspars orthoclase, sanidine and adularia ($KAlSi_3O_8$); the

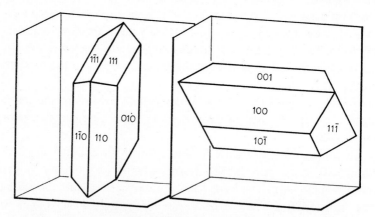

Fig. 109 Crystals of left: gypsum (forms present; prisms {110} and {111}, and pinacoid {010} and right: epidote (forms present; pinacoids {001}, {100} and {$\bar{1}$01}; prism {$\bar{1}$11}; class 2/*m*. For other crystals belonging to this class see Figs. 50 and 117.

micas muscovite and lepidolite and the chlorites. Other minerals include azurite $Cu_3(CO_3)_2(OH)_2$, borax $Na_2B_4O_5(OH)_4.8H_2O$, chondrodite

$Mg(OH.F)_2.2Mg_2SiO_4$, cryolite Na_3AlF_6, gypsum $CaSO_4.2H_2O$, harmotome $BaAl_2Si_6O_{16}.6H_2O$, heulandite $(Ca,Na_2)Al_2Si_7O_{18}6H_2O$, stil-
bite $(CaNa_2K_2)$ $Al_2Si_7O_{18}.7H_2O$, jamesonite $2PbS.Sb_2S_3$, malachite
$CuCO_3.Cu(OH)_2$, monazite $(Ce,LaY(PO_4))$, orpiment As_2S_3, realgar
AsS, sapphirine $(MgFe)_2Al_4O_6[SiO_4]$, talc $Mg_3Si_4O_{10}(OH)_2$ and
sphene $CaTiSiO_4(O,OH)$ (Fig. 109.)

Class m ($=\bar{2}$) Monoclinic domatic

In this class the only symmetry element is a plane of symmetry perpendicular to the principal or b axis. The symmetry may be expressed in
another way as an inversion diad axis, for it has already been demonstrated (p. 98) that the two are equivalent morphologically. The inversion diad is always chosen as the b axis. (Fig. 110).

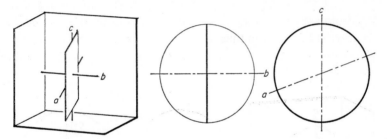

Fig. 110   The symmetry elements and crystallographic axes; class *m*.

SPECIAL FORMS
$\{100\}, \{\bar{1}00\}$ ⎫
$\{001\}, \{00\bar{1}\}$ ⎬ *Pedions*
$\{h0l\}, \{h0\bar{l}\}$ ⎭

These faces are all similarly related to the symmetry elements in that
they project on the plane of symmetry, although at different angular
distances to the crystallographic axes. In such a position the symmetry
element does not cause repetition of the face and the forms are pedions
(Fig. 111).

$\{010\}$ *Pinacoid*

The face (010) is repeated by the plane of symmetry so as to produce a
pinacoid.

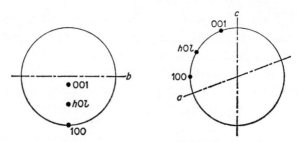

Fig. 111   The pedions {100}, {*h0l*} and {001}; class *m*.

GENERAL FORMS

{*hk0*}, {*h̄k0*} ⎫
{*0kl*}, {*0kl̄*} ⎬ *Domes*
{*hkl*}, {*hkl̄*} ⎭

These three forms are generally related to the symmetry elements and differ from each other only in their inclination to the crystallographic axes (Fig. 112). They can thus be described by the general index {*hkl*}, remembering that {*hk0*} and {*0kl*} are simply more specially related to the crystallographic axes.

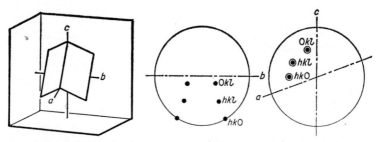

Fig. 112   Left: The monoclinic dome {*hkl*}.
Right: The domes {*hk0*}, {*0kl*} and {*hkl*} in stereographic projection. The forms are shown in the positions they would occupy if a form of constant interfacial angle were rotated about the *b* axis.

The single plane of symmetry causes the face (*hkl*) to be repeated once so as to form a roof-shaped form similar to that called a *dome* in the orthorhombic system. The term dome is thus logically applied to this form also. There is for each positive form a corresponding one with a negative index. If the nomenclature based on the orthorhombic form were used, then {*hk0*} becomes a hemi-prism, {*0kl*} a hemi-dome or

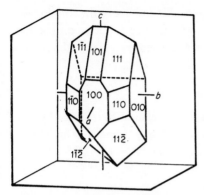

Fig. 113 A possible crystal belonging to class *m*. Forms present; domes {110}, {$\bar{1}$11} and {11$\bar{2}$}; pinacoid {010}; pedions {101}, {100}, {$\bar{1}$00} and {$\bar{1}$01}.

hemi-prism and {*hkl*} a hemi-bipyramid. Such terms are clearly unsatisfactory and should not be used.

EXAMPLES

Examples of minerals crystallizing in this class are not common but among them are clinohedrite $H_2CaZnSiO_5$, scolecite $CaAl_2Si_3O_{10}.3H_2O$ and some authorities include the micas biotite and phlogopite[18] (Fig. 113).

Class 2, Monoclinic sphenoidal

This class is characterized by a single rotation diad axis, always chosen as the *b* crystallographic axis. There are neither planes nor a centre of symmetry and thus the principal axis, *b*, is polar and the resulting crystals are hemimorphic. The symmetry elements are shown in Fig. 114.

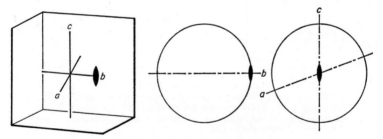

Fig. 114 Symmetry elements and crystallographic axes; class 2.

SPECIAL FORMS

{100} ⎫
{001} ⎬ *Pinacoids*
{*h0l*} ⎭

18. The commonly occurring polymorph of phlogopite and biotite belongs to class *m*; other polymorphs are known with symmetry 2/*m* and 32.

These faces all have [010] as their zone axis and hence the rotation diad axis causes a face to be repeated so as to give a pinacoid. The most general index is {*h0l*}; {100} and {001} are more specially related to the crystallographic axes.

{010}, {0$\bar{1}$0} *Pedions*
Since (010) projects on the symmetry axis it cannot be repeated by it and is thus a pedion. In class *m* the form {010} is a pinacoid and {*h0l*} a pedion.

GENERAL FORMS

{*hk*0}, {*h$\bar{k}$*0} ⎫
{0*kl*}, {0$\bar{k}$*l*} ⎬ *Sphenoids*
{*hkl*}, {*h$\bar{k}$l*} ⎭

From Fig. 115 it is seen that these forms consist of a pair of faces meeting in an edge and developed by rotation about an axis. Thus, although

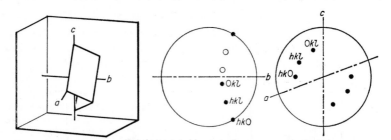

Fig. 115   Left: The monoclinic sphenoid {*hkl*};
Right: Stereographic projection of the monoclinic sphenoids {*hk*0}, {0*kl*} and {*hkl*}. The forms are not in zone, they are shown in the position they would occupy if a form of constant interfacial angle were rotated about the *b* axis.

it is morphologically similar, the form differs in its generation from the dome {*hkl*} of class *m* which is produced by reflection across a plane of symmetry. A distinctive name is therefore needed and the term *monoclinic sphenoid* is in fairly common use.

The name sphenoid has already been used to describe a wedge-shaped, four-faced closed form occurring in the tetragonal and orthorhombic systems and the general form of class 2 does not resemble either of them. Exception has been taken therefore to the use of the same name for dissimilar forms, although if care is taken to distinguish them by adding the prefixes tetragonal-, orthorhombic- or monoclinic-, little confusion should result. A solution adopted by some crystallographers is to use the term *sphenoid* for the two-faced monoclinic form and to call the tetragonal and orthorhombic forms *bisphenoids* because they have four faces. The prefix *bi-* is used in crystallography to denote reflection by a plane of symmetry and, whilst this is true of the form in class $\bar{4}2m$, there are no planes of symmetry in classes $\bar{4}$ and 222. If this departure from convention is accepted, then another name needs to be found for the general form of class $\bar{4}2m$, for this is very commonly called the tetragonal, or better, the ditetragonal bisphenoid. The difficulties may to some extent be overcome by using the name ditetragonal scalenohedron for this form.

Yet another scheme has been suggested in which the term *dihedron* is used to describe the monoclinic sphenoid, thus obviating the need to alter the names of other forms. The term *dihedron* as used by American crystallographers is a general one referring to two planes inclined to one another. It can, therefore, be applied equally to the form that we have called a dome. Whilst this is quite logical, it is felt that the distinction between dihedron (dome) and dihedron (sphenoid) is one that should be retained. Table 4 summarizes the systems of nomenclature.

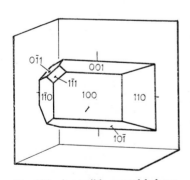

It should be emphasized that none of these systems is 'correct' in that the others are 'wrong'. Each has something to commend it. It is suggested that the term sphenoid be used for the general form of this class, provided it is clearly distinguished by referring to it always as the *monoclinic sphenoid*.

Fig. 116 A possible crystal belonging to class 2 (sucrose). Forms present; pinacoids {100}, {001}, {$\bar{1}$01}; sphenoids {0$\bar{1}$1}, {1$\bar{1}$0}, {1$\bar{1}$1} and {110}.

EXAMPLES

There are very few representatives of this class: afwillite $Ca_3Si_2O_7.3H_2O$, mesolite $Na_2Ca_2(Al_2Si_3O_{10})_3.8H_2O$

TABLE 4

ALTERNATIVE SCHEMES OF NOMENCLATURE FOR CLASSES CONTAINING SPHENOIDAL FORMS

System & Class	Monoclinic 2	Orthorhombic 222	Tetragonal $\bar{4}$	Tetragonal $\bar{4}2m$ {hhl}	Tetragonal $\bar{4}2m$ {hkl}
Nomenclature					
1.	Monoclinic sphenoid	Orthorhombic sphenoid	Tetragonal sphenoid	Tetragonal sphenoid	Ditetragonal bisphenoid†
2.	Monoclinic sphenoid	Orthorhombic bisphenoid*	Tetragonal bisphenoid*	Tetragonal bisphenoid	Ditetragonal scalenohedron†
3.	Monoclinic dihedron	Orthorhombic sphenoid	Tetragonal sphenoid	Tetragonal sphenoid	Ditetragonal bisphenoid†

*Prefix 'bi-' incorrectly used;
there are no planes of symmetry.
†The names ditetragonal bisphenoid and
ditetragonal scalenohedron are
unobjectionable alternatives.

and pickeringite $MgSO_4.Al_2(SO_4)_3. 22H_2O$ are best known, although pickeringite may belong to class $2/m$ (Fig. 116).

Stereographic projection of a monoclinic crystal using a Wulff net
In all monoclinic crystals the diad axis is chosen as the *b* crystallographic axis and the first step in plotting a crystal is to locate the symmetry axis and hold the crystal so that this axis runs horizontally and from left to right. Remember that monoclinic crystals may be elongated along the *a, b* or *c* axes.

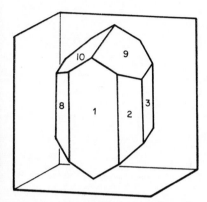

Having chosen the *c* axis and set it vertically, the *a* axis is held conventionally so that it slopes downwards and towards the observer and thus the augite crystal in Fig. 117 might be held as shown as a first approximation.

Fig. 117 A possible orientation of a crystal of augite prior to plotting a stereographic projection.

The interfacial angles between faces $\widehat{1\ 2}$, $\widehat{2\ 3}$ ... $\widehat{7\ 8}$ are measured and recorded (Table 5) and plotted on the stereogram. If the plane of the projection is normal to the *c* axis the poles to these faces will lie on

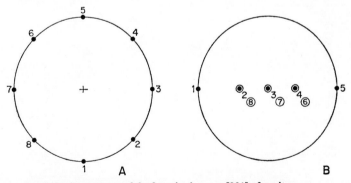

Fig. 118 Stereogram of the faces in the zone [001] of augite;
A. Plane of stereographic projection perpendicular to *c* axis;
B. Plane of stereographic projection perpendicular to *b* axis.

TABLE 5

CONTACT GONIOMETER READINGS OF INTERFACIAL ANGLES OF THE CRYSTAL SHOWN IN FIG. 117

face 1	face 5			
>46°	>46°			
2	6			
>44°	>44°			
3	7			
>44°	>44°			
4	8			
>46°	>46°			
5	1			
	─────			
	360°			

face $1 \wedge 9 = 76°$	face $1 \wedge 10 = 76°$	face $1 \wedge 11 = 103°$	face $1 \wedge 12 = 103°$
$2 \wedge 9 = 60°$	$8 \wedge 10 = 60°$	$2 \wedge 11 = 79°$	$8 \wedge 12 = 79°$
$3 \wedge 9 = 61°$	$7 \wedge 10 = 61°$	$3 \wedge 11 = 61°$	$7 \wedge 12 = 61°$

the primitive (Fig. 118A), but if the selected projection is that normal to the *b* axis, then the poles will lie on a great circle passing through the principal axis (Fig. 118B).

The inclined faces 9, 10, 11 and 12 are next plotted using the small circle method. The interfacial angles between faces $\widehat{1\ 9}, \widehat{2\ 9}, \widehat{3\ 9}$ etc. are measured and recorded (Table 5). Small circles of appropriate radii are constructed about the poles of vertical faces already plotted. This is quite straightforward for the projection normal to *c* and the small circles are shown in Fig. 119A. The pole to face 9 lies at the intersection of the small circles.

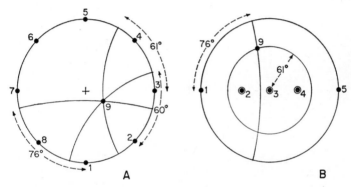

Fig. 119   Stereographic projection of face 9 (Fig. 117) by small circle plotting.
A. Plane of projection perpendicular to *c* axis;
B. Plane of projection perpendicular to *b* axis.

Because face 1 plots on the primitive circle of the projection perpendicular to *b*, the small circle that represents the path described by the pole to face 9 on rotation about the pole to face 1 can be constructed in the same way as that in Fig. 119A. If now the crystal were rotated about the normal to face 3, then the pole to face 9 would describe another small circle which projects as a circle of radius 61° and which is concentric with the primitive. No such small circle is marked on a Wulff net but it can be readily constructed by counting out 61° from the pole to face 3 along a diameter and drawing in the circle with compasses using the pole to face 3 as the centre of the circle. The position of face 9 is at the point of intersection of the two small circles that is in the upper left-hand quadrant. The intersection in the lower left-hand quadrant is ignored because there is no face in such a position on the crystal.

It is clear that a small circle about face 3 is concentric with the primitive because face 3 plots at the centre of the projection. The small circle described by the pole to face 9 on rotation about the pole to face 2 is not so readily constructed. It cannot be obtained by drawing with compasses a circle of appropriate radius about the pole to face 2. Details of the construction of such small circles are given in Chapter 12.

Thus, whilst the projection normal to *b* may be favoured in some

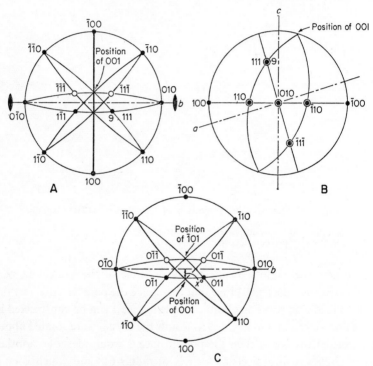

Fig. 120 Stereographic projections of augite in the orientation shown in Fig. 117.
A. Plane of projection perpendicular to *c* axis, symmetry elements inserted. Indices are consistent with face 9 as (111).
B. Plane of projection perpendicular to *b* axis; indices allocated as for A.
C. Plane of projection perpendicular to *c* axis; indices consistent with face 9 as (011). Angle $\beta = 90° + x°$.

instances, it may require more plotting skill than that with the c axis as
its centre.

The completed stereograms are given in Fig. 120, with zones and
symmetry elements inserted. The crystal belongs to class $2/m$.

Allocation of Miller Indices

Once the symmetry has been determined, Miller indices may tentatively
be assigned. The only form that can be a parametral form is the form
comprising faces 9, 10, 11 and 12. This can either be the general form
$\{hkl\}$ or $\{0kl\}$ according to whether or not the edge between faces 9 and
10 is taken to be parallel to the slope of the a axis.

Suppose as a first attempt, the index $\{111\}$ is given to this form; then
the resulting indexed stereograms will be those given in Fig. 120A and B.
Notice that the face indexed as (111) lies in zone with (110) and similarly face $(1\bar{1}1)$ lies in zone with $(1\bar{1}0)$ and that both zones intersect in
the plane of symmetry. From zonal considerations, the index of the face
at the intersection of these two zones is (001), but this is absurd, for it
plots *backward* of the c axis. The face (001), by definition, lies parallel to
the a axis, and it must therefore plot *forward* of c.

Suppose now that the form (9, 10, 11, 12) is given the index $\{011\}$
(Fig. 120C). A possible face at the intersection of the zones containing
this form and the prism faces (110) and $(1\bar{1}0)$ would have the index $(\bar{1}01)$
which is a suitable index for a face whose pole plots backward of the c
axis. The pole to a possible face (001) lies at the intersection of the plane
of symmetry and the zone containing (010) and (011). Angle β is
obtained by adding to $90°$ the angle $x°$ which is read directly from the
stereogram. Angle β, measured in this way, is $106°$ which is in good
agreement with the value obtained from structural studies. From the
morphological standpoint, therefore, this orientation is satisfactory.

Augite is an example of a mineral whose simplest morphological
orientation has to be modified in the light of structural information. A
study of the structure of augite, including its twinning and cleavages,
has shown that the usual form that terminates the crystals and which has
been called $\{011\}$ above, is, in fact, the form $\{\bar{1}11\}$. The stereogram has
therefore to be rotated through $180°$ about its c axis in order to bring it
into the corrected position shown in Fig. 121. In its new setting, the

possible face marked (Ī01) in Fig. 120C becomes (001) in Fig. 121A. If now angle β is measured, it is again found to be 106°. This apparently

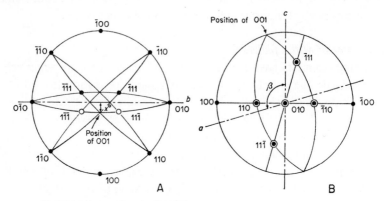

Fig. 121   Stereographic projections of augite in the correct orientation consistent with structural data.
A. Projection perpendicular to *c* axis; angle β = 90° + *x*°.
B. Projection perpendicular to *b* axis.

remarkable coincidence is due to the fact that the interfacial angles (011) (0Ī1) and (Ī11) (ĪĪ1) differ by only six minutes of arc. It is often impossible therefore to choose on morphological grounds between the two orientations, but occasionally a parting parallel to {001} enables a decision to be made.

The student should notice that the change of orientation of the crystal does not affect the names of the forms. The inclined general form is a prism whether its index is {Ī11} or {011}. This is not so if the informal nomenclature is used, for then {Ī11} is called the negative hemi-bipyramid and {011} the clinodome.

Calculation of crystallographic constants
Angle β can be obtained directly from the stereograms given in Fig. 121. In Fig. 121B it is very obviously the angle between the *a* and *c* axes, and in Fig. 121A it is 90° + *x*° = 106°.

The calculation of the axial ratios is a little more involved than previously owing to the inclination of the *a* axis. Fig. 122 is a spherical projection showing the disposition of the poles to common faces in the

monoclinic system. In the tetragonal and orthorhombic systems the unit
intercept on the *a* axis is given by the distance *x*, i.e. the distance be-

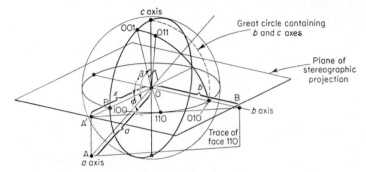

Fig. 122   The monoclinic crystallographic axes and poles to faces of
low Miller index shown in spherical projection.

tween the centre of the projection O and the point of intersection (A′) of
the tangent to (110) and OP produced. From Fig. 122 it is apparent that
in the monoclinic system the unit intercept on the *a* axis is given by *a*,
the distance OA, where A is the point of intersection of the *a* axis and
the plane (110). A simple relationship exists between *x* and *a* such that

$$\frac{x}{a} = \cos\phi, \text{ where } \phi = \beta - 90°$$

$$\therefore x = a.\cos(\beta - 90°) \tag{1}$$

Consider now the positive quadrant of the stereographic projection
plotted with *c* as its centre. (Fig. 123). In this right angled triangle

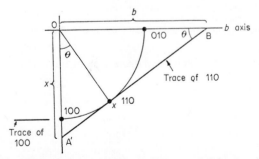

Fig. 123   Determination of axial ratios of a monoclinic crystal: part
of a stereographic projection on the plane perpendicular to the *c*
axis.

$$\frac{x}{b} = \tan \theta = \tan \widehat{OBA'}. \tag{2}$$

By similar triangles $\widehat{OBA'} = \widehat{XOA'} = \widehat{(100)}\ \widehat{(110)}$

Substituting now for x from (1) we have:

$$\frac{a.\cos(\beta - 90°)}{b} = \tan \widehat{(100)}\ \widehat{(110)} \tag{3}$$

$$\therefore \frac{a}{b} = \frac{\tan \widehat{(100)}\ \widehat{(110)}}{\cos(\beta - 90°)} \tag{4}$$

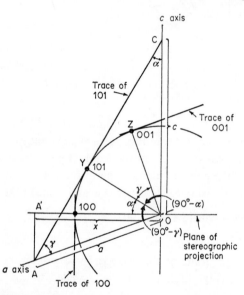

Fig. 124 Determination of axial ratios of a monoclinic crystal: a vertical section of the spherical projection in the plane containing the *a* and *c* crystallographic axes.

In the orthorhombic system because the pole to (011) lies on the great circle containing the *b* and *c* axes, its angular relationship to them can be used to determine the axial ratio. From Fig. 122 it is clear that no such relationship holds in the monoclinic system because the pole to (011) plots forward of the great circle containing *b* and *c*. In calculating *c/b*, it is first necessary to evaluate *c/a* and then determine *c/b* by cross multiplying with equation (4).

Fig. 124 is part of the spherical projection in the plane containing the *a* and *c* axes.

In triangle AOC, $\dfrac{a}{\sin \alpha} = \dfrac{c}{\sin \gamma}$

$$\therefore \frac{c}{a} = \frac{\sin \gamma}{\sin \alpha} \tag{5}$$

It is now necessary to express α and γ in terms of interfacial angles.

Since AYO is a right triangle, $\widehat{AOY} = 90 - \gamma°$ and, since $\widehat{AOZ} = 90°$

(OZ is the normal to (001) and therefore normal to OA) it follows that $\widehat{YOZ} = \gamma$, and $\widehat{YOZ} = (101)\widehat{}(001)$. (6)

The same reasoning applies to the right triangle CYO, where
$$\widehat{COY} = 90^\circ - a^\circ \text{ and thus } \widehat{A'OY} = a = (100)\widehat{}(101) \tag{7}$$

Cross multiplying (4) with (5) gives $\dfrac{c}{a} \times \dfrac{a}{b} = \dfrac{c}{b}$;

$$\frac{\sin \gamma}{\sin a} \times \frac{\tan (100)\widehat{}(110)}{\cos (\beta - 90)} = \frac{c}{b}$$

Further substituting for a and γ from (6) and (7) gives

$$\frac{\sin (101)\widehat{}(001)}{\sin (100)\widehat{}(101)} \times \frac{\tan (100)\widehat{}(110)}{\cos (\beta - 90)} = \frac{c}{b}$$

Graphical determination of axial ratios

The axial ratios may, alternatively, be determined graphically, from the stereographic projection. Use has again to be made of projections in the planes perpendicular to b and to c.

The ratio a/b is determined by using the pole (110), Fig. 125A. Draw

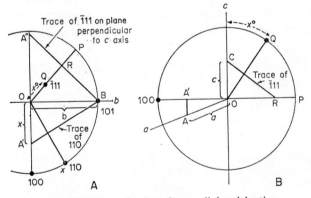

Fig. 125 Graphical determination of monoclinic axial ratios.
A. Constructions on the stereographic plane perpendicular to c axis.
B. Vertical sections through the spherical projection; left of the c axis — in the plane containing a and c axes; right of the c axis — in the plane containing the c axes and the pole to (111).

the line OX from the centre of the projection O to the pole (110). Let b be the unit intercept on the b axis (OB). From B draw the line BA′ perpendicular to OX. The distance OA′ gives the intercept of the plane (110) not on the a axis, but on its projection in the plane of the primitive. The distance OA' corresponds to distance x of Fig. 124.

The true intercept on a is determined by reference to Fig. 125B which is a spherical projection in the plane containing the a and c axes. The distance OA' is transferred from Fig. 125A and the correct unit distance a (OA) is given by dropping a perpendicular from A'. The distance a is read relative to b as unity.

The length of the c axis is determined using the face $(\bar{1}11)$. On Fig. 125A, a line is drawn from the centre O through the pole $(\bar{1}11)$ to meet the primitive at P. A line perpendicular to OP is now drawn from B, where OB is the unit distance b. The point A″ is the intersection of the trace of $(\bar{1}11)$ with the rearward extension of the line perpendicular to OB in the horizontal plane.

Consider now the right-hand half of Fig. 125B as a section through Fig. 125A along the line OP. The distance OR is transferred from Fig. 125A to the horizontal line on Fig. 125B, this being the intercept of $(\bar{1}11)$ on the horizontal plane. Next, measure the angular distance from O-$(\bar{1}11)$, $(x°)$, mark this as shown on Fig. 125B, and join the point Q to the centre O. Now construct from R the line perpendicular to OQ. The distance OC is the unit length c of the c axis expressed relative to b as unity.

The axial ratios can be used to determine the index of any projected face either graphically or by calculation.

CHAPTER 8

THE TRICLINIC SYSTEM

There is only one Bravais lattice that forms the structural basis of all triclinic crystals, the triclinic P lattice. It has the form of a non-orthogonal parallelepiped with three sets of edges of unequal length. Accordingly, triclinic crystals are referred to three crystallographic axes of unequal length, none of which is at right angles to the plane containing the other two (Fig. 126). As is customary, the c axis is held vertically

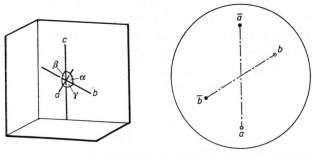

Fig. 126   Drawing and stereogram of triclinic crystallographic axes.

and stereographic projections of triclinic crystals are plotted on the plane perpendicular to c (Fig. 126).

As in the monoclinic system the a axis is conventionally held so that it slopes downwards and towards the observer and the angle between the positive end of the a and c axes is again called angle β and is obtuse. On the stereographic projection the a axis is plotted in the same position as in monoclinic crystals.

The angle between the positive ends of the c and b axes, no longer 90°, is called angle α, and that between the positive ends of the a and b axes (also $\neq$ 90°) is called angle γ. Apart from the conventions already stated, there is no general agreement on the arrangement of triclinic axes. Many authorities suggest that angle α should be obtuse like angle β, but this is by no means universally accepted. Fig. 126 is drawn as though all angles α, β and γ are obtuse, but whether or not this is so, it is clear that the *b* axis will not project in the plane of the primitive and that it will not be at right angles to *a*.

The same lack of agreement applies to the lengths of the crystallographic axes, which may be chosen parallel to any three sets of edges on a crystal.

There are two conventions. One of them makes the *c* axis parallel to the principal zone axis of the crystal, with the *b* axis the longer of the remaining two. The other convention follows orthorhombic practice in making the relative lengths of the axes $b > a > c$. Where possible, both angles α and β are obtuse. Not infrequently, if a crystal has a tabular habit, then the largest face is chosen as (010), and the *a* and *c* axes are chosen so as to be parallel to its most prominent edges. Some crystallographers borrow the orthorhombic nomenclature and call the *a* axis the brachy axis and the *b* axis the macro axis but as in the orthorhombic system itself, the continued use of these terms cannot be justified, for in some crystals the *a* axis is longer than *b*.

The mineral axinite, one of the best known of triclinic crystals, serves to illustrate the wide choice of orientation open to the crystallographer for at least ten different positions have been selected.

Triclinic crystals like axinite (Fig. 127) have a most distinctive appearance, almost as though they are crystals with a higher symmetry that have been accidentally flattened. Other minerals, for example the

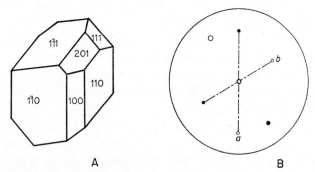

A   B

Fig. 127 A. A crystal of axinite (class $\bar{1}$) with faces indexed in accordance with the Dana setting.
B. A stereogram of the crystallographic axes, symmetry element and the general form (pinacoid) of class $\bar{1}$.
The heavy circle at the centre of the projection represents a centre of symmetry.

plagioclases and some of the potash feldspars, have lattices that are monoclinic within the limits of goniometric measurement and their true triclinic character is apparent only after the most careful analysis by X-rays. Pseudosymmetry therefore is not uncommon in triclinic crystals and when it occurs it is customary to choose an orientation that affords a close comparison with that of its higher symmetry counterpart. At times it is convenient, as in the case of the feldspars, to choose a non-primitive unit cell for the triclinic mineral and this means that the best-developed crystal faces will not necessarily have the simplest Miller indices. It must be emphasized that this is simply a matter of convenience so as to afford easy comparison between genetically related minerals; it does not invalidate the general principle that faces tend to develop parallel to the planes of low index.

Class $\bar{1}$, Triclinic holosymmetric, triclinic pinacoidal, axinite type

The only symmetry element present in this class is an inversion identity axis and in Chapter 4 we saw that this is equivalent to a centre of symmetry. It follows therefore that if there is only a centre of symmetry, then there can be no unique orientation of a triclinic crystal; the crystallographic axes are chosen parallel to prominent edges, bearing in mind the conventions outlined above. Thus, although the inversion identity axis is projected as the principal axis and coincident with c, the symmetry would be equally satisfied if a or b were chosen as the axis of inversion. Thus although the concept of the centre of symmetry is replaced by the more uniform adoption of inversion axes, in this class it remains as a most useful means of viewing the symmetry.

Fig. 127B is a stereographic projection of the crystallographic axes of this class and of the general form. The centre of symmetry causes a given face to be repeated so that the resulting form is a pair of parallel faces. No matter what the orientation of a face, the symmetry element causes its repetition in the same way and the term *pinacoid* is correctly used to describe such a form. It follows therefore that all the forms of this class are pinacoids, regardless of their Miller index. They are all generally related to the symmetry element and therefore general forms, and they can accordingly be referred to by the general index $\{hkl\}$. There are no special forms.

A less logical nomenclature, carried over, as it were, from the orthorhombic system, is still in use. The name of a triclinic form is that of the orthorhombic holosymmetric form having the same Miller index but, where necessary, modified by a prefix. The terms applied are:

{100}, {010}, {001}   pinacoids
{$hk0$}   hemi-prisms
{$h0l$}, {$0kl$}   hemi-prisms or hemi-domes
{hkl}   quarter-bipyramids or tetarto-pyramids.

There seems nothing to be gained by the use of this nomenclature; all the forms are pinacoids and can be distinguished by their Miller indices.

EXAMPLES

Many common minerals crystallize in this class. They include the feldspars microcline $KAlSi_3O_8$, anorthoclase $(NaK)AlSi_3O_8$ and the plagioclases; the pyroxenoids wollastonite $Ca_2Si_2O_6$, rhodonite $Mn_2Si_2O_6$ and bustamite $(MnCaFe)_2Si_2O_6$ and the minerals axinite[19]

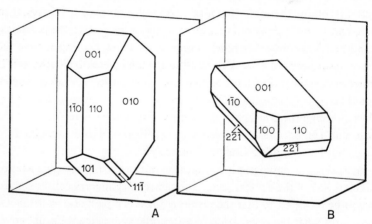

Fig. 128   Minerals belonging to class $\bar{1}$; A. Albite; B. Rhodonite. All the forms present are pinacoids.

$(CaMnFe^{2+})_3Al_2BO_3$ $(Si_4O_{12})(OH)$, chalcanthite $CuSO_4.5H_2O$, kyanite Al_2SiO_5 and polyhalite $2\ CaSO_4.MgSO_4.K_2SO_4.2H_2O$ (Fig. 128).

19. Structurally, axinite appears to belong to class $\bar{1}$, but it sometimes exhibits pyroelectricity.

Class 1, Triclinic pedial, asymmetric

Crystals belonging to this class have no symmetry and every form consists of a single face or *pedion*. As in the holosymmetric class, there can be no special forms and crystallographic axes are chosen parallel to prominent edges of the crystal.

The alternative borrowed orthorhombic nomenclature is as follows:

{100}, {010}, {001}   pedions
{$hk0$}   quarter- or tetarto-prisms
{$h0l$}, {$0kl$}   quarter- or tetarto-prsims or domes
{hkl}   ogdo-bipyramids or eighth-bipyramids

These ugly names are of no real value; the simple term pedion for all faces is preferable.

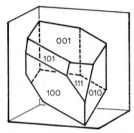

Fig. 129 A hypothetical crystal belonging to class 1. The forms 'out of sight' at the rear of the crystal are {$0\bar{1}0$}, {$\bar{1}\bar{1}0$}, {$00\bar{1}$} and {$\bar{1}00$}. All forms are pedions.

EXAMPLES

Kaolinite $Al_4Si_4O_{10}(OH)_8$ and parahilgardite $Ca_8B_{18}Cl_4.4H_2O$ (Fig. 129).

Stereographic projection of a triclinic holosymmetric crystal using a Wulff net

Since the crystallographic axes are chosen parallel to prominent edges, the crystal to be plotted is examined and a prominent zone of faces selected as those parallel to the *c* axis. The interfacial angles in this zone are measured and the faces plotted in the usual way round the primitive of the stereogram (Fig. 130A). The positions of the other faces are now determined by measuring the angles between the selected face and two of the faces that plot on the primitive, constructing the appropriate small circles and marking their intersections. The completed stereogram is drawn in Fig. 130B.

The prominent face that is selected as (010) lies parallel to the *a* axis and since this is conventionally plotted in the same position as the monoclinic *a* axis, the pole to (010) plots in its usual position on the primitive. Owing to the inclination of the *b* axis, however, the poles to other faces are displaced from the positions that they usually occupy in more symmetrical classes. The positions of those of simple Miller index are marked on Fig. 130C and it should be noted that zonal relationships

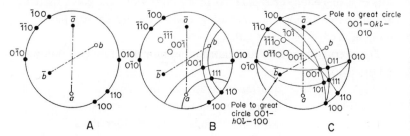

Fig. 130   Stereographic projections of a triclinic crystal.
A. Positions of faces in the zone [001] showing their relation to the crystallographic axes.
B. The plotting of inclined faces by the small circle method.
C. A stereogram of a triclinic crystal showing zonal relationships of faces of simple Miller indices.

still hold good. Examination and measurement of the stereogram shows that each face represented has another face parallel to it and hence the crystal appears to belong to the holosymmetric class of the triclinic system.

Having selected the parametral form, the crystallographic axes may now be inserted on the stereogram. The *c* axis, by convention, is held vertically. This has to be assumed from the outset or plotting could not begin. The *a* axis runs from front to back and, since by convention angle *β* is obtuse, its positive end intersects the lower hemisphere of the projection. All faces in the zone (001)–(0*kl*)–(010) lie parallel to the *a* axis; in other words the *a* axis is the zone axis [100] of this zone, and its location on the stereogram is the pole to the great circle passing through (001)–(0*kl*)–(010). This zone and its pole (*ā*) are marked in Fig. 130C. The same reasoning applies to the *b* axis which is the zone axis [010] of the zone (001)–(*h0l*)–(100), and its position is therefore located as shown on Fig. 130C.

Calculation of the axial ratios and interaxial angles
The crystallographic constants of a triclinic crystal are the axial ratios $\frac{a}{b} : \frac{b}{b} : \frac{c}{b}$ and the values of angles *α*, *β* and *γ*.

(1)   *Determination of angles α, β and γ*

Fig. 131A shows a simple triclinic crystal with axes inserted. In monoclinic crystals, angle β is simply related to the interfacial angle between
(001) and (100). This is not the case in the triclinic system as Fig. 131

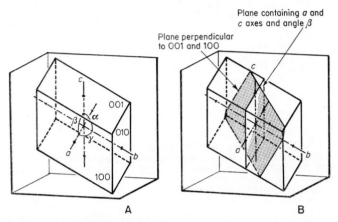

Fig. 131   A. A simple triclinic crystal.
B. The relationship between the plane containing *a* and *c* and the
plane perpendicular to (100) and (001).

shows, for the plane perpendicular to both (001) and (100) lies at an
angle to the plane containing the *a* and *c* axes and therefore to angle β.
Clearly the same is true of angles α and γ which have no simple relationship to the interfacial angles (001)⌢(010) and (100)⌢(010) respectively.

Imagine planes parallel to (100), (010) and (001). These intersect at a
point (Fig. 132A), and therefore angles α, β and γ are disposed as shown,
because the intersections of the planes define the directions of the
crystallographic axes. It follows therefore that the same angles α, β and γ
will be subtended by the three planes containing the normals to (100),
(010) and (001). These three planes are shown in stereographic projection on Fig. 132B. Angle α is subtended by two planes, one containing
the poles to (001) and (100) and the other the poles to (010) and (100).
These two planes are great circles on the stereogram; the one containing
the poles to (010) and (100) is the primitive circle. The angle between
them is marked as angle α on the stereogram. Similarly, angle β is
subtended by the planes containing the poles to (001) and (010) on the

one hand and (010) and (100) on the other. Angle γ is subtended by the planes containing poles to (001) and (100), and the poles to (001) and (010).

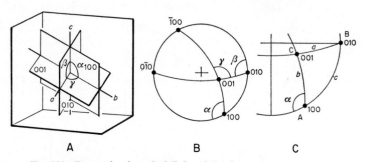

Fig. 132 Determination of triclinic axial ratios.
A. Intersection of planes containing the crystallographic axes.
B. Stereogram of the planes containing the normals to the planes shown in Fig. 132A.
C. The triangle (001) (010) (100).

Consider now the spherical triangle (100)–(010)–(001) labelled ABC in Fig. 132C. The sides a, b, c of this spherical triangle are known and the angle A is given by the formula

$$\tan \frac{A}{2} = \sqrt{\frac{\sin (s-b). \sin (s-c)}{\sin s. \sin (s-a)}}$$

where $s = \dfrac{a+b+c}{2}$

Now in triangle ABC, angle $\alpha = 180° - A$

$$\text{Whence } \tan \frac{A}{2} = \sqrt{\frac{\sin (s - \widehat{(001)\ (100)}). \sin (s - \widehat{(100)\ (010)})}{\sin s. \sin (s - \widehat{(001)\ (010)})}}$$

The only unknown is A and hence angle α is found directly.

The solutions for angle β ($= 180° - B$) and angle γ ($= 180° - C$)

$$\text{are } \quad \tan \frac{B}{2} = \sqrt{\frac{\sin (s-a). \sin (s-c)}{\sin s. \sin (s-b)}}$$

$$\text{and } \quad \tan \frac{C}{2} = \sqrt{\frac{\sin (s-a). \sin (s-b)}{\sin s. \sin (s-c)}}$$

(2) *Determination of the axial ratios*

The parametral plane (111) intersects each crystallographic axis at a unit distance. Fig. 133A shows a simple triclinic crystal with the face (111)

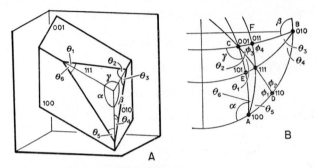

Fig. 133 Determination of triclinic axial ratios.

inserted and Fig. 133B is a projection on which the same faces are marked. Consider now the plane triangle on (001) (Fig. 134).

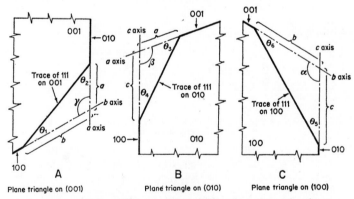

Fig. 134 Determination of triclinic axial ratios: plane triangles on faces (001) (010) and (100) of Fig. 133A.

By the sine formula

$$\frac{a}{\sin \theta_1} = \frac{b}{\sin \theta_2}, \text{ whence } \frac{a}{b} = \frac{\sin \theta_1}{\sin \theta_2} \tag{1}$$

The angle θ_1 is the angle between the trace of (111) on (001) and the edge between (001) and (100) and θ_2 is the angle between the trace of (111) on

(001) and the edge between (010) and (001). They therefore correspond to the angles between these zones on the stereogram and these angles are marked on Fig. 133B. Notice that $\gamma + \theta_1 + \theta_2 = 180°$.

The faces (100) and (010) can be treated in the same way (Fig. 134 B & C). From the plane triangle on (010) it is apparent that

$$\frac{a}{\sin \theta_4} = \frac{c}{\sin \theta_3} \text{ and hence } \frac{a}{c} = \frac{\sin \theta_4}{\sin \theta_3} \tag{2}$$

Also from the plane triangle on (100)

$$\frac{b}{\sin \theta_5} = \frac{c}{\sin \theta_6} \text{ and hence } \frac{c}{b} = \frac{\sin \theta_6}{\sin \theta_5} \tag{3}$$

Consider now the stereographic projection Fig. 133B.

In triangle ACD, $\dfrac{\sin \theta_1}{\sin AD} = \dfrac{\sin \phi_1}{\sin AC}$

$$\therefore \sin \theta_1 = \frac{\sin AD. \sin \phi_1}{\sin AC} \tag{4}$$

In triangle BCD, $\dfrac{\sin \theta_2}{\sin BD} = \dfrac{\sin \phi_2}{\sin BC}$

$$\therefore \sin \theta_2 = \frac{\sin BD. \sin \phi_2}{\sin BC} \tag{5}$$

Substituting now equations (4) and (5) in equation (1)

$$\frac{a}{b} = \frac{\sin \theta_1}{\sin \theta_2} = \frac{\dfrac{\sin AD. \sin \phi_1}{\sin AC}}{\dfrac{\sin BD. \sin \phi_2}{\sin BC}}$$

Now $\phi_2 = 180° - \phi_1$,

$$\therefore \frac{a}{b} = \frac{\sin \theta_1}{\sin \theta_2} = \frac{\dfrac{\sin AD}{\sin AC}}{\dfrac{\sin BD}{\sin BC}} = \frac{\sin AD. \sin BC}{\sin AC. \sin BD}$$

$$\therefore \frac{a}{b} = \frac{\sin (100)\,\widehat{\,}\,(110). \sin (00\overline{1})\,\widehat{\,}\,(010)}{\sin (100)\,\widehat{\,}\,(001). \sin (010)\,\widehat{\,}\,(110)}$$

To determine $\dfrac{c}{b}$ consider triangle CAF (Fig. 133B).

$$\frac{\sin \theta_6}{\sin CF} = \frac{\sin \phi_3}{\sin AC}$$

$$\therefore \sin \theta_6 = \frac{\sin CF. \sin \phi_3}{\sin AC} \tag{6}$$

In triangle FAB:

$$\frac{\sin \theta_5}{\sin BF} = \frac{\sin \phi_4}{\sin AB}$$

$$\therefore \sin \theta_5 = \frac{\sin BF. \sin \phi_4}{\sin AB} \qquad (7)$$

Substituting (6) and (7) in equation (3)

$$\frac{a}{b} = \frac{\sin \theta_6}{\sin \theta_5} = \frac{\dfrac{\sin CF. \sin \phi_3}{\sin AC}}{\dfrac{\sin BF. \sin \phi_4}{\sin AB}}$$

Again, $\phi_3 = 180° - \phi_4$

$$\therefore \frac{c}{b} = \frac{\sin \theta_6}{\sin \theta_5} = \frac{\dfrac{\sin CF}{\sin AC}}{\dfrac{\sin BF}{\sin AB}} = \frac{\sin CF. \sin AB}{\sin AC. \sin BF}$$

$$\therefore \frac{c}{b} = \frac{\sin (001) \widehat{} (011). \sin (100) \widehat{} (010)}{\sin (100) \widehat{} (001). \sin (011) \widehat{} (010)}$$

This calculation, although rather unwieldy, is included in order to show that axial ratios may be derived for triclinic crystals using only simple trigonometry. The concept of the polar lattice and the use of Napier's device for the solution of right angled spherical triangles greatly simplifies these calculations. The student is referred to the texts at the end of the chapter.

Alternatively if angles α, θ_5 and θ_6, and γ, θ_1 and θ_2 are known, then a unit length can be chosen and the two appropriate plane triangles constructed graphically and the unit lengths of a and c measured.

Suggestions for further reading
The following texts give further details of the derivation of triclinic crystallographic constants, employing spherical trigonometry and the concept of the polar lattice.
Phillips, F. C., *An Introduction to Crystallography*, Longmans Green & Co. Ltd., London, 3rd Edition, 1963.
Terpstra, P. and Codd, L. W., *Crystallometry*, Longmans Green & Co. Ltd., London, 1961
Tunell, G. and Murdoch, J., *Introduction to Crystallography — a Laboratory Manual for Students of Mineralogy and Geology*, W. H. Freeman, London, 2nd Edition 1959

CHAPTER 9

THE CUBIC SYSTEM

There are three cubic Bravais lattices; the cubic primitive (P), face-centred (F) and body centred (I) lattices. Each lattice has edges at right angles and the spacing of lattice points is the same along any lattice row parallel to an edge of the Bravais lattice. Consequently cubic crystals are referred to three orthogonal crystallographic axes of equal length and called a_1, a_2 and a_3, where a_1 and a_2 are in the horizontal plane and a_3 is vertical. The a_1 axis is held so that it runs from front to back. The alternative name *isometric system* emphasizes the equal lengths of the axes. It is also sometimes called the *regular system*.

Crystals with a cubic P lattice have a unit cell of the same shape and dimensions as the Bravais lattice itself, whereas for the F and I lattices a simple unit cell can be chosen with the shape of a rhombohedron (see Fig. 11). This difference between unit cell and Bravais lattice has been mentioned previously in Chapter 1, but in order to avoid the unnecessary complication of using different crystallographic axes for cubic P and cubic F or I crystals, the Bravais lattice outline is adopted as the unit cell, although it is a multiply primitive unit cell in many cases.

We can therefore readily imagine a cube of galena or rock salt as being the outward expression of the inner cubic space lattice. It is a valuable exercise to determine, with the aid of a model, the symmetry elements of a cube. It will be found that there are nine planes and thirteen axes, (four triads, three tetrads and six diads), plus a centre (Fig. 135). Of these elements, the four triad axes are characteristic of the cubic system; every class possesses this set of elements and it is not present in crystals belonging to any other system. It will be noticed from Fig. 135, however, that the triad axes do not coincide with the crystallographic axes and as a result special conventions need to be introduced when deriving the Hermann-Mauguin symbol.

As in other systems, the symbol for the principal axis (here a crystallographic axis) is written first. It is necessary next to distinguish between the two sets of planes of symmetry illustrated in Fig. 135. One set of planes lies parallel to the cube faces and so passes through the crystallographic and diad axes but *not* through the triads; these planes are often called the *axial planes*. The other set of planes, often called *diagonal planes*, passes through both the principal and triad axes.

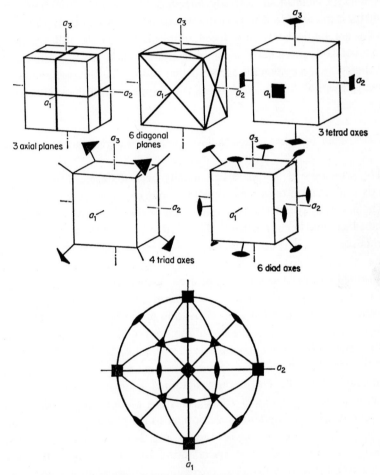

Fig. 135   The symmetry elements of a perfect cube.

Now, since every cubic crystal possesses triad axes, the number 3 must always appear in the International Symmetry Symbol, and the two sets of planes are distinguished by writing the symbol *m* before or after the 3.

Thus, if n represents the principal axis, the position of m in the symbol $nm3$ refers to the axial planes whereas the position of m in $n3m$, indicates the diagonal planes.

In the cubic system more so than in any other, the presence of one symmetry element of necessity introduces others. The common symmetry element of four triads cannot exist on its own, at least three diad axes are immediately introduced. For this reason the full symmetry symbol can conveniently be abbreviated without in any way altering its validity. In the systematic accounts that follow, the International Symmetry Symbol is given first with a fuller statement of the symmetry in brackets.

* **Class $m3m$ ($4/m3m$), Cubic holosymmetric, hexakisoctahedral, galena type**

The symmetry of this class has already been deduced. The principal axis is a rotation tetrad and thus the symmetry symbol begins with 4. The planes of symmetry that do not include the triads lie parallel to the cube faces and hence normal to the tetrad axis and thus the symbol continues as $4/m3$. The next index symbol is that for the planes containing the triad axes giving the symbol $4/m3m$. In American literature it is customary to expand this symbol even further to $4/m\bar{3}2/m$. It is clear from Fig. 135 that the diad axes are normal to the diagonal planes of symmetry and this explains the derivation of the $2/m$ notation. There is nothing contradictory in the use of the symbol $\bar{3}$. In two classes of the cubic system (the other is the pyrite class $2/m3$ or $2/m\bar{3}$) the disposition of the faces about the triad axis is consistent with an inversion triad, whereas in the other classes only rotational symmetry is satisfied. This becomes more apparent if stereograms are plotted with a triad axis instead of a crystallographic axis normal to the plane of the projection (Fig. 136). The distinction between 3 and $\bar{3}$ is thus a real one but, because the triad axis must always occur in combination with other symmetry elements, it loses the morphological distinction it would have if it were present on its own. The distinction is not made in the *International Tables* and the accepted symbols are $m3m$ and $m3$ respectively.

However fully the symmetry symbol may be written, it is usually abbreviated to $m3m$ because these three symmetry elements alone are sufficient to account fully for the observed crystal forms. That they cannot exist on their own is apparent; other elements are introduced. However, for the purpose of writing what amounts to crystallographic shorthand, it is possible to consider that they do have an independent existence.

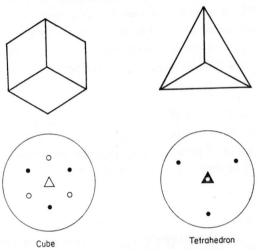

Cube   Tetrahedron

Fig. 136   A cube and tetrahedron drawn and projected with a triad axis arranged vertically. The pole to the fourth tetrahedron face is represented by the circle at the centre of the triad axis flag.

Let us turn now to the development of crystal faces and in this connection it will be helpful to make use of the stereographic projection of symmetry elements (Fig. 135).

SPECIAL FORMS
{100} *Cube*
The symmetry elements cause the face (100) to be repeated so as to give the familiar cube.

{100} *Rhombdodecahedron*
The pole to the face (110) projects on a diagonal plane of symmetry and is repeated so as to produce a twelve-faced closed form each face of which is a rhombus. The name is thus logically derived because dodecahedron means 'twelve faced'.

{hk0} *Tetrakishexahedra* (*tetrahexahedra*)

The index ($hk0$) is appropriate to any face whose pole projects on the primitive between (100) and (110). The diagonal planes of symmetry repeat the face so as to produce a twenty-four-faced closed form that looks as though a four-faced pyramid is raised on each of the cube faces (Fig. 137). A cube has six faces (a hexahedron) on each of which four more are raised and hence the name tetrahexahedron is quite appropriate. It is sometimes colloquially rendered as the 'four-faced cube' and, like many colloquialisms, it is inaccurate.

{111} *Octahedron*

The normals to the form {111} are coincident with the triad axes and project at the points of their emergence. The form is an eight-faced closed form which, if perfectly developed, has each face an equilateral triangle. It can be regarded as developed by truncating the corners of a cube.

{hll} *Icositetrahedra*

The index (hll) is appropriate for any face lying in zone between (100) and (111). There will be a suite of such faces with indices like (211), (311), (411), (322), (433), etc. The elements of symmetry cause their repetition so that there are three faces in each octant of the stereogram, making twenty-four faces in all. Each face has the shape of a trapezium and the edges between the faces in each octant meet to form a letter Y. The point at which the edges meet is the point of emergence of the triad axis. An alternative name is the *trapezohedron*. It is justified from the shape of the faces, but it should be remembered that the name trapezohedron is also given to the general form of the tetragonal holoaxial class 422 and the trigonal holoaxial class 32.

{hhl} *Triakisoctahedra* (*trisoctahedra*)

A suite of faces in zone between (111) and (110) will have the general index (hhl) in which the intercepts on a_1 and a_2 are the same, and different from the intercept on a_3. The resulting form is such that three faces appear in each octant of the stereogram and the appearance of the form is that of an octahedron on each face of which three additional faces are

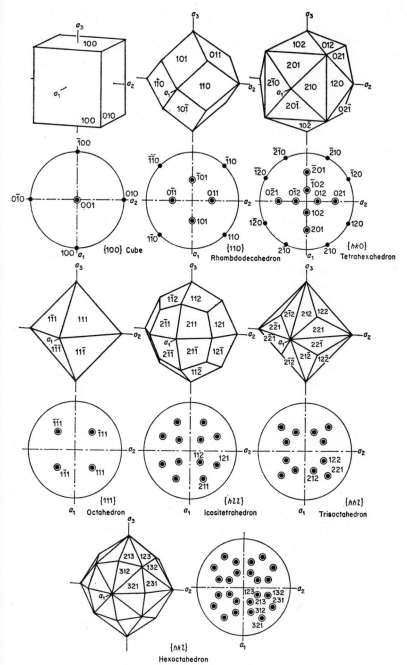

Fig. 137 Drawings and stereograms of forms of class *m3m*.

raised. The faces meet in edges describing an inverted Y (Fig. 137).

GENERAL FORMS

{*hkl*} *Hexakisoctahedra* (*hexoctahedra*)

Each of the special forms projects on one or other of the symmetry elements but the general form {*hkl*} shows a general relationship to them and is repeated so as to give a forty-eight-faced form with the appearance of six faces raised on each octahedron face.

EXAMPLES

There are very many crystals belonging to the cubic holosymmetric class, among them many metals, their oxides, halides and sulphides. Mineralogical examples include galena PbS, halite NaCl, fluorite CaF_2, the garnet group and the spinels (Fig. 138).

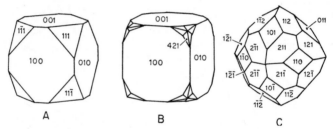

Fig. 138   Crystals belonging to class *m3m*; left: galena (cube {100} and octahedron {111}); centre: a habit of fluorite; a cube modified by the hexoctahedron {421}; right: garnet; a combination of rhombdodecahedron {110} and icositetrahedron {211}.

* **Class *m3* (2/*m3*) Cubic diakisdodecahedral, pyrite type**

Crystals of pyrite, the common representative of this symmetry class, may form either simple cubes or more highly developed crystals, as in Fig. 139. If the highly developed form is examined (Fig. 139A), it is clear that the four triad axes characteristic of the cubic system are present but the diad axes of the holosymmetric class are absent and the principal axes perpendicular to the cube faces are no longer tetrad axes but diads. Similarly, the only planes of symmetry are those passing through the principal axes; there are none that include both the triads and the principal axes. The symmetry symbol may thus be written 2/*m3*. It is important to realize that although pyrite can crystallize in simple forms like the cube, the underlying atomic arrangement does not possess the full symmetry of, say, a cube of galena. This is demonstrated by the striations that are present on the cube faces of many pyrite crystals and illustrated in Fig. 139B. The arrangement of the striations is such that

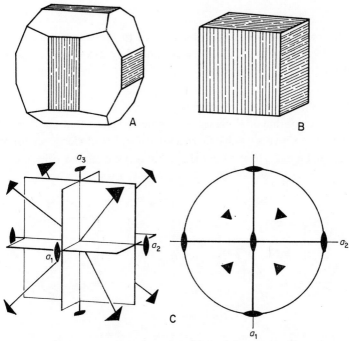

Fig. 139 A and B. Drawings of pyrite crystals with striated cube faces.
C. The symmetry elements and crystallographic axes, class *m*3.

the only symmetry elements are four tetrad axes, three crystallographic diads and axial planes of symmetry. This is evident because the striations are the result of oscillation between the cube and pentagonal dodecahedron faces during growth. Even if the cube faces were perfectly smooth planes the underlying structure would still have a low symmetry.

It is common American practice to write the symmetry symbol as $2/m\bar{3}$ and if a stereographic projection is made of a crystal belonging to this class with a triad axis as the principal axis of the projection then the faces are arranged in a manner appropriate to an inversion triad (see Fig. 136). It is customary British practice to use the symbol $2/m3$ or to use the International Symmetry Symbol $m3$.

SPECIAL FORMS
{100} *Cube*

{110} *Rhombdodecahedron*

The stereographic projection of the poles to these forms lie on symmetry elements present in this class and they are therefore possible forms.

{$hk0$}, {$kh0$} *Pentagonal dodecahedra*

The absence of diagonal planes of symmetry means that the face ($hk0$) is repeated to give a twelve-faced closed form (a dodecahedron) each face of which has a pentagonal shape but is not a regular pentagon (Fig

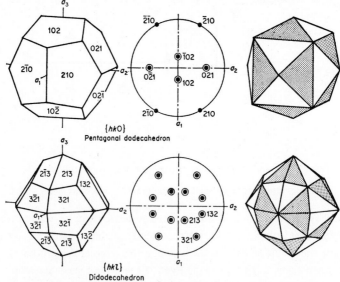

Fig. 140   Drawings and stereograms of the forms {$hk0$} and {hkl} of class $m3$.

140). This form has half the faces of the tetrahexahedron of the holosymmetric class; it can be imagined as produced by developing the shaded pairs of faces of the tetrahexahedron in Fig. 140. If the unshaded faces were developed another tetrahexahedron {*kh*0} would be formed. These have been distinguished as positive and negative forms, but this is unnecessary as they can readily be identified by their Miller indices. Another, but less satisfactory name for the form is the *pyritohedron*.

{111} *Octahedron*

{*hll*} *Icositetrahedra*

{*hhl*} *Trisoctahedra*

Each of these forms is the same morphologically as that occurring in the holosymmetric class and is represented here because only the triad axis and axial planes are needed for their repetition.

GENERAL FORMS

{*hkl*}, {*hlk*} *Diakisdodecahedra (didodecahedra)*

This form may be regarded as produced by developing alternate faces of the holosymmetric hexakisoctahedron (Fig. 140). There is a corresponding form {*hlk*}. Another name for the form is the *diploid*.

EXAMPLES

The commonest mineral in this class is pyrite FeS_2 but others that belong here are the alums and cobaltite $CoAsS$.[20]

Class $\bar{4}3m$ Cubic hexakistetrahedral, tetrahedrite type

A group of economically important copper minerals called the fahlerz series varies in composition between two end members tennantite $Cu_{12}As_4S_{13}$ and tetrahedrite $Cu_{12}Sb_4S_{13}$. Crystals of these minerals commonly have the form shown in Fig. 141, in which the dominant form is a regular tetrahedron, each face of which is an equilateral triangle. Examination of this form reveals the presence of four triad axes perpendicular to the faces of the tetrahedron, which place the crystals in the cubic system. Notice also that these axes are rotation axes and are uniterminal and polar. The principal axes have diad symmetry and

20. Cobaltite has a structure similar to pyrite. If, however, the As and S atoms are regularly distributed throughout the lattice (or *ordered*), the symmetry changes to class 23.

the only planes present are diagonal ones that pass through both the principal and triad axes. There are six such planes.

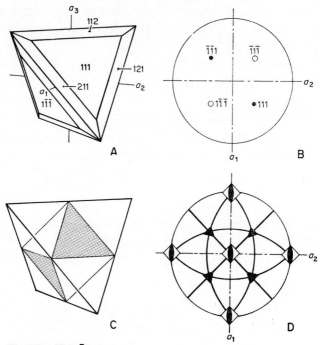

Fig. 141   Class $\bar{4}3m$:
A. A crystal of tetrahedrite comprising the forms tetrahedron {111} and the tristetrahedron {211}.
B. A stereogram of the tetrahedron {111}.
C. The derivation of the tetrahedron from the octahedron.
D. The symmetry elements and crystallographic axes.

If the symmetry of the crystal structure is studied, however, the principal axes are seen to have the higher symmetry appropriate to a inversion tetrad. This is shown by the stereographic projection of the tetrahedron in Fig. 141B, and the form can be compared with the sphenoid of the tetragonal system class $\bar{4}2m$.

On morphological grounds alone, the crystals show twofold symmetry about their principal axes. The International Symmetry Symbol for this class can be written $\bar{4}3m$, the letter m following 3 denoting the presence only of those planes that pass through both triad and principal axes.

SPECIAL FORMS

{100} *Cube*

{110} *Rhombdodecahedron*

The symmetry elements cause the repetition of the faces (100) and (110)
to produce forms that are present both in the holosymmetric and class
$2/m3$.

{*hk*0} *Tetrahexahedra*

The presence of diagonal planes of symmetry in addition to the axial
elements causes the repetition of the face (*hk*0) so as to produce the
tetrahexahedron that is present also in the cubic holosymmetric class.

{111}, {1$\bar{1}$1} *Tetrahedra*

The inversion tetrad axis repeats the face (111) so as to produce the
tetrahedron. It can be regarded as being produced by developing
alternate faces of the octahedron (Fig. 141C).

{*hll*}, {*h$\bar{l}l$*} *Triakistetrahedra (Tristetrahedra)*

The pole to the face (*hll*) projects on a diagonal plane of symmetry and
thus is repeated by the triad axis to give two additional faces symmetrically disposed about it. All three faces are repeated as a group by the
inversion tetrad so that the resulting form appears as though three
triangular faces are raised on each tetrahedron face. The name tristetrahedron is thus entirely appropriate and it should be noted that the edges
between the faces form a letter Y (Fig. 142A).

{*hhl*}, {*h$\bar{h}l$*} *Deltoid dodecahedra*

The pole to the face (*hhl*), like (*hll*), also projects on a diagonal plane of
symmetry and is thus repeated in a similar manner to give three faces
symmetrically disposed about the triad axis. The edges between the
three faces meet in an inverted letter Y. The inversion tetrad causes the
repetition of the group of three faces in a 'tetrahedral' arrangement so
that the resulting form has twelve faces (Fig. 142B). Like the tetrahedron
and tristetrahedron, the form {*hhl*} has a corresponding form with the
index {*h$\bar{h}l$*}.

GENERAL FORMS

$\{hkl\}$, $\{h\bar{k}l\}$ *Hexakistetrahedra (hexatetrahedra)*

Because the pole to the face (hkl) does not project on any symmetry element, both planes and axes affect the number of faces in the full form. From Fig. 142C it is clear that the symmetry elements repeat the

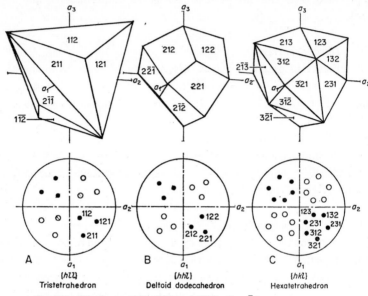

Fig. 142 The forms $\{hll\}$, $\{hhl\}$ and $\{hkl\}$; class $\bar{4}3m$.

face so that there are six faces disposed about the triad and that this group is repeated in other octants by the inversion tetrad so that the form appears as though six faces have been raised on each tetrahedron face.

The hexatetrahedron $\{hkl\}$ has a corresponding form $\{h\bar{k}l\}$.

EXAMPLES

The fahlerz series crystallize in this class and other minerals belonging here include sphalerite or zinc blende ZnS; boracite $Mg_6Cl_2B_{14}O_{26}$ and the helvite group (Fig. 143).

The remaining two classes of the cubic system are both holoaxial classes that have no planes of symmetry.

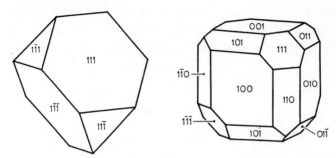

Fig. 143   Crystals of sphalerite (left); a combination of two tetrahedra and (right) boracite with cube and rhombdodecahedron
modified by the tetrahedron {111}. Class $\bar{4}3m$.

Class 432 (43) Pentagonal icositetrahedral

This class has only axial symmetry elements. There are three tetrads
(the principal axes), four triads and six diads. The symmetry can be
regarded as that of the holosymmetric class minus the planes of symmetry. A full expression of the symmetry is given by the symbol 432 but
this is sometimes shortened to 43 since these elements necessarily introduce the diads.

SPECIAL FORMS

{100} *Cube*

{110} *Rhombdodecahedron*

{*hk*0} *Tetrahexahedra*

{111} *Octahedron*

{*hll*} *Icositetrahedra*

{*hhl*} *Trisoctahedra*

The similarity between this class and the holosymmetric class is emphasized by the fact that the special forms are the same for both classes.

GENERAL FORMS

{*hkl*}, {*khl*} *Pentagonal icositetrahedra*

The absence of the planes of symmetry affects only the general form
which has twenty-four faces each of which is an irregular pentagon (Fig.
144). The form is also called the *gyroid* and the form {*hkl*} has an
enantiomorphous form {*khl*}.

N

EXAMPLES

Cuprite CuS_2 is usually placed here but it may be holosymmetric. Another mineral placed here is petzite $(Ag,Au)_2$ Te, but this is equally doubtful.

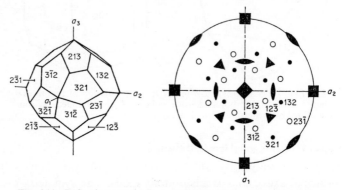

Fig. 144 Left: the general form (pentagonal icosetetrahedron) of class 432 and right, a stereogram of the form {321} with symmetry elements and crystallographic axes.

Class 23 Tetrahedral pentagonal dodecahedral

The only symmetry elements are three diad axes (the principal axes) and four triad axes. It may therefore be regarded as having the symmetry of the pyrite class $2/m3$ minus the planes of symmetry.

SPECIAL FORMS

{100} *Cube*

{110} *Rhombdodecahedron*

{hk0}, {kh0} *Pentagonal dodecahedra*

This form is the same morphologically as that in the pyrite class $m3$, and its development is independent of the planes of symmetry. The appearance of the pentagonal dodecahedron in this class is an argument against the use of the term pyritohedron because the form occurs not only in the pyrite class itself ($m3$) but also in this class of lower symmetry.

{111}, {1$\bar{1}$1} *Tetrahedra*

{hll}, {h$\bar{l}$l}   *Tristetrahedra*

Although $\bar{4}$ and 2 are structurally distinct, they can produce forms that are morphologically similar. For this reason the form {*hll*} is morphologically the same as that occurring in class $\bar{4}3m$. The absence of planes of symmetry does not affect the resulting form because the face (*hll*) is specially related to them.

{*hhl*}, {*hh̄l*} *Deltoid dodecahedra*
For the reasons given above it follows that the special forms {*hhl*} and {*hh̄l*} will be the same morphologically as those with the same indices in class $\bar{4}3m$, namely deltoid dodecahedra. Again there are two groups of forms related to one another by rotation through 90° about the a_2 axis.

GENERAL FORMS
{*hkl*}, {*khl*} *Tetrahedral pentagonal dodecahedra*
The absence of planes of symmetry results in the general form having only twelve faces: a dodecahedron. Each face is an irregular pentagon, and the form as a whole has a distinctly tetrahedral look. Thus, although

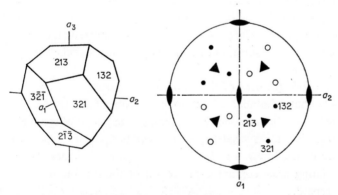

Fig. 145 Left: the general form (tetrahedral pentagonal dodecahedron) of class 23 and right a stereogram of the form {321} with symmetry elements and crystallographic axes.

the name of this form sounds long-winded, it has the merits of being logical and descriptive. One could wish that all crystallographic forms were as appropriately named.

The two groups of forms {*hkl*} and {*khl*} are enantiomorphs (Fig. 145).

EXAMPLES

The minerals ullmanite NiSbS, cobaltite CoAsS and langbeinite $K_2Mg_2(SO_4)_3$ crystallize in this class together with the salts sodium chloride and sodium bromate.

Comparative table of cubic symmetry classes

The number of forms in the cubic system and their distribution among the five symmetry classes can be a burden on the memory. The forms are set out in Table 6 in a way that groups them together and, more important, emphasizes the underlying symmetry on which the development of a particular form depends. Each of the classes of the cubic system has its own unique general form that is generated by the operation of the particular combination of symmetry elements on the face (*hkl*).

In Table 6 notice that the cube and rhombdodecahedron occur in all five classes. The only symmetry elements common to all the classes are the four triad axes that characterize the cubic system. The presence of the cube and rhombdodecahedron therefore depends solely on these symmetry elements. The presence of four triads immediately introduces other elements of course, but the triads alone are sufficient to generate these two forms.

All the special forms of the holosymmetric class *m3m* occur also in class 432 that is tabulated next to it in Table 6. Class 432 may be regarded as the holosymmetric class minus the planes of symmetry and it follows that the special forms of these two classes depend on the presence of triad, tetrad and diad axes and not on planes. Time spent manipulating a stereographic projection of these cubic forms will be amply repaid.

The next two columns of the table give the forms of class *m3* (the pyrite class) and class 23. The relationship between the two is similar to that between the holosymmetric class and class 432 in that class 23 can be considered as class *m3* minus its planes of symmetry. Notice, however, that apart from the cube and rhombdodecahedron, only the pentagonal dodecahedron is common to both classes. The presence of a diad instead of a tetrad as the principal axis shows itself in the morphology when there are no planes of symmetry. The tetrahedron {111},

TABLE 6

COMPARATIVE TABLE OF FORMS OF THE CUBIC SYSTEM. FOR EXPLANATION, SEE TEXT

Class / Form	GALENA *m3m*	432	PYRITE *m3*	23	TETRAHEDRITE *4̄3m*
{100}	Cube	Cube	Cube	Cube	Cube
{110}	Rhomb-dodecahedron	Rhomb-dodecahedron	Rhomb-dodecahedron	Rhomb-dodecahedron	Rhomb-dodecahedron
{hk0}	Tetrahexahedron	Tetrahexahedron	Pentagonal dodecahedron	Pentagonal dodecahedron	Tetrahexahedron
{111}	Octahedron	Octahedron	Octahedron	Tetrahedron	Tetrahedron
{hll}	Icositetrahedron	Icositetrahedron	Icositetrahedron	Tristetrahedron	Tristetrahedron
{hhl}	Trisoctahedron	Trisoctahedron	Trisoctahedron	Deltoid dodecahedron	Deltoid dodecahedron
{hkl}	Hexoctahedron	Pentagonal icositetrahedron	Didodecahedron	Tetrahedral pentagonal dodecahedron	Hexatetrahedron

tristetrahedron {*hll*} and deltoid dodecahedron {*hhl*} of class 23 are the hemihedral representatives of the octahedron {111}, icositetrahedron {*hll*} and trisoctahedron {*hhl*} respectively of class *m*3.

There is a definite morphological similarity between class 23 and the tetrahedrite class $\bar{4}3m$. Excluding again the cube and rhombdodeca-hedron, three of the remaining four special forms are common to both classes. This similarity is the result of the close morphological effect of the axes $\bar{4}$ and 2 when they occur in association with the four triads. Once again the effect of the plane of symmetry is seen in class $\bar{4}3m$ in which the tetrahexahedron {*hk*0} is developed in place of the pentagonal dodecahedron {*hk*0} of class 23.

The general form of course, is uniquely developed in each class and serves to distinguish it from any of the other crystal classes.

Stereographic projection of a cubic crystal, using a Wulff net
Although it is possible to plot a stereographic projection of a cubic, or any other crystal, by setting any prominent zone of faces parallel to the *c* axis, it is obvious that much time and effort in subsequently rotating and replotting the projection can be saved if a reasonable orientation is chosen before work begins. In the cubic system it is only necessary to find the four triad axes in order to know the proper orientation. The crystal is held so that these axes run towards the centres of the faces of an octahedron, whether it is present or not.

In spite of its high symmetry, however, a cubic crystal is often diffi-cult to plot stereographically, especially if one is to make no assump-tions as to symmetry or zonal relationships and rely entirely on measured interfacial angles in preparing the projection.

Consider first the garnet crystal shown in Fig. 138C. An inspection of the crystal reveals four triad axes emerging from the point of inter-section of the edges between the larger faces and the crystal is held appropriately. Four of the smaller, rhomb-shaped faces now appear to stand vertically and the projection can commence most logically with these. Let a point on the primitive circle represent the pole to one of these faces and then with a contact goniometer, measure the interfacial angle between this face and the next vertical one and proceed until the starting face is reached again. Tabulate the results and from the angles obtained plot the poles to the faces around the primitive circle of the projection.

The inclined faces can now be plotted by the small circle method. If the crystal is rotated about the normal to one of the vertical faces, the normal to any other face lying at an angle to it describes a small circle about it. The appropriate interfacial angle is measured and the small circle drawn using a Wulff net. If small circles are constructed about two successive vertical faces the position of the required inclined face is located at the point of intersection of the two small circles.

So far, so good; but what of the crystal like that shown in Fig. 146A which has no vertical faces? There is no longer a fixed 'starting point' on the primitive circle from which angular measurements may be taken, but there are several ways of tackling the problem. Inspection of the crystal shows that some faces meet in edges that are continuous round the crystal and that when it is in the correct holding position one such line of edges lies horizontally and two more vertically. All three are apparently at right angles. If the crystal is now held by the corners where two such lines of edges meet, e.g. B, and is rotated about the axis joining them, successive pairs of faces can be brought into the vertical position. If rotation is continued, it is apparent that the poles to these faces describe small circles about the axis of rotation as shown in Fig. 146B. When in the correct reading position the poles to the pair of faces must lie somewhere along these small circles but additional measurements are needed in order to fix their position.

If the crystal is now rotated about the similar axis emerging at A, it is clear that faces 3 and 4 describe a pair of small circles about it and faces 2 and 5 another pair. The crystal appears from inspection to be cubic and the zones of the edges that run round the crystal seem to be at right angles; therefore it is fair to describe this second set of small circles about an axis at right angles to the first (Fig. 146C). Rotate the tracing paper through 90° over the stereographic net until the line bisecting the angle between the first set of small circles lies along the other marked diameter of the net. Measure the interfacial angles as before and sketch in the small circles. The validity or otherwise of this assumption can readily be verified.

The positions of the faces 1, 2, 3, 4, 5 . . . 8 are now fixed at the

appropriate points of intersection of the small circles. The validity of
the assumption that the crystal is cubic can now be checked experimentally. Measure the interfacial angle between faces 2 and 3 or 1 and 8. Now
rotate the tracing paper over the Wulff net until faces 2 and 3 or 1 and 8
lie along the same great circle and read off from the net the interfacial
angle between them. If it agrees with your measured angle within the
limits of measuring and plotting (say ± 1°), then the initial postulate is
correct.

Another way of checking is to measure the interfacial angles over the

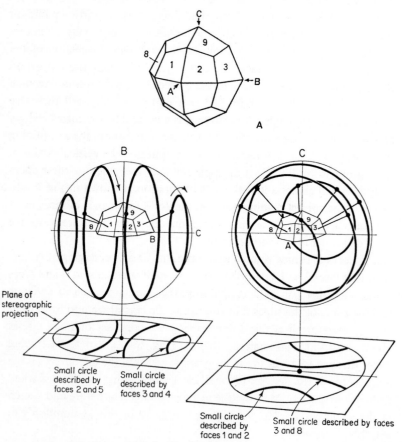

Fig. 146   Cubic crystal plotting technique.

top of the crystal between pairs of faces like 9 and 10 of Fig. 146D. Rotation about the vertical axis causes the poles to these faces to describe small circles about this axis, and in an earlier chapter it was seen that such small circles plot stereographically as concentric circles about the centre of the Wulff net. Some nets show these small circles, in which case the interfacial angles can be plotted directly, but if they are not marked, it is still a simple matter to plot them. The appropriate interfacial angle is read from the centre along one of the diameters of the net, the tracing paper removed from the pin and the small circle drawn in with compasses. If these small circles pass through the points of intersection of the previously constructed small circles, then this is additional proof of the validity of the assumption that the axes are at right angles (Fig. 146E).

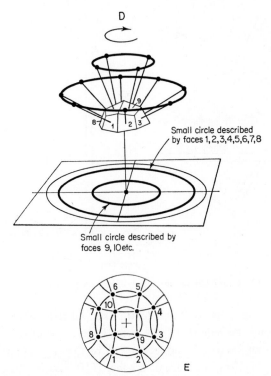

Fig. 146   Cubic crystal plotting technique.

This method of small circle plotting is recommended because it involves a minimum of symmetry assumptions and such as are made can readily be verified by further measurement.

Mathematical relationships

Because the cubic crystallographic axes are equal in length, the axial ratio is 1. This means that the mutual relationships of faces in the cubic system can be readily solved either graphically or by the simple trigonometry of right angled triangles.

The index of any form plotting on the primitive can readily be determined graphically. Fig. 147A is part of a projection of a cubic

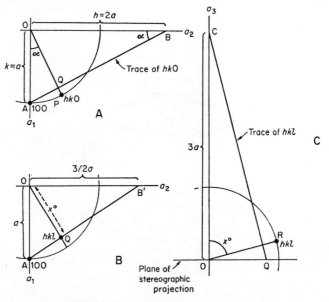

Fig. 147   Graphical determination of indices of cubic crystals.

crystal showing faces (100) and ($hk0$). The Miller index of the latter is required. Join the pole ($hk0$) (the point P) to the centre O. Now draw AB at right angles to OP and let $k = $ OA be the unit distance on the a_1 axis. AB is, in effect, the trace of the face ($hk0$) and in this instance the distance of the intercept on the a_2 axis (h), is 2 OA. The Miller index is thus (210). From Fig. 147A it is also clear that

$$\frac{k}{h} = \tan \alpha = \tan (10\widehat{0)} (hk0),$$

and hence the interfacial angle $(21\widehat{0)} (100)$ is $\tan \dfrac{k}{h} = \tan \tfrac{1}{2} = 26° 34'$.

The calculation of the Miller indices of the general form $\{hkl\}$ is straightforward and may readily be determined graphically. In Fig. 147B the pole (hkl) is shown. Join this point to the centre O and produce the line to the primitive. Now draw AB' at right angles to this line, intersecting it at Q. This line AQB' is, in effect, the trace on the horizontal of the face (hkl). Since OA is the unit intercept on a_1, the intercept on a_2 is given by OB' which is $1\tfrac{1}{2}a_1$, or $\dfrac{3}{2}a$.

Fig. 147C is part of the spherical projection in the plane OQ. The position of (hkl) is given by angle $x°$ taken from Fig. 147B and measured round the sphere. The line OR is the pole to the face (hkl) and the trace of the face itself is, of course, at right angles to this. In Fig. 147B the face intersects the horizontal plane at Q and hence the distance OQ is transferred to Fig. 147C and the line QC constructed from Q normal to OR. The distance OC is thus the intercept on a_3 and in this instance is $3a$.

The intercepts are hence $1 : \dfrac{3}{2} : 3$ and the Miller index of the face is hence (321).

CHAPTER 10

THE HEXAGONAL
AND TRIGONAL SYSTEMS

The study of hexagonal and trigonal crystals has been left until last because they present problems that are not encountered in the other systems. For example, their atomic arrangement is complex and the choice of unit cell is by no means easy.

The most obvious hexagonal lattice would seem to be one having the shape of a hexagonal prism (Fig. 148A), but translation of this lattice

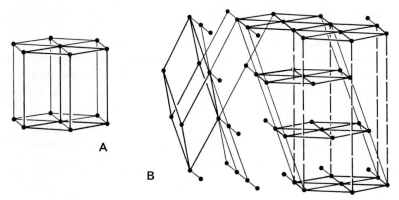

A

B

Fig. 148 (A) Hexagonal P and (B) trigonal R space lattices.

parallel to any of its edges in the horizontal plane immediately introduces another lattice point at the centre of the hexagon. A simpler hexagonal unit cell can be chosen having the shape outlined boldly in Fig. 148A. This is the hexagonal P lattice drawn previously in Figs. 8 and 9.

Imagine several hexagonal nets, stacked one above the other, so that the array of points in the fourth net lies directly above that of the first and with the two intermediate nets evenly displaced between them (Fig. 148B). The simple primitive cell in such a structure has a rhombohedral shape and is the trigonal P space lattice. Because of its shape it is usually called the trigonal R lattice. It has all edges of equal length and although the angles α between the edges can vary from crystal to crystal, they are of course constant in any one mineral species.

It would be convenient if the space lattice could be used to distinguish unambiguously between hexagonal and trigonal crystals. This is not so, however, for whilst all hexagonal crystals have the hexagonal space lattice, trigonal crystals can have either the hexagonal or the trigonal R type structure. Crystals that occur in the same crystal class may have different lattice structures and this further emphasizes the close similarity between the two systems.

It is, however, always possible to choose a rhombohedral lattice for a hexagonal or trigonal substance, but such cells would be multiply primitive and their choice would run counter to the concept of selecting a Bravais lattice that enables the structure to be understood in the simplest possible way. It is worth while digressing to emphasize this point. In the cubic system the cubic I and cubic F lattices are multiply primitive. The primitive lattice in each case is a rhombohedral lattice; in the former it has an inter-edge angle of 109°28′ and in the latter, 60° (Fig. 149). Although these are primitive lattices, neither is chosen,

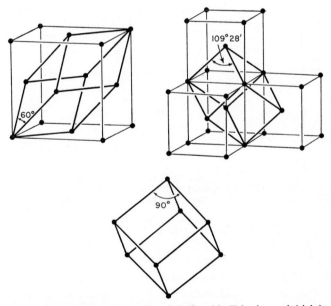

Fig. 149 Rhombohedral cells of (left) cubic F lattice and (right) cubic I lattice. Below: C. The cubic P lattice drawn with a triad axis arranged vertically.

because the multiply primitive cubic Bravais lattices enable the structure to be appreciated more readily. The cubic P lattice, incidentally, can be considered either as a cube or as a rhombohedron with an inter-edge angle of 90°.

The symmetry of the Bravais lattices of hexagonal and trigonal crystals is such that they can all be referred to four crystallographic axes that are chosen parallel to the cell edges of a hexagonal lattice. Three of these axes are of equal length and are symmetrically disposed in the horizontal plane with an inter-axial angle of 120°, whereas the fourth axis differs in length from the other three and is normal to them (Fig. 150A). The horizontal axes are here described as a_1, a_2, a_3 and the vertical axis as c. The relationship of the horizontal axes to the primitive hexagonal lattice is shown in Fig. 150B and the axes are conventionally

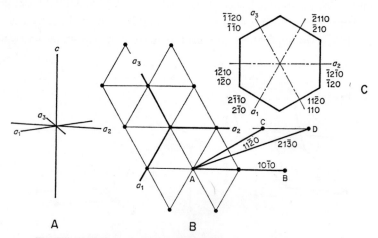

Fig. 150   (A) Hexagonal and trigonal axes.
(B) The relationship of crystallographic axes to the hexagonal P lattice.
(C) A plan view of the hexagonal prism {11$\bar{2}$0} with each face indexed in full and in abbreviated form.

arranged so that the a_2 axis runs from left to right with its positive end at the right. The positive ends of the other axes are symmetrically arranged and thus the positive and negative ends of the crystallographic axes alternate around the axial cross. In structural crystallography the axes here called a_1, a_2, a_3, c, are denoted by x, y, u and z.

Notice that the axial set of hexagonal and trigonal crystals is very similar to that of the tetragonal system in that the horizontal axes are equal in length and the vertical axis is arranged normal to the plane containing them. This similarity is reflected in the crystal forms and the morphology and symmetry of the three systems can be compared directly.

Because there are now four crystallographic axes it follows that the index of any crystallographic plane or face will, if referred to these axes, contain four digits. Such indices are *Miller-Bravais* indices, so called because Bravais adapted the Miller notation for use in the hexagonal and trigonal system. The most general Miller-Bravais index may be written as $(hkil)$ in which h, k, i and l refer to the reciprocal of the ratio of the intercepts of the face on the a_1, a_2, a_3 and c axes in that order.

Look again at Fig. 150B. The trace of the face AB makes a unit intercept on a_1 and on $\bar{a}_3$ but lies parallel to a_2 and c. Its Miller-Bravais index is hence $(10\bar{1}0)$. Face AC has intercepts $1a_1$, $1a_2$, $\frac{1}{2}a_3$, and $\infty\, c$ and thus its index is $(11\bar{2}0)$; face AD has the index $(21\bar{3}0)$ because its intercepts are $1, 2, \frac{2}{3}$ and ∞.

Strictly speaking, the index referring to the intercept on a_3 is redundant because it is controlled by the intercepts on a_1 and a_2. Any change in the intercepts on these axes produces a sympathetic change in the a_3 intercept and this interdependence is shown by the Miller-Bravais index in which $h + k + i = 0$.

There is therefore no real need to use the a_3 intercept and some crystallographers do, in fact omit it, but the crystallography of hexagonal and trigonal crystals will be the more readily understood if the full Miller-Bravais indices are used, at least initially. This scheme is adopted throughout this book.

Fig. 150C is a plan view of the hexagonal prism $\{11\bar{2}0\}$ with each face indexed in full and in its abbreviated form. From the full index of any face it is clear that it belongs to the form $\{11\bar{2}0\}$, but this relationship is obscured when the index is contracted by omitting the a_3 index, as shown by the lower figure.

The contracted notation is, however, of prime importance in determining a zone symbol for hexagonal or trigonal crystals. Since the co-ordinates employed in determining the zone symbol are not applicable to more than three axes, the contracted symbol is used, the missing index (i) being indicated by a full stop, e.g. ($hk.l$). Thus the symbol for the zone containing faces ($hk.l$) and ($h'k'.l'$) is obtained by cross multiplying these in the manner outlined in Chapter 3. The resulting zone symbol is [$uv.w$], but the missing index cannot now be obtained by taking $u + v$ and changing the sign.

The index of a face common to two zones [$uv.w$] and [$u'v'.w'$] can be obtained by cross multiplying in the usual way. The missing figure in the resulting index ($hk.l$) can now be inserted since, for any *face*, $h + k + i = 0$.

There is, therefore, a very strong similarity between the hexagonal and trigonal systems, so much so that some authors describe them as sub-groups of the hexagonal system. Certainly this is so if the crystallo-graphic axes alone are chosen as the basis of defining a system. We have seen, however, that structurally the division is not as sharp as one would wish, but nevertheless the hexagonal and trigonal systems are separable on the nature of the principal axis. All crystals with a vertical hexad axis (6 or $\bar{6}$) are included in the hexagonal system whereas all trigonal crystals have a vertical triad (3 or $\bar{3}$). This distinction can always be made, although the lattice structure of trigonal crystals may be either hexagonal or trigonal. In the following sections certain trigonal crystals will be seen to have a hexagonal morphology, but the distinction between the two can always be made on the basis of the principal axis.

HEXAGONAL SYSTEM

* **Class 6/*mmm*, Hexagonal holosymmetric, dihexagonal bipyramidal, beryl type**

A holosymmetric hexagonal crystal like that of Fig. 151 has seven planes of symmetry, (one horizontal and six vertical), seven axes (one vertical hexad and seven horizontal diads) and a centre. Compare this symmetry set with that of the holosymmetric tetragonal class. The International Symmetry Symbol is derived from a rotation hexad axis normal to a plane of symmetry and at the intersection of two sets of vertical planes, each of which comprises three planes disposed symmetrically. One set of planes contains the horizontal crystallographic axes and the other set bisects the angles between them.

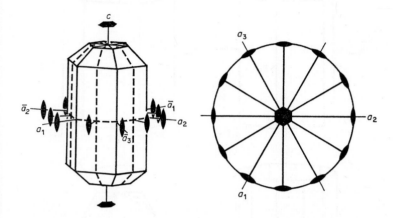

Fig. 151   The symmetry elements and crystallographic axes of class 6/*mmm*. There are two sets of vertical planes of symmetry and two sets of diad axes; one set is coincident with the crystallographic axes; the other set bisects the angles between them.

The elements listed above introduce the six horizontal diads and it is common American practice to write the symbol 6/*m* 2/*m* 2/*m* which emphasizes this.

SPECIAL FORMS

$\left.\begin{array}{l}\{10\bar{1}0\}\\\{11\bar{2}0\}\end{array}\right\}$ *Hexagonal prisms*

Faces with indices $(10\bar{1}0)$ and $(11\bar{2}0)$ are repeated by the symmetry elements so as to produce a six-faced open form parallel to the *c* axis and called a hexagonal prism. The forms $\{10\bar{1}0\}$ and $\{11\bar{2}0\}$ have been distinguished in the past as first- and second-order prisms respectively but they are completely identified by their Miller-Bravais indices.

{hki0} *Dihexagonal prisms*

The face *(hki0)* projects between the planes of symmetry and is hence repeated by them to produce a twelve-faced form called a dihexagonal prism (Fig. 152).

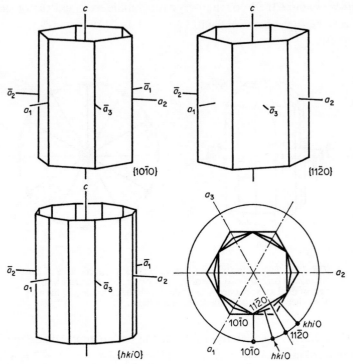

Fig. 152   Prism forms of class 6/*mmm*.

{0001}   *Pinacoid*

$\left.\begin{array}{l}\{h0\bar{h}l\} \\ \{hh\overline{2h}l\}\end{array}\right\}$ *Hexagonal bipyramids*

The inclined forms in zone with the hexagonal prisms are twelve-faced closed forms produced by reflection of the hexagonal pyramid across a horizontal plane of symmetry. A stereographic projection of the unit forms {10Ī1} and {11Ī1} is given in Fig. 153. Notice that the poles of the form {10Ī1} lie closer to the centre of the projection than those of {11Ī1}.

GENERAL FORMS

{*hkil*}   *Dihexagonal bipyramids*

The general form is a twenty-four-faced form that is related to the dihexagonal prism in the same way that the hexagonal bipyramids are

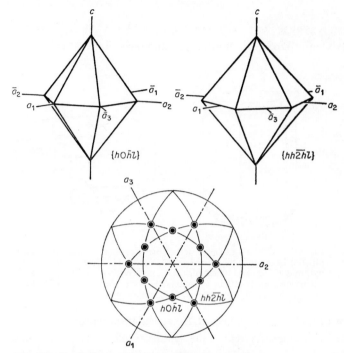

Fig. 153   The forms $\{h0\bar{h}l\}$ and $\{hh\overline{2h}l\}$; class $6/mmm$.

related to the hexagonal prisms. The class as a whole should be compared with the tetragonal holosymmetric class $4/mmm$ (Fig. 154).

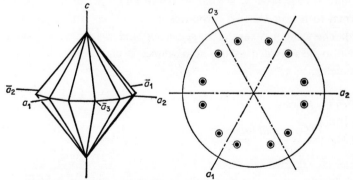

Fig. 154   The general form $\{hkil\}$ of class $6/mmm$: the dihexagonal bipyramid.

EXAMPLES

Crystals assigned to this class include beryl $Be_3Al_2Si_6O_{18}$, covellite CuS, molybdenite MoS_2, pyrrhotite FeS[21] and niccolite NiAs (Fig. 155).

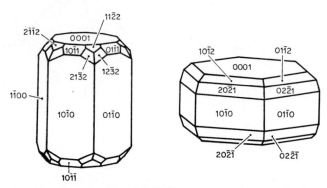

Fig. 155 Crystals of beryl (left) (forms present; hexagonal prism $\{10\overline{1}0\}$; hexagonal bipyramids $\{10\overline{1}1\}$ and $\{11\overline{2}2\}$; dihexagonal bipyramid $\{21\overline{3}2\}$ and pinacoid $\{0001\}$, and pyrrhotite (forms present; hexagonal prism $\{10\overline{1}0\}$ hexagonal bipyramids $\{10\overline{1}2\}$ $\{20\overline{2}1\}$ and pinacoid $\{0001\}$ (see footnote p. 212); class 6/*mmm*.

Class 622, Hexagonal holoaxial, hexagonal trapezohedral

Stated in elementary terms, the symmetry elements of this class are a vertical hexad axis and six horizontal diad axes, of which three are coincident with the crystallographic axes and three bisect the angles between them. There are no planes and no centre of symmetry. The principal axis is a rotation hexad and the International Symmetry Symbol is 622, because a rotation hexad and a set of three diad axes normal to it immediately introduces a second set of three diads (Fig. 156). The symbol is very often shortened and written as 62. The class can also be regarded as the holosymmetric class minus its planes of symmetry.

SPECIAL FORMS

$\left.\begin{array}{l} \{10\overline{1}0\} \\ \{11\overline{2}0\} \end{array}\right\}$ *Hexagonal prisms*

$\{hki0\}$ *Dihexagonal prisms*

The absence of planes of symmetry does not affect the prism forms

21. Pyrrhotite is actually monoclinic (pseudohexagonal) with angle β 90°05′.

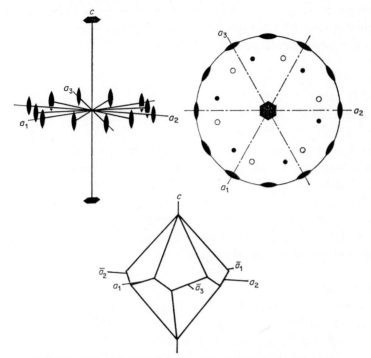

Fig. 156 Symmetry elements, crystallographic axes and a stereo-gram and drawing of the general form (hexagonal trapezohedron) of class 622.

which are the same outwardly as those in the holosymmetric class. The dihexagonal prisms exist because the horizontal diads cause repetition of the face ($hki0$) to produce a twelve-faced open form. As in the holo-symmetric class the hexagonal prisms are readily distinguished by their Miller-Bravais indices rather than by the use of the terms first- and second-order prisms.

{0001}   *Pinacoid*

$\left.\begin{array}{l} \{h0\bar{h}l\} \\ \{hh\overline{2h}l\} \end{array}\right\}$ *Hexagonal bipyramids*

The two forms $\{h0\bar{h}l\}$ and $\{hh\overline{2h}l\}$ are specially related to the symmetry elements in that their poles project on the horizontal diad axes. The diads therefore have the effect of repeating in the lower hemisphere the hexagonal pyramid derived by the action of a rotation hexad, and the resulting form is the hexagonal bipyramid. Like the prisms, these forms are conveniently distinguished by their indices.

GENERAL FORMS

{*hkil*}, {*ikhl*} *Hexagonal trapezohedra*

The absence of planes and centre of symmetry becomes obvious in the general form (Fig. 156). It is a twelve-faced closed form, each face of which is a trapezium. The form should be compared with the general form in classes 422 and 32 of the tetragonal and trigonal systems, to which it is analogous. The hexagonal trapezohedron {*hkil*} bears an enantiomorphous relationship to the form {*ikhl*} and crystals in this class can be right- or left-handed. In fact the general form has not yet been observed in nature and crystals are allocated to this class on structural and optical, not morphological criteria.

EXAMPLES

The best known examples of crystals crystallizing in this class are β-quartz (the high temperature polymorph of quartz stable at atmospheric pressure between 573°C and 870°C) and kalsilite $KAlSiO_4$.

Class $\bar{6}m2$, Ditrigonal bipyramidal

The symmetry elements of this class are an inversion hexad axis (the principal axis) at the intersection of three vertical planes of symmetry that are conventionally placed in the general position bisecting the angles between the horizontal crystallographic axes (Fig. 157). When introducing the concept of inversion axes in Chapter 4 it was pointed out that an inversion hexad axis is morphologically equivalent to a rotation triad normal to a plane of symmetry, although it is structurally distinct and has a higher symmetry. For present purposes, however, this morphological similarity means that the inversion hexad in effect introduces a horizontal plane of symmetry as well as a set of horizontal diad axes that are contained in the vertical planes. The International Symmetry Symbol is thus $\bar{6}m2$.[22] Another consequence is that crystals in this

---

22. A statement as to the significance of the symbol $\bar{6}m2$ is given at the end of the chapter.

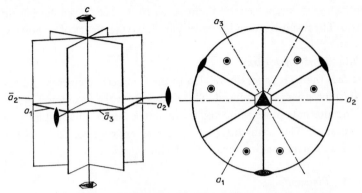

Fig. 157 Symmetry elements, crystallographic axes and a stereogram of the general form (ditrigonal bipyramid) of class 6̄m2.

class have a trigonal appearance because the general form and some of the special forms are of trigonal morphology. There is no ambiguity however; if the student bears in mind the rule that a crystal is assigned always to the highest possible symmetry class on the basis of its structure and that 6̄ has a higher structural symmetry than 3/m, then the apparent difficulties are resolved.

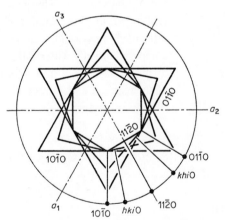

Fig. 158 Prism relationships; class 6̄m2.

SPECIAL FORMS
{101̄0}, {011̄0} *Trigonal prisms*

The operation of the symmetry elements on the face (101̄0) results in it being repeated so as to produce a trigonal prism. There is a corresponding form having the index {011̄0}. The relationships of the various prisms in this class are shown in Fig. 158.

{112̄0} *Hexagonal prism*

Because the face (112̄0) projects on the line bisecting two planes of symmetry, it is repeated by them so as to produce a regular six-sided prism. The resulting form has faces parallel to the planes of symmetry.

{*hki*0} *Ditrigonal prisms*

The face (*hki*0) is generally related to the symmetry elements and again a six-sided prism is produced. This differs from the hexagonal prism in having alternate more acute and more obtuse angles, giving it a trigonal appearance. The term ditrigonal prism is appropriate for this form. There is a corresponding form with the index {*ihk*0}.

{0001} *Pinacoid*
{*h*0$\bar{h}l$}, {0*k*$\bar{k}l$} *Trigonal bipyramids*
{*hh*$\overline{2h}l$} *Hexagonal bipyramids*

GENERAL FORMS
{*hkil*}, {*khil*} *Ditrigonal bipyramids*

The faces that are inclined to both the *a* and *c* axes are simply related to the prism forms and, because of the inversion hexad axis, are all bipyramids. The general form in this class, the ditrigonal bipyramid, can be compared directly with similar forms in classes $\bar{3}m$ and $\bar{4}2m$ of the trigonal and tetragonal systems respectively.

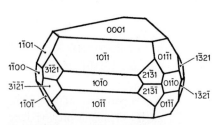

Fig. 159 A possible habit of benitoite; class $\bar{6}m2$. Forms present: trigonal prisms {10$\bar{1}$0}, {01$\bar{1}$0}; trigonal bipyramids {10$\bar{1}$1}, {01$\bar{1}$1}; pinacoid {0001} and ditrigonal bipyramid {21$\bar{3}$1}.

EXAMPLES
Benitoite BaTiSi$_3$O$_9$ (Fig. 159) is one of the few representatives of this class.

Class 6*mm* Dihexagonal pyramidal

Crystals belonging to this class have the symmetry corresponding to a rotation hexad axis at the intersection of two sets of vertical planes of symmetry, each set comprising three planes. One set of planes contains the crystallographic *a* axes and the other set bisects the angles between them (Fig. 160). Stated informally, the symmetry is that of the holo-symmetric class minus the horizontal plane and axes. Consequently the

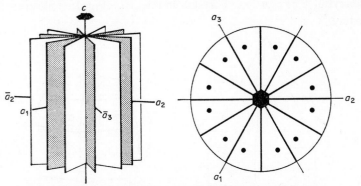

Fig. 160   Symmetry elements, crystallographic axes and a stereo-gram of the general form; (dihexagonal pyramid) of class 6*mm*.

principal axis is polar and some forms in this class are hemimorphic. Again direct comparison should be made with classes 3*m* and 4*mm* in the trigonal and tetragonal systems.

SPECIAL FORMS

$\{10\bar{1}0\}$
$\{11\bar{2}0\}$ } *Hexagonal prisms*

$\{hki0\}$ *Dihexagonal prisms*

The absence of horizontal symmetry elements has no effect on vertical faces whose poles, of course, plot on the primitive circle of the stereo-graphic projection. These forms are therefore morphologically similar to those of the holosymmetric class.

$\{0001\}$, $\{000\bar{1}\}$ *Pedions*

$\{h0\bar{h}l\}$, $\{h0\bar{h}\bar{l}\}$
$\{hh\overline{2h}l\}$, $\{hh\overline{2h}\bar{l}\}$ } *Hexagonal pyramids*

GENERAL FORMS

$\{hkil\}$, $\{hki\bar{l}\}$ *Dihexagonal pyramids*

The uniterminal nature of the principal axis is reflected in the inclined forms which are hemimorphic. If, for example, the form $\{10\bar{1}1\}$ occurs on a crystal, the absence of horizontal symmetry elements means that forms other than $\{10\bar{1}1\}$ can and probably do terminate the other end of the crystal. The sketches of crystals in this class (Fig. 161) illustrate this feature.

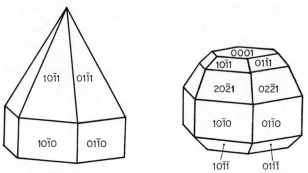

Fig. 161   Possible crystals of zincite (left) (forms present; hexagonal prism $\{10\bar{1}0\}$; hexagonal pyramid $\{10\bar{1}1\}$ and pedion $\{000\bar{1}\}$ and greenockite (right) (forms present; hexagonal prism $\{10\bar{1}0\}$; hexagonal pyramids $\{10\bar{1}1\}$; $\{20\bar{2}1\}$ and $\{10\bar{1}\bar{1}\}$; pedions $\{0001\}$ and $\{000\bar{1}\}$), class 6*mm*.

EXAMPLES

Zincite ZnO, greenockite CdS, wurtzite ZnS and iodyrite AgI are the best known examples, but of these only the first two are at all common. This is another class in which the general form is rarely observed in natural crystals.

Class 6/*m* Hexagonal bipyramidal

There are only two symmetry elements in this class, a rotation hexad axis and a plane of symmetry normal to it. The Hermann-Mauguin symbol is hence 6/*m* (Fig. 162) and comparison should be made with class 4/*m* of the tetragonal system. The symmetry combination 3/*m* is equivalent to an inversion hexad axis $\bar{6}$ and so classes 6/*m* and $\bar{6}$ are directly comparable.

SPECIAL FORMS

$\{10\bar{1}0\}$
$\{11\bar{2}0\}$ *Hexagonal prisms*
$\{hki0\}$

The absence of vertical planes of symmetry and horizontal diad axes precludes the development of the dihexagonal prism. All the prisms in this class are equally generally related to the symmetry elements and can be described by the most general index $\{hki0\}$. The prisms $\{10\bar{1}0\}$ and

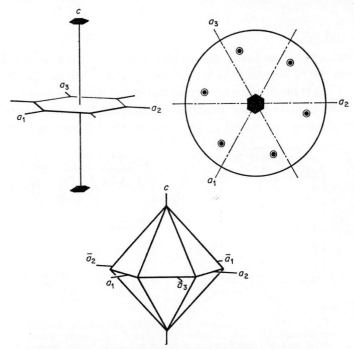

Fig. 162 Symmetry elements, crystallographic axes and the general form (hexagonal bipyramid) of class $6/m$.

$\{11\bar{2}0\}$ are merely more specially related to the a_1, a_2 and a_3 crystallographic axes.

$\{0001\}$ *Pinacoid*

GENERAL FORMS

$\{hkil\}$ Hexagonal bipyramids

Any face that is inclined to the a and c axes will be repeated by the hexad axis so as to produce a hexagonal pyramid and the plane of symmetry causes its repetition in the lower hemisphere to give the hexagonal bipyramid. As with the prisms, the symmetry elements permit only the development of this form and all possible hexagonal bipyramids in this class are general forms and can be described by the index $\{hkil\}$ (Fig. 162). Forms with indices $\{h0hl\}$ and $\{hh\overline{2}hl\}$ have a particular relationship to the crystallographic axes.

EXAMPLES

Minerals that crystallize in this class frequently have a simple habit and appear to belong to a higher symmetry class. Apatite $Ca_5(PO_4)_3$ (OH,F,Cl) is the best-known representative and only occasionally does it exhibit bipyramids other than those in zone with the prism. The usual form of an apatite crystal is illustrated in Fig. 163 and externally it

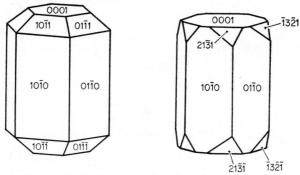

Fig. 163 A crystal of apatite of simple habit (left) (forms present; hexagonal prism $\{10\overline{1}0\}$; hexagonal bipyramid $\{10\overline{1}1\}$ and pinacoid $\{0001\}$, and a possible crystal of vanadinite, showing the general form $\{21\overline{3}1\}$: class $6/m$.

appears to possess the full holosymmetric symmetry. Single crystal X-ray studies would reveal the true structural symmetry and etch-figures on crystal faces are often of value in indicating the lack of vertical planes of symmetry.

Other minerals crystallizing in this class are a group of lead chloro-phosphates, arsenates and vanadinites, called mimetite, pyromorphite and vanadinite (Fig. 163).

Class $\overline{6}$, Trigonal bipyramidal

This is another of the classes of the hexagonal system, the forms of which are morphologically trigonal in aspect. The trigonal appearance is the result of the morphological equivalence of the inversion hexad axis ($\bar{6}$), the only symmetry element of this class, to a rotation triad normal to a plane of symmetry ($3/m$). Crystals belonging to this class would, on their shape, be classified as trigonal but the symmetry of the lattice is such as to place them in the hexagonal system. In practice, however, the problem does not arise, for this class has no known representatives. Comparison should be made with class $6/m$.

SPECIAL FORMS

{*hki*0}   *Trigonal prisms*

As in class $6/m$, the absence of vertical planes of symmetry and horizontal diad axes precludes the development of the ditrigonal prism, and

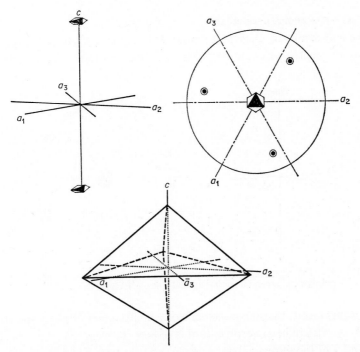

Fig. 164   Symmetry elements, crystallographic axes and the general form (trigonal bipyramid) of class $\bar{6}$.

all forms whose zone axis is [0001] are trigonal prisms. They may therefore be described by the most general index $\{hki0\}$.

$\{0001\}$ *Pinacoid*

GENERAL FORMS
$\{hkil\}$ *Trigonal bipyramids*
Given any inclined face $(hkil)$ the symmetry elements generate always
the trigonal bipyramid (Fig. 164). The general index therefore covers the
forms like $\{h0\overline{h}l\}$ and $\{hh\overline{2h}l\}$ that make simple intercepts on the *a* axes.

EXAMPLES
There are, as already mentioned, no known substances that crystallize
in this class.

Class 6 Hexagonal pyramidal
The only symmetry element is a rotation hexad axis; there are no planes
and no centre of symmetry. The absence of horizontal symmetry

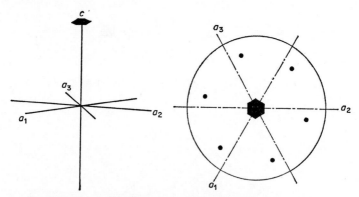

Fig. 165 Symmetry elements, crystallographic axes and a stereogram of the general form (hexagonal pyramid); class 6.

elements means that the principal axis is uniterminal or polar and that
the crystals are hemimorphic. In this respect the class resembles classes
4 and 3 of the tetragonal and trigonal systems with which it should be
compared.

SPECIAL FORMS
{hki0} Hexagonal prisms
The rotation hexad axis causes the repetition of any face lying parallel
to the c axis so as to produce a hexagonal prism. The general index
{hki0} therefore covers all possible forms.

{0001}, {000$\bar{1}$} Pedions

GENERAL FORMS
{hkil}, {hki$\bar{l}$} Hexagonal pyramids
The absence of horizontal symmetry elements means that the general
form is the hexagonal pyramid and not the bipyramid (Fig. 165). All such
pyramids are generally related to the symmetry elements and the index
{hkil} may be used to describe them all.

EXAMPLES
This is another class in which crystals can look deceptively simple; they
appear as though they belonged to class 6*mm*. A structural study would
be necessary in order to assign a crystal of simple morphology correctly
to its class.

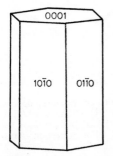 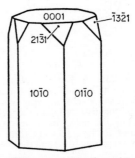

Fig. 166   Left: A common habit of nepheline comprising hexagonal
prism {10$\bar{1}$0} and pedions {0001} and {000$\bar{1}$}; right: A possible
nepheline crystal modified by the general form {21$\bar{3}$1}; class 6.

Nepheline $NaAlSiO_4$ is the best known representative of this class.
Although well-formed crystals are not abundant, most students will be
familiar with the six-sided basal sections that occur in undersaturated
basic lavas like nephelinite (Fig. 166).

Plotting technique and calculation of the axial ratio
Because the same principles are involved in the plotting technique and
calculations for both hexagonal and trigonal systems, they are treated
together at the end of the chapter.

TRIGONAL SYSTEM

* **Class $\bar{3}m$, Trigonal holosymmetric, ditrigonal scalenohedral, calcite type**
Perfect calcite crystals are not difficult to find and the most elementary
collections usually contain crystals of several habits. In the simplest
terms a calcite crystal like that of Fig. 167 can be described as having

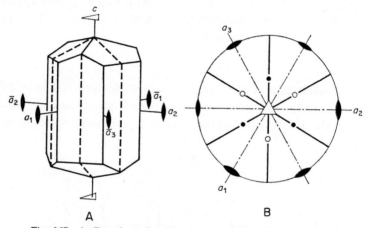

Fig. 167   A. Drawing of a calcite crystal showing symmetry elements and crystallographic axes of class $\bar{3}m$.
B. A stereogram showing symmetry elements, crystallographic axes
and the distribution of the inclined faces of Fig. 167A. (In order to
show the poles more clearly, the form plotted makes twice the
intercept on c than the form in Fig. 167A.) Forms present: hexagonal prism $\{10\bar{1}0\}$ and rhombohedron $\{01\bar{1}2\}$.

four axes of symmetry (a vertical triad and three horizontal diads; all
coincident with the crystallographic axes), three vertical diagonal planes
of symmetry and a centre. In Fig. 167B the inclined faces are plotted on a
stereogram and if this is compared with Fig. 60 it will be seen that they
are arranged in the manner determined by an inversion triad axis $\bar{3}$.
This is the symbol that is used therefore in writing the International

Symmetry Symbol, $\bar{3}m$. The student should check for himself that $\bar{3}m$ introduces horizontal diad axes. In American literature the symbol is often written $\bar{3}2m$ which emphasizes the fact that the diad axes stand normal to the symmetry planes. The International Symmetry Symbol is derived from structural considerations which make $\bar{3}2m$ an incorrect statement of the point group symmetry. An outline of the reasons for this are given at the end of the chapter.

SPECIAL FORMS

$\{10\bar{1}0\}$
$\{11\bar{2}0\}$ $\Big\}$ *Hexagonal prisms*

The poles to faces $(10\bar{1}0)$ and $(11\bar{2}0)$ project either on a symmetry plane or on a diad axis and hence they are repeated by the symmetry elements to give six-sided hexagonal prisms (Fig. 168).

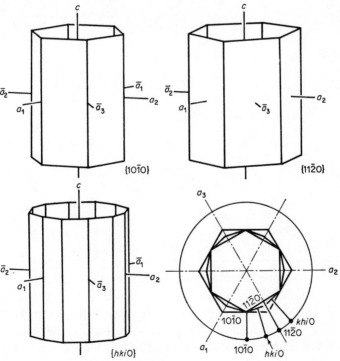

Fig. 168   Prism forms of class $\bar{3}m$.

P

{*hki*0}   *Dihexagonal prisms*

The pole to the face (*hki*0) projects on the primitive circle of a stereogram in a position generally related to the diad axes and planes. The resulting form is a twelve-faced dihexagonal prism.

{0001}   *Pinacoid*

{*h*0$\bar{h}$*l*}, {0*k*$\bar{k}$*l*}   *Rhombohedra*

The operation of the inversion triad axes on the face (*h*0$\bar{h}$*l*) generates the rhombohedron which is a six-faced closed form (Fig. 169) each face of

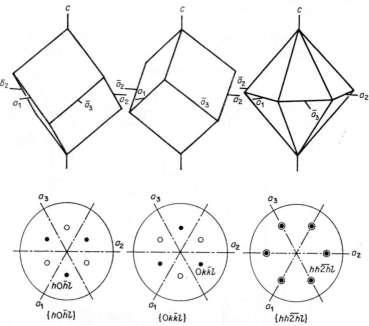

Fig. 169   The forms {*h*0$\bar{h}$*l*}, {0$\bar{k}$$\bar{k}$*l*} and {*hh*$\bar{2}$*hl*}; class $\bar{3}$*m*.

which is a rhombus. There are three upper faces symmetrically disposed about the principal axis and three similar lower faces arranged so that they lie parallel to the upper faces and thus their poles plot as shown on Fig. 169. There is a family of rhombohedra having the index {*h*0$\bar{h}$*l*} and specific forms have indices like {10$\bar{1}$1}, {20$\bar{2}$1}, {40$\bar{4}$1} and so on. It will be seen from Fig. 169 that the face (0*k*$\bar{k}$*l*) is not a possible face of the rhombohedron $\{h0\bar{h}l\}$ but that it is part of another rhombohedron $\{0k\bar{k}l\}$ that is rotated, as it were, 60° from the form $\{h0\bar{h}l\}$. These two families of rhombohedra are distinct, and they are most logically distinguished by their Miller-Bravais indices. In the past the terms *positive* and *negative rhombohedra* have been used for the forms $\{h0\bar{h}l\}$ and $\{0k\bar{k}l\}$ respectively.

Occasionally it happens that the two rhombohedra are developed on the same crystal. The structural difference between them is nevertheless maintained, although if both rhombohedra were developed equally, the crystal would resemble the hexagonal bipyramid. This structural distinction is very clearly shown by calcite in which the perfect cleavage is developed parallel to the rhombohedron $\{10\bar{1}1\}$.

$\{hh\overline{2h}l\}$ *Hexagonal bipyramids*
Because the pole to the face $(hh\overline{2h}l)$ projects on a line bisecting the planes of symmetry, the resulting form has twice the number of faces as the rhombohedron and is a hexagonal bipyramid.

GENERAL FORMS
$\{hkil\}$, $\{khil\}$ *Ditrigonal scalenohedra*
The form $\{hkil\}$ is a closed form having twelve faces, but because the face $(hkil)$ is generally related to the symmetry elements, the form differs

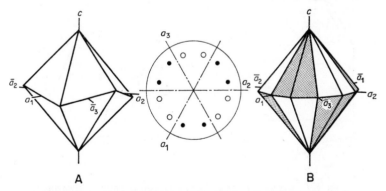

Fig. 170 A. The general form $\{hkil\}$ (ditrigonal scalenohedron) of class $\bar{3}m$.
B. The dihexagonal bipyramid: development of the shaded faces generates the general form.

from the hexagonal bipyramid both in appearance and in its relation to the symmetry elements. Fig. 170 illustrates the form and its stereographic projection. Each of the faces is a scalene triangle and the form has, in effect, six pairs of faces so that the edges between them are alternately sharp and blunt around the crystal. The form may be considered as derived from the dihexagonal bipyramid by developing alternate pairs of faces like those shaded in Fig. 170B. The alternation round the crystal of like and unlike edges is a mark of the ditrigonal nature of the form and the logical name for it is hence the *ditrigonal scalenohedron*. If a comparison is made between this class and class $\bar{4}2m$ of the tetragonal system it will be seen that the general forms are very similar. One of the names applied to the general form in $\bar{4}2m$ is the ditetragonal scalenohedron and it serves to emphasize the relationship between the classes.

EXAMPLES

The commonest representative is the mineral calcite $CaCO_3$ together with the other rhombohedral carbonates magnesite $MgCO_3$, siderite $FeCO_3$, rhodochrosite $MnCO_3$ and smithsonite $ZnCO_3$. Other minerals to crystallize here are the zeolite chabazite $(CaNa_2)Al_2Si_4O_{12}.6H_2O$ corundum Al_2O_3, haematite Fe_2O_3 and brucite $Mg(OH)_2$ (Fig. 171).

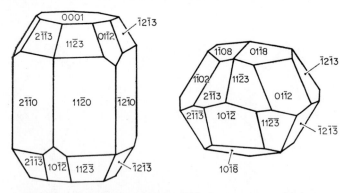

Fig. 171 Crystals of corundum (left) (forms present; hexagonal prism $\{11\bar{2}0\}$; rhombohedron $\{01\bar{1}2\}$; hexagonal bipyramid $\{11\bar{2}3\}$ and pinacoid $\{0001\}$), and haematite (forms present; rhombohedron $\{01\bar{1}2\}$ and $\{01\bar{1}8\}$; hexagonal bipyramid $\{11\bar{2}3\}$); class $\bar{3}m$. See figs. 167 and 184 for drawings of calcite.

Class 32, Trigonal holoaxial, trigonal trapezohedral, quartz type

Quartz is another mineral that occurs abundantly in nature. Well-shaped crystals very commonly line vugs and cavities in rocks and have been known to man since earliest times. A crystal of quartz like that shown in Fig. 172 has a vertical triad axis of symmetry, three horizontal

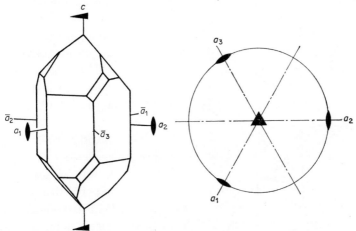

Fig. 172 A quartz crystal showing symmetry elements and crystallographic axes; class 32. The forms present are hexagonal prism {10$\bar{1}$0}, rhombohedra {10$\bar{1}$1} and {01$\bar{1}$1} and the trigonal bipyramid {11$\bar{2}$1}.

diad axes coincident with the crystallographic axes and a centre. It is clear from this crystal that there are no planes of symmetry, but some quartz crystals are simpler than the one illustrated and may give the impression that planes of symmetry are present.

The symmetry may be stated formally as a rotation triad normal to a set of three diads which are chosen as the crystallographic axes. The Hermann-Mauguin symbol is hence 32 and the class can be thought of as the holosymmetric minus its planes of symmetry. Comparison should be made with classes 422 and 622 of the tetragonal and hexagonal systems.

SPECIAL FORMS

{10$\bar{1}$0} *Hexagonal prism*

The pole to the face (10$\bar{1}$0) projects between the horizontal symmetry axes and is hence repeated by them to give the hexagonal prism.

{11$\bar{2}$0}, {2$\bar{1}\bar{1}$0} *Trigonal prisms*

The poles to faces (11$\bar{2}$0) and (2$\bar{1}\bar{1}$0) plot stereographically on the primitive circle at the points of emergence of the symmetry axes. They are repeated therefore to form two enantiomorphous trigonal prisms {11$\bar{2}$0} and {2$\bar{1}\bar{1}$0}. The prisms are shown diagrammatically in Fig. 173.

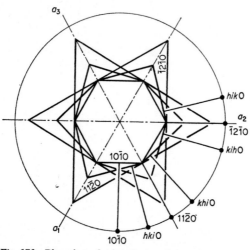

Fig. 173 Plan view of prism forms of class 32.

{*hki*0}, {*ikh*0} *Ditrigonal prisms*

It will be seen from Fig. 173 that the face (*hki*0) is more generally related to the horizontal symmetry elements than are (10$\bar{1}$0) and (11$\bar{2}$0). Thus, although the symmetry axes cause its repetition to give a six-faced prism, it is clear that this is not a regular hexagonal prism, because it has alternate sharp and blunt edges. This prism is related to the trigonal prism in the same way as the dihexagonal prism is related to the hexagonal prism and thus the name *ditrigonal prism* is appropriate. Just as there are enantiomorphous trigonal prisms, there are enantiomorphous ditrigonal prisms.

{0001} *Pinacoid*
{*h*0$\bar{h}l$}, {0*k$\bar{k}$l*} *Rhombohedra*

The combined operation of the triad and diad axes generates the rhombohedra {*h*0$\bar{h}l$} and {0*k$\bar{k}$l*} from inclined faces in zone with (10$\bar{1}$0) and (01$\bar{1}$0) respectively. The quartz crystal drawn in Fig. 172 has both rhombohedra developed, but the difference in size between them emphasizes their separate structural identity. Quite often the two rhombohedra are differently etched in natural crystals; one set of rhombohedral faces being smooth and glassy and the other set pitted and dull. This differential etching is of value in demonstrating that although both rhombohedra may be equally developed and make a crystal look hexagonal it is nevertheless trigonal.

$\{hh\overline{2h}l\}$, $\{2hh\overline{h}l\}$ *Trigonal bipyramids*

The forms $\{11\overline{2}0\}$ and $\{2\overline{1}\overline{1}0\}$ are trigonal prisms. The forms $\{hh\overline{2h}l\}$

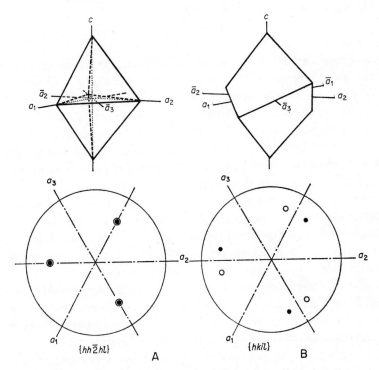

Fig. 174 The form $\{hh\overline{2h}l\}$ and the general form $\{hkil\}$ (trigonal trapezohedron); class 32.

and $\{2hh\overline{h}l\}$ are in zone with them and $\{0001\}$ and they are six-faced closed forms illustrated in Fig. 174A.

GENERAL FORMS

$\{hkil\}$, $\{ikhl\}$ *Trigonal trapezohedra*

The general form is illustrated in Fig. 174B and is a six-faced closed form having three upper and three lower faces. This is true also of the rhombohedron and trigonal bipyramid, but the general form differs from them in that each face has an irregular, four-sided outline. It is as though the upper and lower faces of the trigonal bipyramid had been twisted slightly out of alignment by rotating them counter to one another about the *c* axis. The term *trapezohedron* is appropriate and has been used also for similar forms in the tetragonal and hexagonal systems. Again enantiomorphous forms occur.

EXAMPLES

The best-known example of this class is α-quartz, the polymorph of SiO_2 that is stable at atmospheric pressure below 575°C. Most crystals are combinations of the hexagonal prism and both rhombohedra, the relative development of which can give the crystal a hexagonal or trigonal appearance (Fig. 172). Not infrequently, however, the crystals are modified by trigonal bipyramid and trigonal trapezohedron faces. These occur in untwinned crystals at the corners of every alternate prism face and show clearly the trigonal symmetry of quartz. The trigonal bipyramids appear as parallel-sided, rectangular faces that truncate the corners between the prism and rhombohedron faces and the trigonal trapezohedron (the commonly occurring form is $\{51\bar{6}1\}$) bevels the edge between the trigonal bipyramid and the prism faces. It has only two parallel edges; those against the prism and bipyramid.

The structure of quartz is such that either the forms $\{hh\overline{2h}l\}$ and $\{hkil\}$ or $\{2h\bar{h}\bar{h}l\}$ and $\{hkil\}$ occur. These faces appear either at the upper right- or upper left-hand corner of the hexagonal prism faces and accordingly quartz is described as right- or left-handed.

The internal symmetry confers on quartz another feature of prime industrial importance, that of *piezo-electricity*. All crystals in this class of the trigonal system have *a* axes that are polar and uniterminal. In 1880, J. and P. Curie found that if a compressive force was applied to quartzes parallel to their *a* axes, then the ends of the axes became oppositely charged. They also demonstrated that if an electric field was

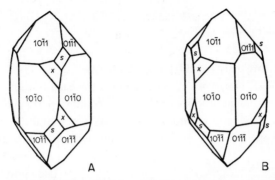

Fig. 175   Right (A) and left handed (B) crystals of quartz. Forms present are hexagonal prism {10Ī0}; rhombohedra {10Ī1} and {01Ī1}; trigonal bipyramid (s) {11Ž1} (A) and {2ĪĪ1} (B) and the trigonal trapezohedra (x) {51ō1} (A) and {6Ī51} (B).

applied to a quartz crystal in this direction then a measurable deformation resulted. For years this phenomenon of piezo-electricity remained a scientific curiosity but eventually it was put to great use in oscillator plates. In an AC field the piezo-electric properties of quartz cause it to deform first one way and then the other so that the crystal oscillates rapidly at a very constant frequency; a property of great value in radio and electrical equipment.

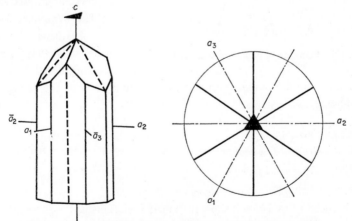

Fig. 176   A tourmaline crystal and stereogram showing symmetry elements and crystallographic axes; class 3*m*. The forms present are trigonal prism {10Ī0}; the hexagonal prism {11Ž0} and the trigonal pyramid {02Ž1}.

The other mineralogical example is cinnabar HgS and the metals selenium and tellurium crystallize here also (Fig. 175).

*   **Class 3m Ditrigonal pyramidal, tourmaline type**

Tourmaline, although not of as common occurrence as calcite or quartz, is a fairly abundant accessory mineral of granites, particularly those of south-west England. If complete crystals are examined, both their trigonal shape and lack of horizontal symmetry elements are at once apparent (Fig. 176). The only elements of symmetry are a rotation triad, the principal axis, at the intersection of a set of three vertical planes of symmetry that are placed in the most general position bisecting the angles between the horizontal crystallographic axes. The symmetry symbol is hence 3m and crystals show hemimorphic forms. Comparison should be made with classes 4mm and 6mm of the tetragonal and hexagonal systems.

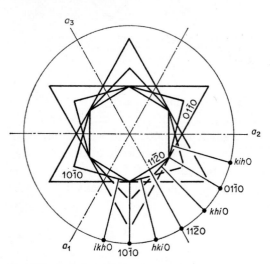

Fig. 177   Plan view of prism forms; class 3m.

SPECIAL FORMS

$\{10\bar{1}0\}$, $\{01\bar{1}0\}$ *Trigonal prisms*

$\{11\bar{2}0\}$ *Hexagonal prism*

$\{hki0\}$, $\{ikh0\}$ *Ditrigonal prisms*

Reference to Fig. 177 will show the mutual relationships of these prisms. Compare Fig. 177 with Fig. 173 and notice that the prism $\{10\bar{1}0\}$ is the hexagonal prism in class 32 and the trigonal prism in class 3m, and that similarly the roles of the forms of $\{11\bar{2}0\}$ in these two classes are reversed.

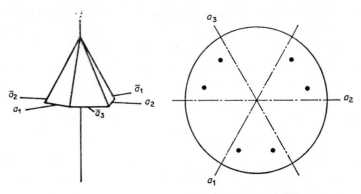

Fig. 178   The general form {*hkil*} (ditrigonal pyramid) of class 3*m*.

{0001}, {000$\bar{1}$} *Pedions*

{*h*0$\bar{h}l$}, {0*k$\bar{k}l$*} *Trigonal pyramids*
These forms are in zone with the trigonal prisms and the pedions. The form is hence a three-faced open form, the *trigonal pyramid*.

{*hh$\overline{2h}l$*} *Hexagonal pyramids*
The pole to the face (*hh$\overline{2h}l$*) projects between the symmetry planes,

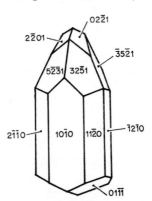

which together with the triad axis, produce a six-faced hexagonal pyramid. The rhombohedron is precluded by the absence of horizontal diads.

GENERAL FORMS
{*hkil*}, {*hki$\bar{l}$*} ⎫
{*ikhl*}, {*ikh$\bar{l}$*} ⎬ *Ditrigonal pyramids*
The absence of horizontal symmetry elements results again in a simple relationship between the prism {*hki*0} and the general form {*hkil*} which is the ditrigonal pyramid. It has the form shown in Fig. 178.

EXAMPLES
Tourmaline is the type mineral of this class

Fig. 179   A crystal of tourmaline (class 3*m*) showing the general form {32$\bar{5}$1}. Other forms are the trigonal prism {10$\bar{1}$0}; the hexagonal prism {11$\bar{2}$0} and the trigonal pyramids {02$\bar{2}$1} and {01$\bar{1}\bar{1}$}.

and a crystal is drawn in Fig. 179. Some tourmaline crystals show the polar nature of the principal axis by being coloured green at one end and pink at the other. Tourmaline has piezo-electric properties and it also shows *pyroelectricity*, so that a crystal acquires opposite electrical charges at the two ends on heating. Other examples are proustite Ag_3AsS_3 and pyrargyrite Ag_3SbS_3.

Class $\overline{3}$ Trigonal rhombohedral

Crystals belonging to this class appear to have a vertical triad axis and a centre of symmetry, but this is equivalent to an inversion triad axis and the symmetry symbol is hence $\overline{3}$ (Fig. 180).

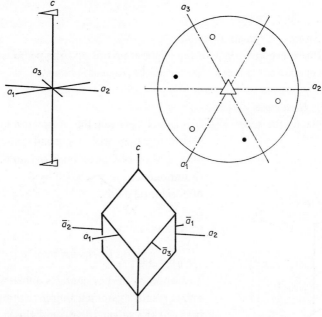

Fig. 180   Symmetry elements, crystallographic axes and the general form (rhombohedron); class $\overline{3}$.

SPECIAL FORMS

{*hki*0}   *Hexagonal prisms*

Because there is only one symmetry element all possible prism forms are equally generally related to it and may be described under the most general index $\{hki0\}$. An inversion triad repeats the face (hki0) so as to produce a hexagonal prism. The prisms $\{10\bar{1}0\}$ and $\{11\bar{2}0\}$ are merely prisms with indices that show a simple relationship to the crystallographic axes.

$\{0001\}$ *Pinacoid*

GENERAL FORMS
$\{hkil\}$ Rhombohedra
As with the prisms, the absence of vertical and horizontal planes and horizontal symmetry axes, means that all possible inclined forms are equally related to the inversion triad. All such forms are rhombohedra. They are similar morphologically to the rhombohedra that occur as special forms in classes 32 and $\bar{3}m$ but differ from them structurally in that they possess neither diad symmetry axes, nor planes (Fig. 180).

EXAMPLES
This is yet another class in which crystals can be deceptively simple in appearance and appear to belong to higher symmetry classes. Frequently

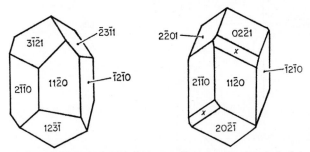

Fig. 181   Crystals belonging to class $\bar{3}$. Left: the rhombohedron $\{3\bar{1}\bar{2}1\}$ in combination with prism $\{11\bar{2}0\}$; Right; prism $\{11\bar{2}0\}$ terminated by rhombohedra $\{02\bar{2}1\}$ and $\{13\bar{4}1\}$ (x) (Dioptase).

additional structural information is required in order to allocate a crystal correctly to its class. Comparison should be made with classes $\bar{4}$ and $\bar{6}$.

Some of the carbonates crystallize in this class, among them dolomite

$CaMg(CO_3)_2$ and ankerite $Ca(Fe^{2+}Mg)(CO_3)_2$. Dioptase $Cu_6Si_6O_{18}$. $6H_2O$ is usually placed here although it may belong to class 3. Phenacite Be_2SiO_4, commonly crystallizes with a flat rhombohedral habit and the related mineral willemite Zn_2SiO_4 occurs here as well. Ilmenite, $FeTiO_3$, an important iron ore and an accessory in basic igneous rocks, also crystallizes in this class (Fig. 181).

Class 3, Trigonal pyramidal

The only symmetry element in this class is a rotation triad axis, always chosen as the principal axis, which is polar and uniterminal.

SPECIAL FORMS

{hki0} *Trigonal prisms*

A face that is parallel to the *c* axis will be repeated by the triad so as to produce a trigonal prism. All possible forms are covered by using the

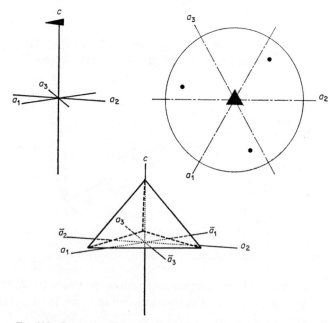

Fig. 182 Symmetry elements, crystallographic axes and the general form (trigonal pyramid); class 3.

most general index $\{hki0\}$; the forms $\{10\bar{1}0\}$ and $\{11\bar{2}0\}$ merely have particularly simple intercepts on the horizontal crystallographic axes.

$\{0001\}$, $\{000\bar{1}\}$ *Pedions*

GENERAL FORMS
$\{hki l\}$, $\{hki\bar{l}\}$ *Trigonal pyramids*
Any face that is inclined to both the *a* and *c* axes will be repeated by the triad to give a trigonal pyramid like that illustrated in Fig. 182 which, on

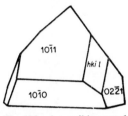

its own, appears to be more symmetrical than in fact it is. Structurally it differs from other trigonal pyramids in that it possesses no planes of symmetry. Direct comparison can be made with forms that occur in classes 4 and 6 of the tetragonal and hexagonal systems.

Fig. 183 A possible crystal belonging to class 3. A combination of the trigonal prism $\{10\bar{1}0\}$ and the pedion $\{000\bar{1}\}$ with the trigonal pyramids $\{10\bar{1}1\}$, $\{02\bar{2}1\}$ and $\{hki l\}$.

EXAMPLES
Mineralogical examples are very few. Parisite, a fluocarbonate of the rare earth metals $[(Ce, La, Di) F_2]_2.Ca(CO_3)_3$, has been placed here as has gratonite $Pb_9As_4S_{15}$, but neither with absolute certainty. A possible crystal is illustrated in Fig. 183.

Stereographic projection of hexagonal and trigonal crystals using a Wulff net
The plotting technique and calculation of crystallographic constants are the same for hexagonal and trigonal crystals and they are described together. Although the worked example is of a trigonal crystal, exactly the same principles apply when plotting hexagonal crystals.

Fig. 184A is a drawing of a calcite crystal. The holding position is at once apparent, because in most hexagonal and trigonal crystals the principal hexad or triad axis is obvious. The crystal is first carefully drawn and the interfacial angles measured and recorded for the faces 1 to 6 in the prism zone. Mark a point on the primitive circle of the tracing paper placed over a Wulff net and let this represent the pole to face 1. The remaining faces 2 to 6 can now be inserted by plotting their interfacial angles successively round the primitive.

The inclined faces 7 to 12 and 13 to 18 are plotted next using the small circle technique. Start with face 7. Measure and record the interfacial

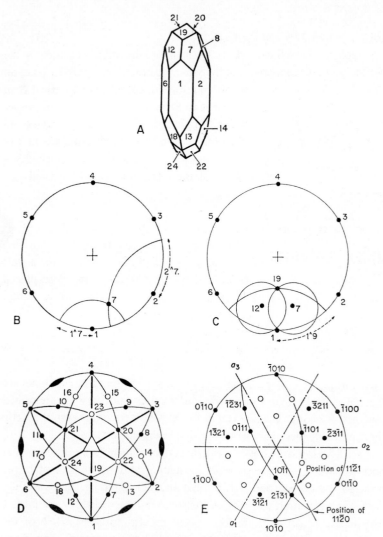

Fig. 184   The stereographic projection of a crystal of calcite.

angles $\widehat{1\ 7}$ and $\widehat{2\ 7}$ taking care to ensure that the goniometer is held at right angles to the edge between the faces being measured and that the arms of the instrument are bedded snugly against the faces.

Move the tracing paper over the Wulff net until the pole to face 1 lies over the origin of the small circles (Fig. 184B). Read off round the primitive the interfacial angle $\widehat{1\ 7}$ and sketch in the small circle as shown. Rotate the tracing paper now until the pole to face 2 lies over the origin of the small circles, read off the interfacial angle $\widehat{2\ 7}$ and sketch in this small circle. The pole to face 7 is at the point of intersection of these two small circles. This procedure is repeated for the remaining faces 8 to 12 and 13 to 18, taking care to measure and plot the interfacial angles $\widehat{1\ 13}$ and $\widehat{2\ 13}$ correctly because it is easy inadvertently to turn the crystal through $60°$.

There are two obvious ways of plotting faces 19 to 21 and 22 to 24. The interfacial angles $\widehat{1\ 19}$ and $\widehat{2\ 19}$ can be measured, recorded and plotted in the usual way by constructing small circles, giving the pole to face 19 at the intersection of the two resulting small circles. The difficulty, however, is that the accurate measurement of the interfacial angle $\widehat{2\ 19}$ requires considerable dexterity and errors can easily be introduced.

An alternative method is to measure the interfacial angles $\widehat{7\ 19}$ and $\widehat{12\ 19}$ and to construct the appropriate small circles about faces 7 and 12 using the method described in Chapter 12 (Fig. 184C). The pole to face 19 lies at one of the points of intersection of the two small circles. It is very obvious from the disposition of the faces of the crystal which of the two intersection points is the one required.

The completed stereogram appears as Fig. 184D and zonal relationships can be sketched in and symmetry planes and axes inserted. There are clearly three vertical symmetry planes and the poles to the prism faces lie on them. No horizontal symmetry plane is present because faces plotting in the upper hemisphere within the primitive are not repeated vertically below. That the principal axis is a triad is obvious from the disposition of faces 19, 20 and 21, but the poles of faces 22, 23 and 24 show that they are part of the same form and that the principal axis is an inversion triad. Inspection of the crystal and stereogram reveal also the presence of three horizontal diad axes emerging, as it were, from the edges between the vertical prism faces and on the stereogram

Q

bisecting the angles between the poles of these faces. The symmetry of the crystal can be expressed by the International Symmetry Symbol $\bar{3}m$ and it is a member of the holosymmetric class of the trigonal system. Notice that no attempt has been made as yet to allocate crystallographic axes. The positions of these are decided after the parametral form is chosen.

Choice of parametral form and allocation of Miller-Bravais indices

As in all other systems, the next step is to select a suitable inclined form as the parametral form. In this example the obvious form to select as the parametral form is that comprising faces 19 to 24 and this is given the index $\{10\bar{1}1\}$. This immediately fixes the positions of the crystallographic axes (Fig. 184E) and allows the other faces to be indexed. The vertical faces are in zone with $\{10\bar{1}1\}$ and must hence constitute the hexagonal prism $\{10\bar{1}0\}$. The steeply inclined faces 7 and 8 are in zone with $\{10\bar{1}1\}$ and the prism $\{11\bar{2}0\}$ which, although not represented on the crystal, would nevertheless plot on the primitive mid-way between the existing prism faces, and on the diad and crystallographic axes. Thus by summation of indices a suitable Miller-Bravais index for the form is $\{21\bar{3}1\}$, making it the general form, the ditrigonal scalenohedron. The parametral form itself is the rhombohedron $\{10\bar{1}1\}$.

It may well happen that the ditrigonal scalenohedron is a steeper form than $\{21\bar{3}1\}$ in which case the pole will not be in zone with $\{10\bar{1}1\}$ and $\{11\bar{2}0\}$. This is the case in Fig. 185A, where the index of the form $\{hkil\}$

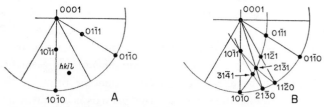

Fig. 185   Determination of Miller indices by zonal methods. For clarity all poles are shown in the upper hemisphere position.

is required. It may be found graphically in the manner illustrated by Fig. 185B. First sketch in the great circle joining $(01\bar{1}1)$ and $(10\bar{1}0)$. This fixes the position of face $(11\bar{2}1)$ at the intersection with the great circle joining (0001) and (11$\bar{2}$0). The position of (21$\bar{3}$1) is fixed also as shown in the figure. Now draw a straight line from (0001) through (21$\bar{3}$1) to the primitive. This is another great circle and the pole on the primitive has the index (21$\bar{3}$0). A great circle from (21$\bar{3}$0) to (10$\bar{1}$1) passes through the face (*hkil*) and the index (31$\bar{4}$1) is appropriate. Sketching in zones like this is a simple matter and indices of forms can be deduced either by summation or by using zone symbols and 'cross multiplying'.

Many hexagonal crystals, particularly those of high symmetry, have two well-developed bipyramids like those illustrated by the stereogram in Fig. 186. Notice that the faces of the forms {10$\bar{1}$1} and {11$\bar{2}$1} lie on

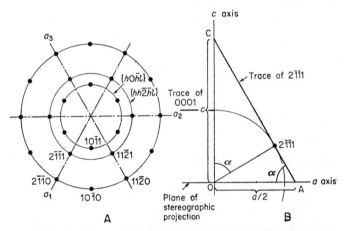

Fig. 186 Determination of axial ratio of hexagonal and trigonal crystals.
A. Relative positions in stereographic projection of forms {*h0h̄l*} and {*hh2̄hl*}.
B. Section through spherical projection in the plane containing the a_1 and *c* crystallographic axes.

small circles concentric about {0001} but that the faces of {11$\bar{2}$1} lie closer to the primitive than those of {10$\bar{1}$1}. This is a most useful guide in selecting the parametral form. Where two such pyramids are developed, make the one that plots nearest the centre of the projection the form {10$\bar{1}$1}, provided of course that it has a reasonable slope and is not obviously an obtuse form like {10$\bar{1}$4} for example. If only one pyramid is developed, then assign to it *first* the index {10$\bar{1}$1}.

Calculation of the axial ratio

In the hexagonal and trigonal systems, as in the tetragonal, the axial ratio is given by a/c. It is seen from Fig. 186A that the pole to face $(2\bar{1}\bar{1}1)$ lies in the plane of the a_1 and c axes and is accordingly more useful than $(10\bar{1}1)$ in determining the axial ratio. Notice also that the intercept on a_1 given by the first digit of the Miller-Bravais index is not a unit intercept but is half the unit value and in the index it therefore appears as the figure 2.

Fig. 186B is part of the spherical projection in the plane containing the a_1 and c axes. It is clear from this that $c/\frac{a}{2} = \tan \alpha = \tan (0001) \overset{\frown}{\ } (2\bar{1}\bar{1}1)$

Thus $c/a = \frac{1}{2} \tan (0001) \overset{\frown}{\ } (2\bar{1}\bar{1}1)$.

The axial ratio can also be calculated from face $(10\bar{1}1)$. Fig. 187A

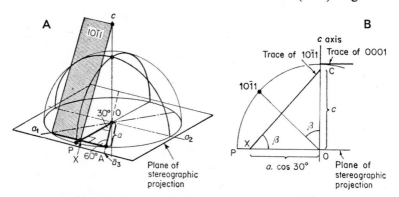

Fig. 187 Determination of axial ratio of hexagonal and trigonal crystals using $\{10\bar{1}1\}$.
A. Part of spherical projection.
B. Section through the spherical projection in the plane containing the c axis and the pole to $(10\bar{1}1)$.

shows the attitude of the face $(10\bar{1}1)$ to the crystallographic axes. Let OA be the unit intercept on $\bar{a}_3$. OX is the intercept made in the horizontal plane by the face $(10\bar{1}1)$ along the line OP which bisects the angle between the crystallographic axes a_1 and $\bar{a}_3$. The intercept OX is given by $a.\cos 30°$ since OA is the unit length a of the $\bar{a}_3$ axis.

Fig. 187B is part of the spherical projection in the plane containing c and OX, from which it is apparent that $\dfrac{c}{a.\cos 30°} = \tan \beta = \tan (0001) \overset{\frown}{\ } (10\bar{1}1)$.

Thus $c/a = \tan (0001)\widehat{}(10\bar{1}1) \cdot \cos 30°$, and $\cos 30° = \sqrt{\dfrac{3}{2}}$ since OAX is a 90°, 60°, 30° triangle.

Graphical determination of the axial ratio

It is a relatively simple matter to determine graphically the axial ratio of a hexagonal or trigonal crystal, given a stereogram having the poles (10$\bar{1}$1) or (11$\bar{2}$1) (or other faces of these forms) shown. Fig. 188A is a

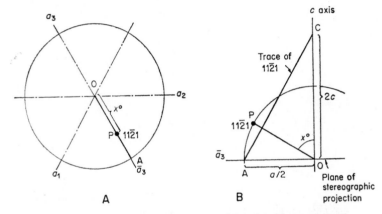

Fig. 188 Graphical determination of axial ratio of hexagonal and trigonal crystals.

stereogram showing the pole of face (11$\bar{2}$1) and the length OA is the intercept of this face on the $\bar{a}_3$ axis. This is however only half the unit intercept, because the third digit in the Miller-Bravais index is a figure 2. Fig. 188B is part of the spherical projection in the plane containing c and $\bar{a}_3$. The position of the pole (11$\bar{2}$1) (P) is marked on the trace of the sphere and the line OP drawn in. A line from A drawn at right angles to OP gives the slope of the face and it is produced to intersect the c axis at C. The distance OC is thus twice the unit intercept on c because OA is a half the unit intercept on a.

Graphical determination of the index of a face, when the axial ratio is known

Fig. 189 is part of a stereographic projection of a calcite crystal showing the pole of a face x whose Miller-Bravais index is required. First a line is drawn from the centre of the projection through x and produced to the primitive and next another line is drawn perpendicular to the first with its origin at the point of emergence of the a_1 axis and the line extended to intersect a_2 produced. This line marks the intersection of the plane whose pole is x with the horizontal plane and the reciprocals of the relative intercepts on the a_1, a_2 and a_3 axes will give the first three integers of the Miller-Bravais index. The intercepts are 1, 2 and $\frac{2}{3}$ respectively.

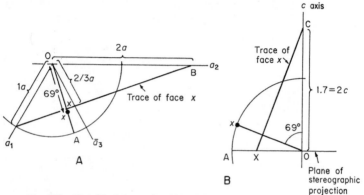

Fig. 189   Graphical determination of Miller indices.

Fig. 189B is a vertical section in the plane OXA. The position of the pole x is plotted on the section of the sphere, $69°$ from the zenith of the projection, and the line xO inserted. Next the distance OX is transferred accurately from Fig. 189A since this is the distance at which the face x intersects the horizontal in the line OA. From X construct a line perpendicular to Ox and produce it to intersect OC. This gives the slope of the face x and the distance OC gives the intercept on the c axis which in this instance is $1\cdot7$. The morphological axial ratio of calcite, however, is $0\cdot85$ and hence the intercept on the c axis is twice the unit intercept. Writing now the intercepts in full, they are $1a_1$, $2a_2$, $\frac{2}{3}a_3$ and $2c$ which gives the Miller-Bravais index $(21\bar{3}1)$.

Comparative table of tetragonal, hexagonal and trigonal systems
In describing the tetragonal, hexagonal and trigonal systems constant reference has been made to similarities between them. This is to be

expected, particularly between the tetragonal and hexagonal systems because the tetrad and hexad axes have very similar effects upon morphology.

Table 7 sets out the forms of these three systems side by side so that the important similarities and differences may be more readily appreciated.

In all but two instances there is a direct comparison, form for form, between similar classes in the tetragonal and hexagonal systems; the morphology of one is the morphology of the other. The two exceptions are those classes of the hexagonal system having inversion hexad axes. Attention has often been drawn to the trigonal aspect of such crystals. The inversion hexad ($\bar{6}$), for example, is morphologically equivalent to a triad normal to a plane ($3/m$) and, although structurally they are hexagonal, for morphological purposes they have a very close affinity with the trigonal system, as will be seen later.

The fact that 3 is odd and a prime number explains some of the differences in morphology between trigonal and hexagonal and tetragonal crystals belonging to similar classes. The presence of vertical planes of symmetry has a greater effect, morphologically, on trigonal than tetragonal and hexagonal crystals and direct comparison between all three, form for form, is only possible in classes 422, 622 and 32, and 4, 6 and 3 in which the principal axis is a rotation axis and does not occur in combination with vertical planes (see columns 2 and 7 of Table 7). Direct morphological comparison is also possible between classes $4/m$, $6/m$ and $\bar{6}$ because $\bar{6}$, as we have seen above, is equivalent morphologically to $3/m$. For this reason these classes are similarly signalled in Table 7. A very close comparison is possible on the same basis between classes $4/mmm$, $6/mmm$ and $\bar{6}m2$. This is apparent if $\bar{6}m$ is written alternatively as $3/mm$. Exactly similar forms do not exist in all systems however, because in $\bar{6}m2$ the horizontal diads are not perpendicular to the planes of symmetry as they are in $4/mmm$ and $6/mmm$ (see Table 8). The general forms of the three classes have similar names however and again the classes are similarly signalled in Table 7 for easy comparison and reference.

Classes $4mm$ and $6mm$ are similar to $3m$, the differences between them reflecting the lower symmetry of the odd triad compared with the even

TABLE 7

Comparative table of forms of the tetragonal, hexagonal and trigonal systems.

Class	4/mmm ZIRCON*	422	4mm
System & Form			
TETRAGONAL {100} {110}	} tetragonal prism	} tetragonal prism	} tetragonal prism
{hk0}	ditetragonal prism	ditetragonal prism	ditetragonal prism
{001}	pinacoid	pinacoid	pedions
{h0l} {hhl}	} tetragonal bipyramid	} tetragonal bipyramid	} tetragonal pyramids
{hkl}	ditetragonal bipyramid	tetragonal trapezohedra	ditetragonal pyramids

	6/mmm BERYL*	622	6mm
HEXAGONAL {10$\bar{1}$0} {11$\bar{2}$0}	} hexagonal prism	} hexagonal prism	} hexagonal prism
{hki0}	dihexagonal prism	dihexagonal prism	dihexagonal prism
{0001}	pinacoid	pinacoid	pedions
{h0$\bar{h}$l} {hh$\bar{2}$hl}	} hexagonal bipyramid	} hexagonal bipyramid	} hexagonal pyramids
{hkil}	dihexagonal bipyramid	hexagonal trapezohedra	dihexagonal pyramids

	3/mm≡$\bar{6}$m2	32 QUARTZ	3m TOURMALINE
TRIGONAL {1010} {1120}		hexagonal prism trigonal prisms	trigonal prisms hexagonal prism
{hki0}		ditrigonal prisms	ditrigonal prisms
{0001}		pinacoid	pedions
{h0$\bar{h}$l} {hh$\bar{2}$hl}		rhombohedra trigonal bipyramids	trigonal pyramids hexagonal pyramid
{hkil}		trigonal trapezohedra	ditrigonal pyramids

NOTES	Direct comparison of forms in 4/mmm and 6/mmm. General form of $\bar{6}$m2 comparable; special forms show the effect of the inversion hexad.	Direct comparison of forms in 422 and 622. General form of 32 comparable; special forms show the effect of a triad. Enantiomorphism.	Direct comparison of forms in 4mm and 6mm. General form of 3m comparable; special forms show the effect of a triad.

TABLE 7 contd.

4/m†	4̄2m	4̄	4
} tetragonal prisms pinacoid	} tetragonal prisms ditetragonal prisms pinacoid — tetragonal bipyramid	} tetragonal prisms pinacoid	} tetragonal prisms pedions

} tetragonal
  bipyramids
	tetragonal sphenoid
	————
	ditetragonal
	scalenohedra[1]
		} tetragonal
		  sphenoids
			} tetragonal
			  pyramids

6/m†	6̄m2*	6̄†	6
} hexagonal prisms pinacoid	trigonal prisms hexagonal prism ditrigonal prisms pinacoid — trigonal bipyramids	} trigonal prisms pinacoid	} hexagonal prisms pedions

} hexagonal
  bipyramids
	hexagonal bipyramid
	————
	ditrigonal bipyramids
		} trigonal
		  bipyramids
			} hexagonal
			  pyramids

3/m≡6̄	3̄m CALCITE	3̄	3
	} hexagonal prisms dihexagonal prisms pinacoid rhombohedra hexagonal bipyramid	} hexagonal prisms pinacoid	} trigonal prisms pedions
	———— ditrigonal scalenohedra	} rhombohedra	} trigonal pyramids

Direct comparison of forms throughout since 3/m≡6̄.	6̄m2 should be compared with 6/mmm and 4/mmm. Classes 4̄2m and 3̄m are comparable; note the similarly of the rhombohedron and sphenoid. [1]ditetragonal bisphenoid is an alternative name.	6̄ should be compared with 4/m and 6/m. Classes 4̄ and 3̄ are directly comparable.	Direct comparison of forms throughout. Enantiomorphism.

tetrad and hexad axes. The same is true if on the one hand $\bar{4}2m$ and $\bar{3}m$, and on the other hand classes $\bar{4}$ and $\bar{3}$ are compared. (We have already referred to the effects of $\bar{6}m2$ and $\bar{6}$). Study of the table again shows how closely similar the forms are and serves also to emphasize the close resemblance of the rhombohedron and the tetragonal sphenoid. A case can clearly be made for the use of the term ditetragonal scalenohedron for the general form of class $\bar{4}2m$ in order to emphasize the similarity with the ditrigonal scalenohedron.

A word or two needs to be said about the International Symmetry Symbols $\bar{4}2m$, $\bar{6}m2$ and $\bar{3}m$. All have inversion axes, one set of planes and horizontal diad axes and yet the figure 2 denoting the diads appears before the letter m in $\bar{4}2m$, after it in $\bar{6}m2$ and not at all in $\bar{3}m$. This is because the structural crystallographer needs to distinguish clearly between several possible space groups in these three classes.

The figure 2 preceding m implies that the planes of symmetry are not perpendicular to the crystallographic axes. This is true for $\bar{4}2m$, but it does not hold good for $\bar{3}m$ in which the crystallographic axes, although diads, are perpendicular to the planes of symmetry. For this reason the symbol $\bar{3}m$ is used. The symbol $\bar{6}m2$ in which the 2 follows m, implies that the diad axes are perpendicular to the crystallographic axes and also that the planes of symmetry are perpendicular to the axes (Fig. 190). There are space groups corresponding to $\bar{4}m2$ and $\bar{6}2m$.

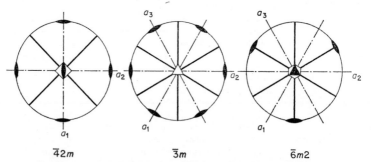

$\bar{4}2m$ $\bar{3}m$ $\bar{6}m2$

Fig. 190 A comparison of the symmetry elements of classes $\bar{4}2m$, $\bar{3}m$ and $\bar{6}m2$.

Suggestions for further reading
Phillips, F. C., *An Introduction to Crystallography*, Longmans Green & Co. Ltd., London, 3rd Edition, 1963 Especially Chapter 11.

SYNOPTIC TABLE OF CRYSTAL CLASSES

An attempt is made in Table 8 to show the thirty-two symmetry classes in tabular and diagrammatic form. The classes within a crystal system are arranged horizontally and the tetragonal, hexagonal and trigonal systems are grouped for ease of reference. Similarly the orthorhombic, monoclinic and triclinic systems are placed together so that cross reference can more readily be made.

Similar classes are arranged vertically. The International Symmetry Symbol, a stereogram of the symmetry elements and the name of the general form are given for each of the thirty-two classes. The name of the characteristic mineral is given for each of the eleven classes of symmetry with which the elementary student is concerned.

Suggestions for further reading
   The following texts refer largely or in part to morphological crystallography:
Berry, L. G., and Mason, B., *Mineralogy*, W. H. Freeman & Company, San Francisco, California, 1959.
Buerger, M. J., *Elementary Crystallography*, John Wiley & Sons Inc., New York 1956.
de Jong, W. F., *General Crystallography*, W. H. Freeman & Company, San Francisco, 1959.
Phillips, F. C., *An Introduction to Crystallography*, Longmans, Green & Co. Ltd., London, 3rd Edition 1963.
Read, H. H., *Rutley's Mineralogy*, Allen and Unwin (Murby), London, 24th Edition, 1948.

TABLE 8

THE THIRTY-TWO CRYSTAL CLASSES

TYPE OF SYMBOL AND NOTES / CRYSTAL SYSTEM	n/mm	$n2$	$\bar{n}m$	nm	n/m	$\bar{n}$	n
(notes)		Crystals display enantiomorphism		Principal axis is polar and uniterminal crystals hemimorphic			Crystals display enantiomorphism. Excepting class 23 principal axis is polar and uniterminal crystals hemimorphic
ORTHORHOMBIC	$mmm = 2/mmm$ Orthorhombic bipyramidal, BARYTES *	222 Orthorhombic sphenoidal	$\bar{2}m = mm$ Orthorhombic See above	$mm2 = mm = 2m$ Orthorhombic pyramidal	$2/m$ Monoclinic See below	$\bar{2}$ Monoclinic See below	2 Monoclinic See below
MONOCLINIC	$2/mmm$ Orthorhombic See above	222 Orthorhombic See above	$\bar{2}m = mm$	mm Orthorhombic See above	$2/m$ Monoclinic prismatic, GYPSUM *	$m = \bar{2}$ Monoclinic domatic	2 Monoclinic sphenoidal
TRICLINIC	$1/mm = mm$	$12 = 2$	$\bar{1}m = 2/m$	$1m = m = \bar{2}$	$1/m = m = \bar{2}$	$\bar{1}$ Triclinic pinacoidal, AXINITE *	1 Triclinic pedial

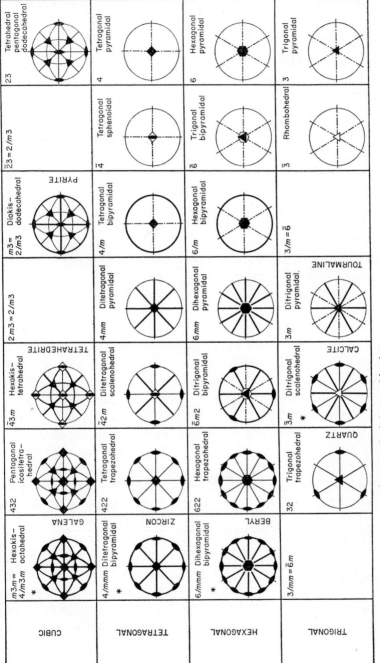

*denotes the holosymmetric class

CHAPTER 11

CRYSTAL GROWTH AND COMPOSITE CRYSTALS

In the previous chapters attention has been focused on ideal and regular crystals. It has been assumed that crystals are ideally shaped and are the expression of a perfectly uniform and regular atomic arrangement. The reader will probably be sufficiently familiar with nature to appreciate that neither concept is invariably correct. The examination of a mineral collection will bring to light many crystals in which the faces are not equally developed. Attention was drawn to this in Chapter 1 and Fig. 1 illustrates some of the shapes assumed by the rhombdodecahedron and octahedron owing to unequal facial development. This does not alter the truth of the law of constancy of angle.

Domains

Imperfections on the atomic scale are revealed by X-ray structural studies. When X-ray films are developed it is very commonly the case that the spots caused by the diffraction of X-rays by a set of lattice planes are not sharp but are somewhat diffuse. This is because the structure is not perfect throughout the crystal but is composed of small blocks or *domains* that are perfect within themselves but slightly out of line with the neighbouring domains. In two dimensions the effect is like a terrazzo floor laid by an inexperienced amateur. The small blocks, although perfectly shaped, are laid in lines that are nearly, but not perfectly straight and give a surface that is nearly, but not perfectly level (Fig. 191). Just as a beam of light would be scattered to some extent by the terrazzo floor, so diffracted X-rays are scattered about a mean position by the mosaic structure of crystals.

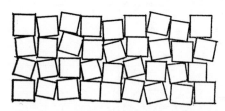

Fig. 191 A diagrammatic and much exaggerated representation of mosaic structure.

Crystal growth

Before considering the effects of such defects it is necessary to have some idea of the way in which crystals grow. If a solution or melt is cooled, crystallisation commences with the formation of *nuclei* consisting of a number of regularly arranged ions or atoms and capable of growing into a larger unit or crystal by addition of more atoms or ions. Initially the crystal nucleus has a large surface energy and will be unstable and tend to dissolve unless it can grow quickly to a size at which its surface energy is small when compared with the total energy of the crystal as a whole. Thus, although the free energy of the crystalline state is less than that of the supersaturated solution, a crystal has to surmount an energy barrier before it can grow to a large size. Once it reaches and passes a critical size at which its free energy is equivalent to that of the melt or solution, it is stable and can continue to grow, for beyond this point it has a lower free energy than the solution. Moreover it has been found that the number of nuclei per unit volume of solution increases markedly in the temperature range of supercooling or supersaturation. The number of nuclei formed has, in turn, an effect on the type of crystal produced; the higher the degree of supersaturation, the more nuclei are produced and the greater the tendency to form many small crystals. The largest and 'best' crystals are produced either under conditions of small supersaturation or by reducing the number of nuclei artificially. If particularly perfect crystals are required, they are grown very slowly from undisturbed solutions from which the nucleus-forming particles have been removed.

From the nucleus stage a crystal grows by attracting to itself ions or atoms from the solution or melt so as to build up orderly layers and form a larger crystal. Initially several independently formed nuclei may aggregate and thus rapidly surmount the energy barrier.

The atoms or ions in motion in a solution or melt may be pictured as colliding with a growing crystal face and moving along it until they become fixed in a vacant lattice site where there are strong unsatisfied attractive forces. Fig. 192 is a sketch of a simple growing crystal with the sodium chloride structure. The upper layer is shown as containing a 'pit' caused by a vacant site and an ion of the appropriate charge wandering over this surface would be attracted strongly to the unfilled site (*a*) where it would be bound by electrostatic forces, so filling the pit and completing the layer. Other ions moving over the surface could fill vacant sites at the edge of the layer, or elsewhere, but it will be apparent that the attractive forces will not all be the same. The attractive force depends on the number of filled sites that are the nearest neighbours of the unfilled ones; the greater the number of filled sites, the greater the

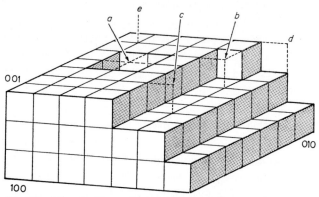

Fig. 192   Diagram illustrating the growth of a crystal lattice.

attractive force. Vacant site (*b*) although having a weaker attraction than (*a*), will be stronger than (*c*) and (*d*). Site (*e*) has the weakest attractive force of all and, in terms of energy, starting a new layer is little better than starting a new nucleus. There is therefore a tendency for a face like (001) in Fig. 192 to extend laterally rather than for new layers to be added.

As more and more ions wander over the surface of such faces as (100), (010) and (001) to become fixed in vacant sites at their edges, it follows that the rhombdodecahedron faces (110), etc., grow forwards more rapidly than the cube faces, which, for energy considerations, grow laterally. Thus from Fig. 193 it will be appreciated that the lateral growth of the cube faces (001) and (100) will eventually result in the disappearance of the rhombdodecahedron face (101). There is, therefore, a tendency for crystals to eliminate during growth faces of high Miller index and low atomic density. The bulk of the crystals studied by the student will be found to have faces of low index, and when forms of higher index are found they are usually small faces.

The rate of migration of particles across a growing crystal face depends upon factors like the viscosity of the solution or melt and the size of the face. These factors determine whether a particle reaches the edge of a face and if they should be such as to prevent its doing so, then

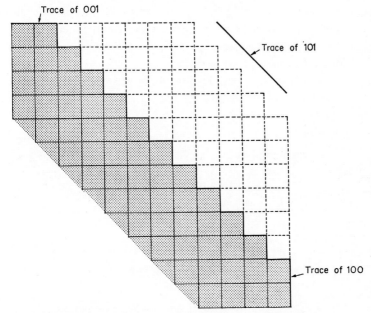

Fig. 193   The elimination of (101) by lateral growth of (001) and (100).

the habit of the crystal will be changed as a result. It will be appreciated therefore, that although there is the tendency for crystals to develop large faces of low index, this tendency may be to some extent offset by growth conditions. Crystals of sodium chloride, for example, form cubes when grown from the pure solution[23], but the addition of urea causes the octahedron to develop. The petrologist is familiar with the different habits shown by natural crystals that have formed under different conditions. Apatite and amphibole when they occur in pegmatitic diorites or appinites have a slender or acicular habit that contrasts with the more equant crystals of 'normal' diorites.

23. Better cubes are formed if the solution contains a trace of lead.

R

Dislocations

We have mentioned already that X-ray studies show that most crystals have a mosaic structure in which the small, slightly disoriented blocks are bounded by dislocation arrays, across which the crystal structure is to some extent imperfect. A dislocation is a line of atoms, each of which has a co-ordination differing from that normally adopted by those atoms in the structure. Modern work has shown that these dislocations play a most important role in crystal growth.

There are two main types of dislocation called *edge dislocations* and *screw dislocations*. Edge dislocations have the effect of introducing additional planes of atoms into the regular atomic array, as shown in Fig. 194A.

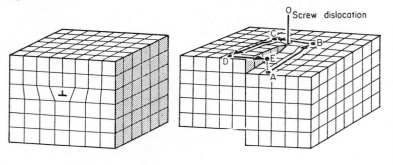

A   B

Fig. 194   A. Edge dislocation.
B. Screw dislocation.

Screw dislocations are more important than edge dislocations in controlling crystal growth and an example is illustrated in Fig. 194B. Their effect is perhaps best illustrated by analogy. Imagine a soft rectangular eraser on all sides of which is drawn a regular grid of lines. Now imagine this being cut half-way through from front to back and the front edge on one side of the cut being displaced upwards one grid square relative to the other side of the cut. In Fig. 194B, E is one grid square vertically above A and it is possible to go from A to E by travelling always on the same plane and without climbing a step. The crystal structure is uniform and unbroken in going from A-B-C-D-E. The effect is like climbing a spiral ramp about O, the origin of the screw dislocation.

It has been pointed out earlier that considerable energy is required to start a new layer on a perfectly flat existing crystal face; in fact the energy requirements are only a little more favourable than starting a new nucleus. But if a screw dislocation is present, a crystal can grow upwards by growing always laterally around the screw dislocation. This method of growth is energetically much more favourable than starting a new layer for, in effect, all new atoms being bound to the crystal form one surface.

Dendritic and hopper crystals

In all the foregoing discussions in this book it has been assumed that crystals are solids bounded by plane faces that meet in salient angles. But not all crystals are ideally formed in this sense.

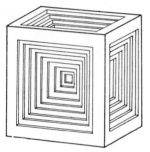

Fig. 195   A hopper cube.

The Keuper Marl of the English Midlands contains many halite crystals (now pseudomorphs) that were formed during periods of desiccation. Very many of these crystals have hollow faces and are appropriately called *hopper crystals* (Fig. 195). If particularly perfect examples are studied it is seen that a step-wise structure is present in the hollow.

Modifications of crystal habit occur if crystals form under conditions in which their growth in certain directions is limited. For example, ice crystals forming in the thin film of water on a window pane show skeletal, branching forms and similar *dendritic* crystals as they are called

Fig. 196   A dendritic snow crystal (after Bentley).

can be produced in shallow droplets of liquid in the laboratory. Perhaps the most familiar of all dendrites are snow crystals found in the feathery flakes of winter snow storms (Fig. 196). In certain crystals, particularly those of ionic or metallic character, there is a tendency for atoms to be particularly strongly attracted to the corners and edges of the crystal owing to the largely non-directional character of the bonds. If such crystals can grow rapidly, as from supersaturated solutions, then the growth at the corners and edges outstrips the rate of growth at the centres of faces and either dendrites or hopper crystals result.

Striated faces

Crystals like tourmaline, quartz and pyrite, very often display a marked contrast between faces which are quite plane and those that are very strongly striated (Fig. 197). If these striated faces are examined closely

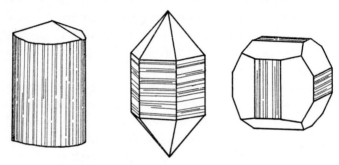

Fig. 197   Striated crystals of (left to right) tourmaline, quartz and pyrite.

it will be seen that they are step-like and composed of a regular oscillation of small plane faces. In quartz the oscillation is between the prism and the rhombohedron, giving rise to horizontal striations on the prism faces. Where only one rhombohedron is present three of the prism faces may be quite plane and the other three, those in zone with the rhombohedron, are strongly striated and often curved. In tourmaline the striations are usually very marked and caused by oscillatory combination of the faces in the prism zone. It is rare to find a tourmaline crystal with plane prism faces. In pyrite there is pronounced oscillatory combination between the cube and the pentagonal dodecahedron and pyrite crystals with a cubic habit usually show strong striations that indicate the symmetry class to which it belongs.

Etch figures

We have seen that crystals grow in a regular and orderly manner.

Crystals can also dissolve, and solution is really the reverse of crystallization. It would not be surprising therefore if it were found that crystals dissolved in a manner that was to a large extent controlled by their structure.

In the early stages of solution, the plane surface of a crystal face becomes etched by a solvent and small depressions, called *etch pits*, form in its surface. These etch pits are controlled by the atomic arrangement and are bounded by new crystal faces that often have high Miller indices. Such faces are of great use in determining the symmetry class to which a mineral belongs and etch pits can be used to allocate crystals with only simple forms to their correct symmetry class. Apatite, for example, crystallizes in the hexagonal system but usually as simple crystals with only the pinacoid {0001} and prisms developed. The shape of the etch pits on the prism faces (Fig. 198) show that there are no vertical planes

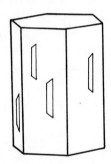
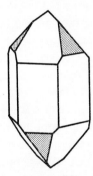

Fig. 198   Left: Diagrammatic representation of apatite (class $6/m$) etched with HCl.
Right: Diagrammatic representation of the differential etching of rhombohedra of quartz (class 32).

of symmetry and that apatite cannot be holosymmetric but belongs to class $6/m$. Nepheline is also hexagonal and, like apatite, forms simple crystals. Its etch figure shows that there are neither vertical nor horizontal planes of symmetry and that it belongs to class 6.

The rhombohedral faces of quartz are frequently differentially etched and serve to show that quartz is trigonal, although the facial development may give it a hexagonal appearance. A more detailed study of the shape of the etch pits will often reveal the difference between right- and left-handed crystals in the absence of the trigonal trapezohedron or trigonal bipyramid faces.

Twinned crystals

We have just examined some of the ways in which crystals with re-entrant angles may be produced. There also exists an important group of composite crystals that very often, but not always, show re-entrant angles. These are called *twinned crystals* and they consist of two or more individuals either in contact or intergrown in such a way that the individual parts are related to one another in a definite structural manner. In different examples of the same twin, the individual parts of the twin have always the same mutual orientation.

An understanding of twinned crystals is best obtained by considering the ways in which they may develop.

Growth twins, as their name implies, have grown as such with the two parts of the twin present from an early stage of growth, perhaps even from the nucleus. Nearly all the twinned crystals of mineral collections belong to this category. But it is soon apparent that some minerals are hardly ever found as twinned crystals whereas others are commonly twinned. It follows that there must be some structural factor that influences whether or not a particular mineral can occur as a twin. Perhaps the most important restriction is one of energy. A twin will only form if the energy of the twin is similar to that of the untwinned crystal and this in turn is a function of the dimensional properties of the crystal lattice.

In the consideration of crystal structure in Chaper 2, it was noted that crystals are regarded as comprising atoms or ions that pack together so that a positive ion is surrounded by several negative ions to which it is co-ordinated. In considering ionic crystals it was seen that the co-ordination number of an ion (i.e. the number of ions of opposite charge that pack around it) depends upon the ratio of the radii of the positive and negative ions and that ionic structures can be regarded as co-ordination polyhedra of anions (the larger) surrounding a central smaller cation.

A single crystal represents the least energy state, for in it the co-ordination polyhedra about each cation are identical and undisturbed. The charge of the cation can be regarded as being shared equally and mainly with the anions immediately surrounding it (the first co-ordination sphere) and that the influence of the central cation on anions beyond the immediate neighbours is relatively slight.

If there is any disturbance of this ideal state, then the resulting crystal would have a higher energy than the perfect crystal. But clearly the greatest energy term is that between a cation and the anions immediately surrounding it in the first co-ordination sphere, and any disturbance of this co-ordination would probably be sufficient to make the structure unstable. However, a rearrangement of the anions beyond the first co-ordination sphere would add only slightly to the energy of the crystal provided it left unchanged the arrangement of anions immediately surrounding a cation. If this energy condition is satisfied, then growth twinning can occur.

A very good illustration of this is provided by the orthorhombic calcium carbonate, aragonite, the structure of which is illustrated in Fig. 199. It is essentially a close-packed arrangement of the flat triangular CO_3^{2-} anion groups and Ca^{2+} cations such that the CO_3's form rows parallel to the *a* axis in which all the triangles point the same way. Each calcium has six oxygen nearest neighbours forming the first co-ordination sphere.

Twinning takes place because an arrangement of the structure of the type shown in Fig. 199 can occur and yet leave the first co-ordination sphere almost unaltered. That part of the structure between the dashed lines of Fig. 199 is common to both halves of the twin with the result that the twinned crystal has only a slightly higher energy state than the untwinned crystal. Ions of calcium or carbonate when moving over growing crystal faces can thus either continue the existing perfect structure or take up the twin position which is only slightly less favourable energetically. Even if the twin positions is taken up there will be a tendency for atoms to move into their normal, low-energy lattice sites but if this tendency is overcome, say by rapid growth, then both parts of the crystal can continue to grow in the usual way and give rise to twins on (110) like that of Fig. 199B. Twinning that is energetically as favourable as this will take place readily and aragonite often occurs as twins that may be simple, repeated, or complex and interpenetrant.

A tiny crystal nucleus is particularly prone to develop stacking faults

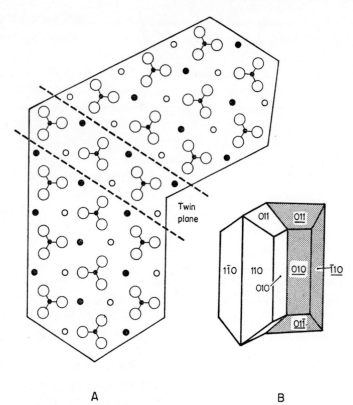

A   B

Fig. 199 Growth twinning of aragonite.
A. Diagrammatic representation of the structure projected on (001).
The triangular arrangement of small black circles and large open
circles represent CO_3 molecules; the other black and open circles
represent Ca atoms at different heights. The structure between the
dashed lines is consistent with both halves of the twin (After Bragg).
B. A drawing of aragonite twinned on {110}.

because the small size of the crystal means that the forces favouring the
retention of atoms in the correct sites for perfect growth are smaller than
in well-developed crystals.

The atomic arrangement of quartz has SiO_4 tetrahedra linked by their
corners to form spirals which run parallel to the *c* crystallographic axis.
These spirals are either left-handed or right-handed and in perfect
crystals the entire structure has a screw pattern of the same hand
throughout. Some crystals, however, grow with parts of the structure in

a left-hand and parts in a right-hand spiral and are called *Brazil* or
Optical twins. They are growth twins and the two orientations have
always been present during the growth of the crystal. This twinning
usually shows in the development of the trigonal bipyramid and trapezohedron faces in both the left- and right-hand corners of the prism
faces (Fig. 200A). It can also be detected by suitably etching a section
cut parallel to (0001) when the two individuals are seen to be inter-
penetrating and to be bounded by plane surfaces (Fig. 200B). Compare
this with the Dauphiné twins illustrated in Fig. 202.

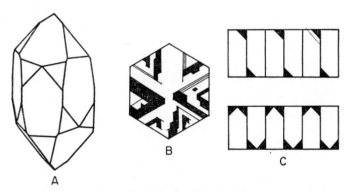

Fig. 200   Growth twinning (Brazil twinning) of quartz.
A. The morphology of a Brazil twin: forms present; prism $\{10\bar{1}0\}$;
rhombohedra $\{10\bar{1}1\}$ and $\{01\bar{1}1\}$ and trigonal trapezohedra $\{51\bar{6}1\}$.
B. An etched basal section showing plane composition surfaces.
C. A diagrammatic representation of the position of the trigonal
trapezohedron faces of (above) a right-handed crystal, (below) a
Brazil twin. The prism faces are drawn as though flattened out.

Growth twins, in the early stages of their development, are particularly unstable. Their continued growth is favoured by a supersaturated
solution but should saturation conditions approach equilibrium, the
twinned crystal will dissolve and a normal, low-energy crystal will form.
Twinned crystals frequently reach a large size and are preserved for very
long periods. This is so because a twin, growing in a supersaturated
solution, will reach and pass a size beyond which the extra energy of the
twin layer itself is so small in relation to the surface energy of the growing
faces that it has no effect on them even if the saturation should fall to an
equilibrium level. Twins can be thought of as passing a point of no
return in terms of size.

Transformation twins

Some substances show *polymorphism* in that, although retaining the same chemical composition, they assume different structures under different temperature and pressure conditions. Calcium carbonate can exist as trigonal calcite or orthorhombic aragonite, and titanium dioxide forms the minerals rutile (tetragonal 4/*mmm*), anatase (4/*mmm*) and brookite (orthorhombic *mmm*). Silica can exist in the forms cristobalite, tridymite and quartz as well as in high-pressure modifications coesite and stishovite. The series cristobalite-tridymite-quartz reflects the changes within the Si-0 lattice structure with falling temperature and the transformations have been thoroughly studied experimentally. Each member exists in two modifications, a high temperature β form and a low temperature α modification. β-quartz, under anhydrous conditions, is stable below 870°C. It is hexagonal and belongs to class 622. Its

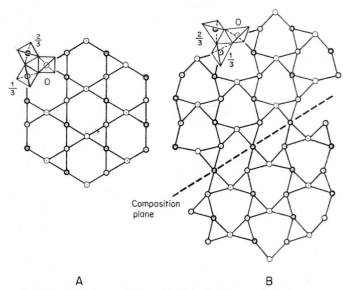

A   B

Fig. 201   Transformation twinning (Dauphiné twinning) of quartz.
A. The structure of β quartz projected on to (0001).
B. The structure of α quartz projected on to (0001) showing the composition plane between two individuals. The circles represent Si atoms; the tetrahedral arrangement of oxygen atoms around the silicons is shown diagrammatically at the top left of each diagram. The light, medium and heavy outline of the silicons represent those atoms at relative heights 0, $\frac{1}{3}$ and $\frac{2}{3}$ respectively. (After Bragg).

structure is illustrated diagrammatically in Fig. 201A. If cooling is continued, at 575°C the structure changes to that of the α form, which has trigonal holoaxial symmetry 32 and is illustrated in Fig. 201B.

This transformation from β to α-quartz takes place rapidly and involves only a slight distortion of the lattice. The bonds themselves remain unbroken. A perfect crystal of β-quartz would be entirely left- or entirely right-handed. At 575°C the change from hexagonal to trigonal symmetry begins at several points in the lattice and spreads rapidly through it. The trigonal symmetry of the α-quartz lattice means that it can take up either of the orientations of Fig. 201B. The transformation starting at different points may take up different orientations and they result in a transformation twin like that of Fig. 201B. The boundaries between the members of the twin are irregular in consequence of the largely random spread of the transformation through the lattice. Etched basal sections of these *Dauphiné* or *Electrical* twins, as they are called, show interpenetration twinning with the individuals bounded by irregular surfaces (Fig. 202). Morphologically the crystals are either double

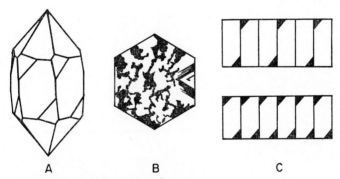

A   B   C

Fig. 202 Dauphiné twinning of quartz.
A. The morphology of a Dauphiné twin.
B. An etched basal section showing irregular composition surfaces. Brazil twinning shown to right.
C. Diagrammatic representation of the disposition of the trigonal trapezohedron faces of (above) a left-handed crystal and (below) a Dauphiné twin. The prism faces are drawn as though flattened out.

right-handed or double left-handed in that the trigonal bipyramid and trapezohedron faces are present at the corners of every prism face and crystals have the appearance of that in Fig. 202. Transformation twinning is impermanent and can be removed by heating quartz to a temperature above the transformation temperature, when the lattice becomes hexagonal again. If the cooling conditions are very carefully controlled, an untwinned α-quartz crystal can be produced. This technique is used in the production of quartz oscillator plates which must be cut from untwinned material.

Transformation twinning can, of course, be superimposed on growth twinning and Fig. 202B shows both twins present in one crystal.

Deformation twins

Because of differences in atomic arrangement, crystals behave differently when stressed. Some crystals break when a directed stress like a shear couple is applied to them, whereas others will deform plastically. The plastic deformation occurs by gliding on certain planes of atoms, and it can be either *translation gliding* or *twin gliding*. In translation gliding one part of the lattice is displaced laterally a whole number of interatomic distances with respect to the other (Fig. 203A), with the

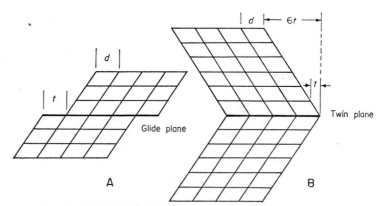

Fig. 203   A. Translation gliding.
B. Twin gliding (deformation twinning).

result that after gliding has ceased the structure is unbroken and uniform across the glide plane.

When twin gliding takes place, the displacement of the lattice is a fraction of an interatomic distance and this results in a change of orientation of the lattice across the glide plane (Fig. 203B). Twins produced by this means are called *deformation twins* or *gliding twins*.

The movement of atoms into new sites that are not equivalent to the normal ones is rather like the atoms in a growth twin taking up alternative lattice positions of slightly higher energy. In deformation, the energy needed to move an atom to the new site is supplied by the force causing the deformation, but only certain crystals exhibit twin gliding and again it is the lattice energy that exerts the control. Atoms occupying their normal low-energy positions in a perfect crystal structure can be regarded as occupying energy pits or hollows. The twin position has a higher energy than the normal position but in order to reach this an energy barrier has to be surmounted (Fig. 204). In very many crystals

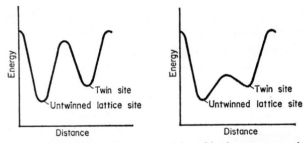

Fig. 204 Hypothetical curves illustrative of lattice energy restrictions on deformation twinning. Left: a considerable energy barrier between the normal lattice site and the twin position — the crystal does not twin easily. Right: a low energy barrier between the normal and twin lattice site — the crystal twins readily.

the energy required to surmount this barrier is sufficient first to break down the lattice and the crystal does not glide but breaks. Those crystals that do glide also exhibit a very strong structural control on the glide direction. There are, as it were, low 'cols' in certain directions that separate the normal from the twin position and twinning will take place preferentially along these lines. The structural control thus extends not only to the glide planes but to the directions within those planes along which gliding can take place. It does not follow that because a mineral develops growth twins on a certain plane that glide twins will develop there too. They are controlled by different structural features.

Look again at Fig. 203. In Fig. 203A the movement is concentrated on one glide plane. To produce the twin shown in Fig. 203B movement has taken place on six glide planes giving a total displacement of $6t$, equivalent to about 2·5 lattice units in our example, requiring a considerable expenditure of energy. Deformation twinning progresses by a series of steps. Initially the twinning occurs along narrow lamellae which gradually widen as more and more atoms adopt the twin position (Fig. 205).

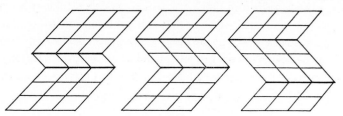

Fig. 205   The progressive development of a deformation twin.

The best mineralogical example of this kind of twinning is calcite which responds to stresses by gliding on $\{01\bar{1}2\}$. The twin lamellae show very clearly in thin sections of metamorphosed limestone. Zinc blende (sphalerite ZnS) twins in a similar way and very many metals exhibit deformation twinning.

Effects of twinning
Most twinned crystals are clearly composite and can be related in a direct way to the simple, untwinned form. This relationship to the untwinned crystal has given rise to a rather complex nomenclature that is useful for descriptive purposes, but goes no way to replacing the genetic classification adopted here. Spinel crystallizes as octahedra and commonly occurs also in the form of twinned octahedra (Fig. 206). One twin may be regarded as being related to the other by rotation through 180° about a triad axis (here perpendicular to (111)) or by reflection across a plane parallel to the octahedron face. The former are called *rotation* and the latter *reflection* twins. The axis of imaginary rotation is the *twin axis* and the reflection plane is termed the *twin plane*. The surface along which the two individuals comprising the twin are in contact is called the *composition surface*. It is a plane in Fig. 206, but in transformation twins of quartz and in many other twins it is a highly irregular surface.

A distinction is sometimes made between *contact* twins like those of Fig. 206 in which the composition surface is a plane and *interpenetration*

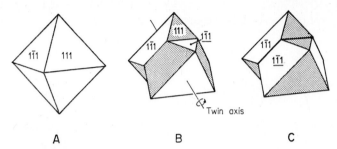

Fig. 206   A. Octahedron.
B. Octahedron — rotation twin.
C. Octahedron — reflection twin.

twins like quartz Dauphiné twins in which the composition surface is irregular. The distinction between the two is of no great importance.

Simple twins have two component parts in related orientation whereas *multiple* twins comprise more than two individuals. If three or more individuals are present with the same twin plane, the name *polysynthetic twin* is used. *Lamellar* twinning is a special case of polysynthetic twinning in which the twin individuals are narrow, plate-like lamellae.

From the foregoing it is clear that there are certain restrictions on twinning imposed by the symmetry of the lattice. A lattice plane that is a plane of symmetry can never be a reflection twin plane for example, nor can any even-fold symmetry axis be a twin axis, for rotation through 180° restores congruence. Only triad or identity symmetry axes can be twin axes.

In the twinned octahedron of Fig. 206 the twin plane and composition plane are identical and the twin axis is normal to it, but this is not always so. The orthoclase twin of Fig. 207A has the *c* axis as the twin axis and {010} as the composition plane; the twin axis here lies *within* the composition plane. In most twins the twin axes and twin planes have simple rational Miller indices but complex twins exist in which, although the twin axis itself may not have a rational index, it is simply related to other axes or planes that are rational. This feature is used to distinguish between (a) *normal twins* (e.g. spinel Fig. 206) in which the twin axis is normal to a possible crystal face; (b) *parallel twins* (e.g. orthoclase Fig. 207) in which the twin axis lies in the composition plane parallel to a zone axis and (c) *complex twins* in which the twin axis again lies in the composition plane but perpendicular to a zone axis.

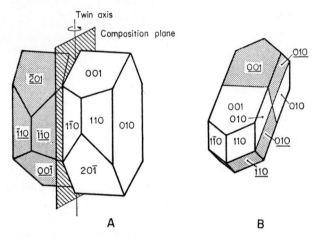

Fig. 207   A. A Carlsbad twin of orthoclase drawn to show the twin axis lying in the composition plane.
B. A pseudotetragonal mimetic twin of harmotome (monoclinic). Twin individuals shaded.

Sometimes twinning appears to confer on a crystal a higher symmetry than it really has. Such twins are called *mimetic* twins and the examples *par excellence* are found in the zeolite group of minerals and in aragonite (Fig. 207B).

The more important types of twinning

The greater the symmetry of a lattice, the greater the restriction on the number of planes and axes about which twinning can occur. The extent to which twinning will occur depends ultimately on the lattice configuration and properties of individual minerals but, in general, the broad principle stated above is seen to hold good when surveying the incidence of twinning in the crystal systems and classes. The greater the symmetry of a crystal system, the more restricted the range of twins possible. Thus a greater variety of twinning is to be expected in the triclinic than in the hexagonal system. Similarly, within any one system, the less symmetrical classes would be expected to show more types of twin than in the holosymmetric class because the lattice symmetry restrictions are fewer.

In the following survey the tetragonal system is considered first and then compared with the hexagonal and trigonal systems with the object of emphasizing these lattice restrictions. Although these three systems are so much alike morphologically, they differ very much in the type and incidence of twinning. The remaining systems are dealt with in the order orthorhombic, monoclinic and triclinic. See Figs. 206 and 213 for cubic twins.

Tetragonal system

The symmetry of the holosymmetric class (4/*mmm*) is such as to preclude

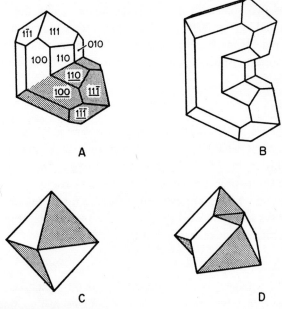

Fig. 208   Tetragonal twins.
A. Rutile: geniculate twin.
B. Rutile: multiple twin.
C. Chalcopyrite: two sphenoids equally developed.
D. Chalcopyrite: reflection twin on (111).

all symmetry axes from being twin axes. The number of planes of symmetry restricts possible twin planes to those with indices $\{hk0\}$, $\{h0l\}$, $\{hhl\}$, and $\{hkl\}$. The most common twins have a face of the bipyramid $\{h0l\}$ as the twin plane and very often it is a face of the form $\{101\}$. Twins of zircon, cassiterite and rutile commonly have the form shown in Fig. 208A and are described as knee- or elbow-twins. The term *geniculate* twin (Latin *genu*, knee) means the same thing. Multiple twinning of this type gives rise to crystals like that of Fig. 208B and in rutile *cyclic* twins are known.

Other types of twin can occur in lower classes of symmetry. For example, in the pyramidal class (4) the absence of a horizontal plane of symmetry means that (001) can be a twin plane. Chalcopyrite crystallizes in the scalenohedral (bisphenoidal) class $\bar{4}2m$, but its morphological axial ratio ($c/a = 0.985$) is so very close to unity that the crystals are pseudo-cubic, and can be compared with the tetrahedrite class ($\bar{4}3m$). Sometimes two sphenoids are well developed, giving the crystals an octahedral habit. (Fig. 208C). Such crystals when twinned on $\{111\}$ look very like spinel twins, but it is possible to be sure that they are reflection twins because the sphenoids can be differentiated (compare Fig. 208D with Fig. 206B & C).

Hexagonal system

The tetragonal and hexagonal systems are very much alike morphologically and it would be expected that they show similar twinning effects. This is so, but twins are rare amongst hexagonal crystals. Pyrrhotite (holosymmetric class $6/mmm$) is an exception and twins on the bipyramid $\{10\bar{1}1\}$, but even so twins are rarely found. As in the tetragonal system, additional twin planes become available in the lower symmetry classes, but again twins are rarely developed.

Trigonal system

Because the principal symmetry axis in trigonal crystals is a triad, it follows that it can act as a twin axis, and twinning is very common among trigonal crystals, so much so that it is possible to give here only a few examples.

Calcite crystallizes in the holosymmetric class of the trigonal system

($\bar{3}m$) in which the plane {0001} is not a plane of symmetry and can function as a twin plane. Twins of the type shown in Fig. 209A are common and have (0001) as the composition plane and the principal axis as the twin axis. The other common twin plane is the rhombohedron. The rhombohedron ($01\bar{1}2$), it will be remembered, is the plane on which

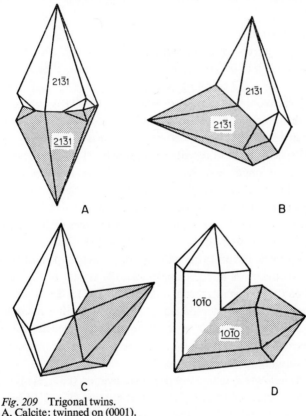

Fig. 209 Trigonal twins.
A. Calcite: twinned on (0001).
B. Calcite: twinned on ($10\bar{1}1$).
C. Calcite: twinned on ($02\bar{2}1$).
D. Quartz: twinned on ($11\bar{2}2$).

glide twinning occurs during deformation, but growth twins may twin equally on rhombohedral planes of different index. Fig. 209B is a twin on ($10\bar{1}1$) and Fig. 209C on ($02\bar{2}1$) and the effect in each case is similar to the geniculate twins of the tetragonal system.

The twinning of quartz has been discussed already and the most common twins are interpenetration Dauphiné and Brazil twins (Figs. 200, 201 and 202). Contact twins of quartz are rare, but of several types, the *Japanese twin* is the best known. The plane $(11\bar{2}2)$, parallel to the trigonal bipyramid face, is the composition plane and the c axes of the two individuals make an angle of 84° 33' (Fig. 209D).

Orthorhombic system

Twinning is very common among orthorhombic crystals. It is possible for any prism face to be a twin plane and reference has already been made in this chapter to the twinning of aragonite on (110). Such twinning is particularly favourable if the prism angle $(110)\,\widehat{\,}\,(1\bar{1}0)$ approaches 60° or 90°, when mimetic twins are produced with a pseudo-hexagonal and pseudo-tetragonal habit respectively. The prism angle of marcasite $(110)\,\widehat{\,}\,(1\bar{1}0)$ is 74°55' and repeated twinning on (110) gives rise to cyclic twins with five members. Pentagonal symmetry is unknown crystallographically and it is curious that such twinning should occur when the prism angle approaches 72° so that $72° \times 5 = 360°$.

Twinning commonly takes place parallel to faces of the forms $\{0kl\}$ and $\{h0l\}$ and is well illustrated by staurolite. Staurolite twins are usually interpenetration twins with an iron cross shape and those with the arms of the cross at right angles like the crystal of Fig. 210A, are twinned on (032). The interfacial angle $(001)\,\widehat{\,}\,(032)$ is 45°41' and the two individuals lie almost at right angles. Some staurolite twins have the individuals set at about 60° to each other and somewhat askew (Fig. 210B) because the twin plane is parallel to a face of the bipyramid form $\{232\}$. Twinning can also occur on (230).

Crystals in lower symmetry classes may twin on (001). Hemimorphite crystallizes in class $mm2$ and twins in this manner (Fig. 210C). If the re-entrant angle is eliminated these twins may even appear to possess full holosymmetric symmetry (Fig. 210D). Twins like this that appear to belong to a class of higher symmetry within the same system are sometimes called *supplementary twins*.

Monoclinic system

The symmetry of monoclinic crystals is such that it is easier to speak of

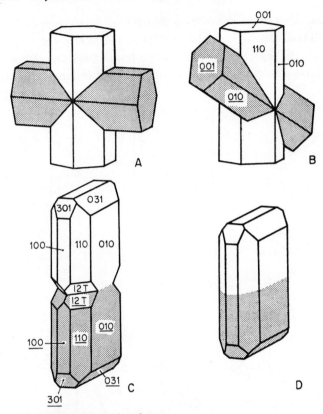

Fig. 210 Orthorhombic twins.
A. Staurolite: twinned on (032).
B. Staurolite: twinned on (232).
C. Hemimorphite (class *mm*2); twin on (001).
D. Hemimorphite: supplementary twin on (001).

those planes and axes that cannot act as twinning elements than of those that can. In the holosymmetric class (2/*m*) only the diad axis and the plane of symmetry normal to it are precluded from being a twin plane or axis and consequently it is not surprising that twinning is very common among monoclinic crystals.

Most crystals twin on planes parallel to the *b* axis and some examples are drawn in Fig. 211. Hornblende is an example of a twin that does not show re-entrant angles. Twinning can occur in several ways in ortho-clase, the monoclinic potash feldspar. *Manebach* twins are usually simple contact twins with (001) as the twin plane and composition plane (Fig. 211D). *Baveno* twins have (021) as the twin plane (Fig. 211E), and since the angle (001) ⌢ (021) is only a few minutes away from 45° the twins have a rectangular cross section. In both instances the twin axis

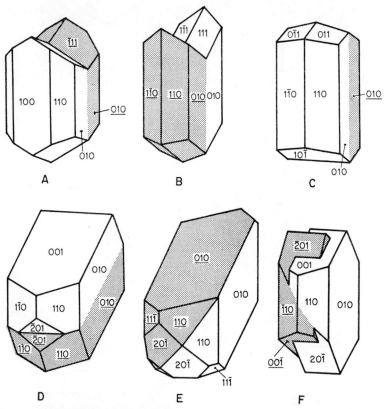

Fig. 211 Monoclinic twins.
A. Augite twinned on (100).
B. Gypsum twinned on (100).
C. Hornblende twinned on (100).
D. Orthoclase: Manebach twin, twin plane (001).
E. Orthoclase: Baveno twin; twin plane (021).
F. Orthoclase: interpenetration Carlsbad twin, twin axis = *c*.

can be regarded as being normal to the twin plane. *Carlsbad* twins are parallel twins in the sense in which the term is used on p. 272. The twin axis (the *c* axis) lies in the composition plane (010). Fig. 211F is an interpenetration Carlsbad twin.

Triclinic system

The absence of symmetry planes and axes means that any lattice plane or lattice row can be a twin plane or twin axis. But the fact that twins are of less importance only in the hexagonal system again emphasizes that factors other than those of crystal geometry are involved in determining the incidence of twinning.

The best-known triclinic twins are those of the plagioclase feldspars, and the relationship between the orientation of the optical indicatrix and a known crystallographic direction shown by a composition plane is of great value in determining the composition of a plagioclase in terms of the end members albite and anorthite. There are many types of twin shown by the plagioclases, the most common of which are the *albite* and *pericline* twins. Both are polysynthetic lamellar twins, the former with (010) as the twin plane and with lamellae parallel to {010} and the latter with *b* as the twin axis. More than one type of twin can occur in a crystal. Thus many plagioclases have two sets of lamellae lying nearly at right angles and others show combined Carlsbad-albite twinning.

Stereographic projection of twinned crystals

The construction of a stereographic projection of twinned crystals presents difficulties not encountered in untwinned crystals. The student with only a contact goniometer at his disposal will find it awkward and in some instances impossible to measure interfacial angles where the two parts of a twin meet in a re-entrant angle. It is in problems of this kind that the two-circle goniometer comes into its own. The construction of the instrument is such that it is possible to determine the position of each face by taking the readings on the two circles of the instrument and plotting the angles directly on a stereographic net. This is a distinct advantage when compared with the single circle goniometer that enables only angles between a zone of faces to be measured without resetting the crystal.

Some twins, like those of hornblende, do not have re-entrant angles and they can be plotted using the contact goniometer and the usual plotting techniques. At one time it was thought possible to assign a new set of Miller indices to the displaced faces on the basis of their relationship to the axes of the untwinned crystal, but this is confusing. We have seen that the orientation of the two parts of a twin is crystallographically controlled and the practice now is to index the faces of the 'displaced' part of the twin by referring them to the crystallographic axes of the displaced part and to distinguish them on the stereogram by underlining them, e.g. ($\underline{111}$). Implicit in this system of indexing is the understanding of the relationship between the two parts of the twin in terms of the twin operation producing them. The underlined index ($\underline{111}$) means in effect, the position adopted by the face (111) when twinning takes place according to the particular law in question.

If the twin axis is known, the twinned position of a face can readily be found because the operation of twinning can be thought of as involving a rotation through 180° about the twin axis. The twinned position of any pole always lies in the plane containing the pole and the twin axis and at the same angular distance from the twin axis as the original pole. Fig. 212 is a spherical projection showing a twin axis and a pole P. The

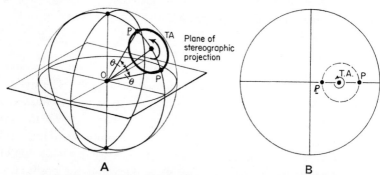

Fig. 212 The effect of rotation twinning on poles in stereographic projection. (A) a spherical projection and (B) a stereogram showing the rotation of pole *p* about a small circle about the twin axis (T.A.) to the twinned position *p*.

operation of twinning 'moves' the pole P through 180° around a small circle with the twin axis as its centre, so that it takes up position $\underline{P}$ which lies in the same plane as the twin axis and P and at an angular distance θ on the other side of the twin axis. Now since the twin axis and the pole

P pass through the centre of the spherical projection O it follows that the projection of this plane is a great circle and the stereographic projection of this operation is shown in Fig. 212B.

Fluorite commonly twins on (111). Fig. 213B is a stereographic projection of the crystal shown in Fig. 213A. The face (100) has its twin

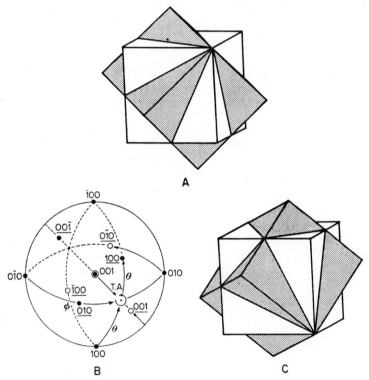

Fig. 213   A. An interpenetration twin of a fluorite cube on [111] as the twin axis.
B. Stereogram of Fig. 213A.
C. The twin redrawn with [Ī Ī 1] as the twin axis in order to show more clearly the twin.

position along the great circle joining it to the twin axis and at an angular distance θ beyond the twin axis. The twin position of the pole to (001) moves similarly but projects in the lower hemisphere. The pole (0Ī0) is some 125° (ϕ) from the twin axis and moves a further 125° along the great circle beyond the twin axis, a move that takes it into the lower hemisphere as shown on the stereogram. Notice that the twin position of this pole must lie 180° from the twin position of the pole (010), and is a useful check on the accuracy of the projection.

Using similar reasoning and construction it is possible from a stereographic projection of a twin to determine the twin axis, particularly when the twins are simple twins.

Suggestions for further reading
Azároff, L. V., *Introduction to Solids*, McGraw-Hill Book Company Inc., New York, Toronto and London, 1960.
Bentley, W. A. and Humphries, W. J., *Snow Crystals*, McGraw-Hill Book Company Inc. New York, 1931.
Buckley, H. E., *Crystal Growth*, John Wiley & Sons Inc., New York, 1951.
Bunn, C. W., *Chemical Crystallography*, University Press Oxford, 2nd Edition 1961.
Bunn, C. W., *Crystals: their role in nature and science*, Academic Press, New York and London, 1964.
Fyfe, W. S., *Geochemistry of Solids*, McGraw-Hill Book Company Inc., New York, San Francisco, Toronto, London, 1964.
Read, W. T. Jr., *Dislocations in Crystals*, McGraw-Hill Book Company Inc., New York 1953.

CHAPTER 12

STEREOGRAPHIC PROJECTIONS —
SOME ADDITIONAL CONSTRUCTIONS

The student will at times find it necessary to construct or interpret a stereographic projection without the aid of a Wulff net. The essential constructions are given below.

The first and obvious step is to draw with compasses the primitive circle. This should be large enough to enable constructions to be done without overcrowding. Circles, it is suggested, should not normally be less than six inches in diameter.

Construction of small circles
The preparation of a stereographic projection necessitates the construction of small circles centred on the pole of a face that may project:

(a) as the central point of the projection
(b) as a point on the primitive circle
(c) as a point lying within the primitive and not the centre of the projection.

Cases (a) and (b) are special cases of the general construction (c).

(a) *Construction of a small circle centred on the central point of the projection*
It is frequently necessary to plot the position of a face like face *b* in Fig 214A, knowing the interfacial angle between it and a face that plots at the centre of the projection. Face *b* will lie somewhere on a small circle whose centre is at O (Fig. 214B) and whose radius *d* is proportional to the interfacial angle θ. We have seen already in Chapter 3 that this relationship is given by $d = r.\tan\dfrac{\theta}{2}$ where r is the radius of the primitive circle. All that is necessary is to set the compasses to the appropriate calculated radius and draw in the circle with O as its centre.

(b) *Construction of a small circle centred on a point on the primitive*
The interfacial angle between faces *b* and *c* is ϕ and the position of the

pole to *b* must lie on the small circle about *c* whose radius is ϕ. The construction is shown in Fig. 214C. The interfacial angle ϕ is measured around the primitive from *c* with a protractor and the radius OB drawn. Next draw a line at right angles to OB and extend it to cut O*c* produced at C. C is the centre and BC the radius of the required small circle.

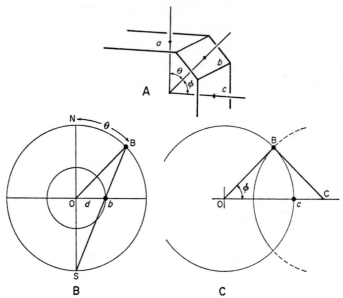

Fig. 214 Construction of small circles about poles plotting at the centre of a stereogram and on the primitive circle.

(c) Construction of a small circle about a point within the primitive

The properties of small circles in stereographic projection were discussed in Chapter 3 and it was seen that any circle drawn on the surface of a sphere projects stereographically as a circle (Fig. 45).

It would seem that a circle drawn on the stereographic net about the projected centre of the circle on the sphere would be the required small circle. A consideration of Figs. 214B and C shows that this is not so. The centres of the circle on the sphere and the projected small circle coincide only when they are the centre point of the projection (Fig. 214B). In all other cases the centre of the projected small circle is displaced outwards towards the primitive relative to the projected centre of the small circle drawn on the sphere. This outward displacement reaches its maximum in the limiting case in which the centre of the small circle projects on the primitive circle (Fig. 214C).

In Fig. 215A the angle between faces b and d is α, and if the crystal is rotated about the normal to b then the normal to d will describe a small circle about b, as shown in the spherical projection Fig. 215B. The

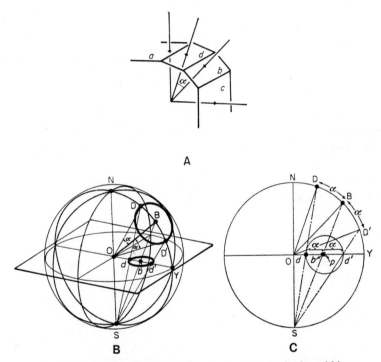

Fig. 215 Construction of a small circle about a pole plotting within the primitive circle.

construction of the small circle involves the spherical projection in the plane containing N, D, B, Y (Fig. 215C) and then reverting to the normal stereographic plane.

First join Ob and produce it to the primitive at Y (Fig. 215C). Next draw NOS perpendicular to this and construct the line SbB. This gives the spherical projection B of the stereographic pole b. With a protractor measure the angle α round the primitive on either side of B. The two points D and D′ mark the limits of the small circle in the plane NBY. Next join these two points to S and mark their stereographic projection points *d* and *d′* on the line O*b*Y. These points mark the limits of the small circle in stereographic projection. Bisect the distance *dd′*, giving *p* which is the centre of the required small circle. Draw the small circle on the stereographic projection with its centre *p* and radius *pd*.

Construction of great circles

Although nearly all crystals can be plotted by the small circle method, the interpretation of the completed projection involves the use of great circles to check zonal relationships between faces. We need to construct great circles when:

    (a) three poles are known

    (b) two poles are known, but one lies on the primitive

    (c) two poles are known, neither of which lies on the primitive.

(a) *Construction of great circle through three known poles*

The three poles are marked *a*, *b* and *c* in Fig. 216A. It is immaterial

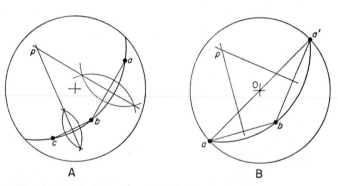

Fig. 216 Construction of great circles through (A) three poles; (B) two poles, one of which lies on the primitive circle.

whether they lie within the primitive or on it; the general case is illustrated. First join *ab* and *bc*. Next construct lines bisecting *ab* and *bc* and perpendicular to them by scribing with compasses overlapping arcs from *a* and *b* and *b* and *c* and joining the intersections. Produce the lines to meet at p which is the centre of the required great circle whose radius is pa.

(b) *Construction of a great circle through two poles, one of which lies on the primitive*

The two poles a and b are marked on Fig. 216B, but before the centre of the great circle can be located a third pole that lies on the great circle has to be found. Since all great circles pass through the centre of the sphere, it follows that the pole a' lying on the primitive 180° away from a must also lie on the great circle. Its position is found by drawing in the diameter aOa'. The centre p of the great circle is then constructed as in case (a) above.

(c) *Construction of a great circle through two poles, neither of which lies on the primitive*

This construction is the general case of construction (b). For any pole, another can be constructed that is diametrically opposite to it and on the same great circle. In order to construct the great circle through poles a and b in Fig. 217A the opposite to one or other of these poles must be located. This then gives three points lying on the same great circle whose centre can be found by using construction (a). The construction again involves using the projection in two ways. In Fig. 217B the stereographic projection of pole a is shown together with its spherical projection A. The point A′ is diametrically opposite to A and it is obvious from the diagram that they lie on the same great circle. The stereographic projection of A′ is a' and it should be noticed that the projection is from the south pole of the sphere. The full projected great circle on which a and a' lie is sketched in.

Fig. 217A is first used as spherical projection in the plane NA′SA of Fig. 217B. First draw the line aO which represents the equatorial plane of the spherical projection. The line NOS at right angles to this is drawn next and from point S, the south pole of the spherical projection, a line is drawn through a to meet the primitive at A. This is the pole of the face in spherical projection. The opposite pole, A′, is diametrically opposite to A, as shown. We require the stereographic projection of A′ and this is

obtained by projecting from S through A′ and producing the line to
meet the equatorial line aO at $a′$. The poles a, b and $a′$ lie on the required
great circle which can now be constructed following the procedure of
construction (a).

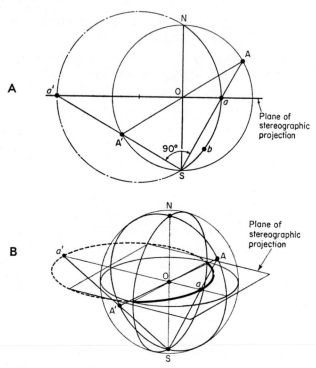

Fig. 217 Construction of a great circle through two poles lying
within the primitive circle.

Other useful constructions

The construction of small circles and great circles allows a stereographic
projection to be drawn and zones inserted. It frequently happens that
additional information is required and this involves other constructions.
For example, let Fig. 218A represent part of a stereogram of a crystal in
which the poles a, b, c and d are in zone. We require the angle between
faces b and c. The first step is to draw in the great circle and then to find
its pole.

(a) *Construction of the pole to a great circle*

A great circle is the projection of a diametral plane of a sphere and the pole to this plane is at 90° from all points on the great circle. Having drawn the great circle, draw next the diameter aOd and the normal to it XOY. It will be clear from Fig. 218B that the stereographic projection

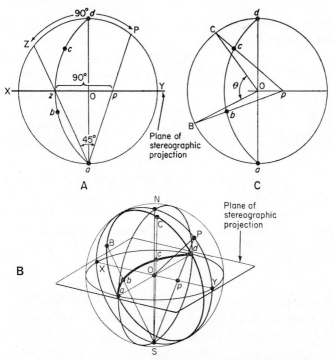

Fig. 218 Determination of the angle between two poles lying within the primitive.

of the pole to the plane projecting as the great circle *abcd* must lie also in the line XOY. Using now Fig. 218A as a vertical projection, draw a line from S through z and produce it to meet the circle at Z. This is the position of the pole z in spherical projection. Now measure 90° round the circle to give the position of P, the pole to the plane. The stereographic projection of this point gives the pole to the great circle and it is obtained by projecting from S, giving the pole p at the intersection with XOY.

T

(b) *Measurement of the angle between two poles on an inclined great circle*
Having found the pole to the great circle the angle between poles *b* and *c*
in Fig. 218A can be measured. From *p* (Fig. 218C) project through *b*
and *c* to the primitive to give the points B and C. The angle between B
and C can now be measured using a protractor centred at O.

(c) *Measurement of the angle between two great circles that intersect at
a point within the primitive*

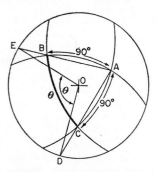

It is sometimes necessary to know the
angle θ between two great circles that
intersect at a point A (Fig. 219) within
the primitive. By using constructions (a)
and (b) above, two points B and C, each
90° from A, can be plotted on the two
great circles. Point A is the pole to the
great circle containing B and C and
$\widehat{B\ C} = \theta$. To measure this, join AC and
produce to D and join AB and produce
to E. Angle D–E is also θ and can be
measured directly with a protractor centred at O.

Fig. 219 Determination of the
angle between two great circles
intersecting at A.

(d) *Rotation of the poles of a projection to a new position (tilting)*
Very occasionally it is necessary to change the attitude of a stereographic
projection. Take the simple case of Fig. 220 as an example. Here a cube
has been plotted with a triad axis as the principal axis and the resulting
stereographic projection appears as in Fig. 220B. It is required now to
rotate the projection about the axis *x* in order to bring the pole to the
cube face to the centre of the projection. When the projection is rotated
about *x* all the poles describe small circles about *x*. The pole to face *a*
projects on the diameter perpendicular to *x* and moves along it through
$\theta°$ to the centre of the projection. The poles *b* and *c* move also $\theta°$ along
the small circles centred on *x* that pass through them and move to the
primitive. Similarly, the lower hemisphere poles move as shown and the
rotated projection is shown in Fig. 220C. In cases like that of Fig. 220D
where the rotation moves a pole through a greater angle than would

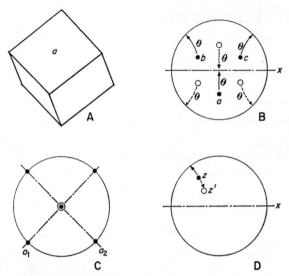

Fig. 220   Rotation of poles in stereographic projection.
A. Cube drawn with triad axis vertical.
B. Stereogram of Fig. 220A.
C. Stereogram of cube after rotation.
D. Rotation of pole through an angle taking it beyond the primitive.
Solid arrow: movement of pole in upper hemisphere.
Broken arrow: movement of pole in lower hemisphere.

take it to the primitive, then it follows the same small circle into the lower hemisphere and projects as z'.

Suggestions for further reading
Phillips, F. C., *An Introduction to Crystallography*, Longmans, Green & Co. Ltd., London, 3rd Edition, 1963.
Terpstra, P, and Codd, L. W., *Crystallometry*, Longmans, Green & Co., Ltd., London, 1961.

CHAPTER 13

CRYSTAL DRAWING

In addition to the construction of an accurate stereographic projection, the student needs also to be able to construct an accurate drawing of a crystal.

A person with some artistic ability can probably produce a creditable formalized drawing from an actual crystal but such a drawing will most likely be a perspective drawing of some kind. Fig. 221 is a drawing of an

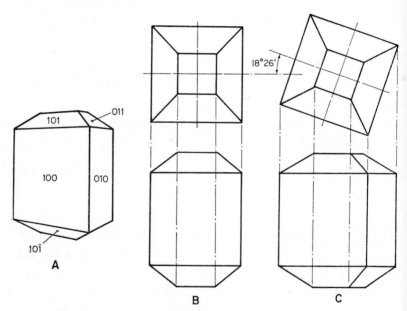

Fig. 221 A. A simple idocrase crystal drawn in two-point perspective.
B. Idocrase in plan and elevation.
C. Fig. 221B rotated $18°26'$ about c axis.

idocrase crystal in two-point perspective. It is artistically correct in that parallel edges on the crystal are drawn converging towards vanishing points on the horizon. Crystallographic drawings should, however, show crystal faces in their correct geometrical position and edges between them that are parallel on the crystal should also be parallel on the drawing. In this way the zonal relationships between faces are apparent in the drawing.

There are two ways of constructing a crystal drawing. The simpler and most useful method from the student's point of view is to construct first an axial cross and from this build up the drawing. The other method, which is the one used by most practised crystallographers, is to construct the drawing from the stereographic projection. This method is most useful when making drawings of richly faceted crystals, but the first method shows most clearly the nature of the axial ratio, the meaning of the law of rational intercepts, the fact that faces in zone meet in parallel edges and the variation in crystal shape caused by variation in development of a particular form.

The engineer and carpenter work from scale drawings that give the shape of an object in plan and elevation. The idocrase crystal is shown this way in Fig. 221B. In order to produce a solid-looking, three-dimensional drawing it is first necessary to turn the elevation slightly to the left and then raise the viewing position slightly in order to look down on the top of the crystal. Such a projection is called a *clinographic projection.*

It is necessary now to construct an axial cross that shows the crystallographic axes in their correct position and length as viewed from this new position. The cubic axial cross is taken first as being the simplest.

Clearly, the angles through which the elevation is rotated and the viewpoint is raised can vary, but for some years it has been customary to rotate through $18°26'$ to the left about the vertical axis and to elevate the viewpoint by $9°28'$. These angles are chosen because their tangents have simple values; $\tan 18°26' = \frac{1}{3}$ and $\tan 9°28' = \frac{1}{6}$. The foreshortening of the horizontal axes is therefore simply related to the vertical axis that is always shown as full length. The derivation of an axial cross for the cube is shown in Fig. 222. The plan view of this cube and the new position when rotated through $18°26'$ about a_3 are given in Fig. 222A. The foreshortening of the length of the a_2 axis is clearly seen in projection at B and the projected elevation is given at C.

It is now necessary to raise the viewpoint by $9°28'$. This will have the effect of tilting the a_1 axis downwards by an amount equal to the tangent of 9°28′. Since tan 9°28′ is $\frac{1}{6}$, the distance d (Fig. 222D) is one sixth of the foreshortened length of a_2.

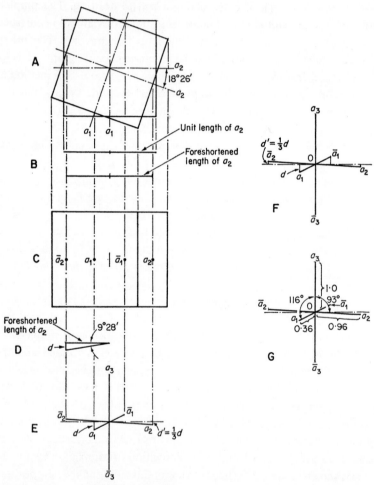

Fig. 222 Construction of clinographic axial cross (after Penfield).

The raising of the viewpoint also has the effect of moving the positive end of a_2 forwards and downwards with respect to the horizontal. This is effectively the same as displacing it downwards by a distance d' (Fig. 222E) that is equal to $\frac{1}{3}d$.

The cross can be constructed very rapidly by first drawing a vertical

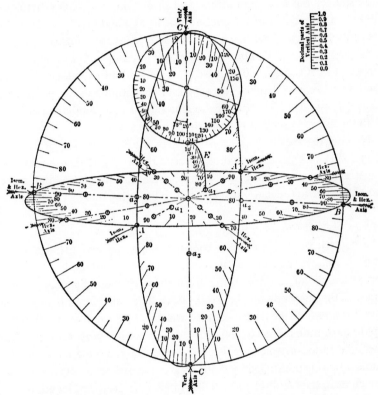

Fig. 223 The Penfield axial protractor (reproduced by permission of J. Wiley and Sons).

line to represent the a_3 axis and marking a point O at its centre. Next draw a construction line perpendicular to a_3 through O and along it on either side of O mark the positions of the ends of the a_1 and a_2 axes as derived in Figs. 222A and B. From these points draw perpendiculars downwards at a_1 and a_2 and upwards $\bar{a}_1$ and $\bar{a}_2$ (Fig. 222F). From a_1, mark off along the perpendicular, distance d which is $\frac{1}{6}$ Oa_2. Join this point through O to the perpendicular from $\bar{a}_1$ and this is the trace of the a_1 axis.

Next, from a_2 mark downwards along the perpendicular a distance d' which is equivalent to $\frac{1}{3}d$. Again join through O and produce to the normal at $\bar{a}_2$. This is the trace of the a_2 axis.

A simpler but less accurate method of drawing the axial cross is to draw first a vertical line to represent the a_3 axis and mark a point O at its centre. Using a protractor centred at O construct angles $a_3\widehat{O}a_1 = 116°$, and $a_3\widehat{O}a_2 = 93°$. Draw the lines $a_1 \, O \, \bar{a}_1$ and $a_2 \, O \, \bar{a}_2$ making the lengths $Oa_1 : Oa_2 : Oa_3 : : 0{\cdot}36 : 0{\cdot}96 : 1$. This method expresses in plane angles and relative lengths the construction outlined in the paragraph above. It is suggested that the student should first familiarize himself with the full construction before using this short cut.

In order to save doing the constructions, the Penfield axial protractor (Fig. 223) can be used as a guide for crystal drawing. This protractor is constructed in accordance with the principles set out above, and it is a simple matter to transfer the axial cross to overlying tracing paper.

Tetragonal and orthorhombic crystals

The construction of an axial cross for tetragonal and orthorhombic crystals follows the same pattern as for the cubic system, but the projected lengths of the axes differ from those of the cubic cross by an amount that depends on the axial ratios. The cubic cross is first constructed and then the length of the a and c axes adjusted by multiplying by the axial ratios. Thus to construct the appropriate cross for forsterite, the axial ratios of which are $0{\cdot}467 : 1 : 0{\cdot}586$, the projected length of the cubic a_1 axis is multiplied by $0{\cdot}467$ to give the orthorhombic a axis and the cubic a_3 axis multiplied by $0{\cdot}586$ to give the projected length of the orthorhombic c axis.

Monoclinic crystals

In addition to the adjustment of the cubic cross for axial ratios, an adjustment has to be made for angle β. This allowance is made by first determining the position of the end of the a axis below the horizontal construction line of Fig. 222F by increasing the distance d. This increase is proportional to angle $(\beta - 90°)$, the dip of a below the horizontal. The length d is thus $\tan(9°28' + (\beta - 90°))$. The correction for the axial ratio is then applied.

Scales are marked on the Penfield axial protractor that allow corrections for angle β and axial length to be made with ease.

Further corrections have to be made to allow for the inclination of the *b* axis of triclinic crystals, but these are complex and they are omitted here for brevity.

Hexagonal and trigonal crystals

The positions of the a_1, a_2 and a_3 axes for hexagonal and trigonal crystals are clearly shown on the Penfield protractor. They may be constructed directly as follows. First draw a cubic axial cross and label the axes, *a*, *b*, *c*, in orthorhombic fashion (Fig. 224). (This is to avoid possible confusion between cubic a_1, a_2 and a_3 and hexagonal a_1, a_2 and a_3

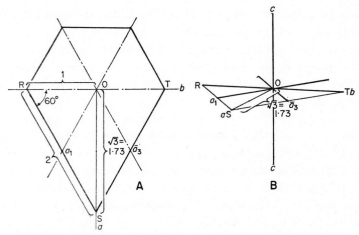

Fig. 224   Construction of hexagonal axial cross.

axes.) If a regular hexagon is constructed in the horizontal plane so that *b* passes through a pair of corners, then the hexagonal a_2 axis is coincident with *b* and the other two horizontal hexagonal axes a_1 and a_3 pass through the other corners of the hexagon. Thus if the regular hexagon is constructed on Fig. 224A then the position and length of the a_1 and a_3 axes are fixed.

Draw a line OS so that it is 1·73 times the unit length of the *a* axis on the cubic axial cross. Join RS and TS. Bisect these lines to give points a_1

and $\bar{a}_3$. Lines from a_1 and a_3 through O give the projected positions and lengths of the a_1 and a_3 axes.

The length of the vertical axis is determined, as in the tetragonal system, by multiplying by the axial ratio.

Plotting faces on the axial cross

Having constructed the appropriate axial cross, the next step is to plot the actual crystal faces.

Fig. 225A shows the cubic axial cross and the construction of the form {111} on it. The face (111), from its Miller index, must make a unit intercept on the positive ends of the a_1, a_2 and a_3 axes. These are the limits of the constructed axes and the shape of the face is obtained by joining these three points.

When the figure 0 forms part of a Miller index, the form has a crystallographic axis as a zone axis. The construction of prism forms in the tetragonal system is illustrated in Fig. 225 B-D. The prism {110} makes unit intercepts on the two horizontal axes and lies parallel to c, or put another way, intercepts it at infinity. The faces of the form therefore meet in edges that lie parallel to c. These edges can be inserted directly on the axial cross as lines parallel to c passing through the unit intercepts of the a_1 and a_2 axes. In order to finish the form, construction lines parallel to a_1 and a_2 are drawn at equal distances above and below O; in Fig. 225B they are drawn through the unit intercept on c. The points ABCD, A'B'C'D' at which these construction lines meet the parallel edges already drawn, mark the arbitrarily chosen upper and lower limits of the form, and they are joined to one another in the manner shown.

A similar procedure is followed in the construction of the form {100}. The edges between the faces are again parallel to c but they do not pass through the a_1 and a_2 axes and the positions of the points ABCD (Fig. 225C) through which they pass must be constructed. This is done by drawing lines DA and CB parallel to a_2 through the unit intercepts on a_1 and the lines DC and AB parallel to a_1 through the unit intercepts on a_2. The intersections of these lines give the points ABCD and the edges between the faces pass through these points and lie parallel to c.

The construction of the ditetragonal prism {$hk0$} introduces another

constructional principle. The construction of this form with the index
{210} is illustrated in Fig. 225D. The first point to bear in mind is that
the Miller index of a face is the reciprocal of its intercepts and hence the
face (210) makes double the unit intercept on a_2. This face can be constructed on the axial cross by marking the appropriate intercepts on the
a_1 and a_2 axes and then drawing in the four faces with similar indices
(210) ($\bar{2}$10) ($\bar{2}\bar{1}$0) (2$\bar{1}$0) by drawing lines parallel to c through points
A,B,C and D.

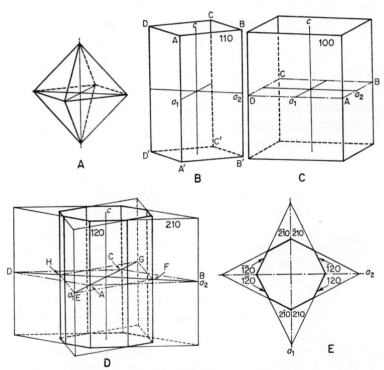

Fig. 225 Construction of some cubic and tetragonal forms of
simple Miller indices on the axial cross.

We know, however, that the ditetragonal prism has eight faces in-
dexed as shown in Fig. 225E. The four faces (120) ($\bar{1}$20) ($\bar{1}\bar{2}$0) (1$\bar{2}$0) can
be constructed similarly to those described above, simply by making the
appropriate intercepts on the a_1 and a_2 axes. The shape of the form is

shown by the heavy lines in Fig. 225D, the edges between faces (210) and (120) being given by the intersections of the 'extended' planes of the faces.

This principle of the truncating of one face by another is of importance when drawing crystals having more than one form. Suppose for example we require to draw a tetragonal crystal that is a combination of forms {110} and {111}, a habit shown by some zircon crystals. The appropriate axial cross for zircon (axial ratio $c = 0.905$) is first constructed and on this the form {111} is drawn. The prism {100} is next inserted, but if it is constructed at the unit intercepts on a_1 and a_2 then the prism and bipyramid would touch only at the points of emergence of the axes. It is necessary therefore to 'move in' the prism faces towards O so that they will intersect the bipyramids. Accordingly, points A, B, C, D, are selected somewhere on the a_1 and a_2 axes so that they are in their correct relative distance from O. Notice that moving these points does not affect the index of the form; it still remains {100}, as it would if they were moved instead outside the unit distance.

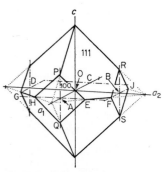

Fig. 226 Construction of a drawing of a crystal of zircon comprising the forms {111} and {100}.

The next step is to construct lines parallel to a_1 and a_2 through points A, B, C and D. (Fig. 226). These give the plan of the form {100} in the plane of the a axes and the points E, F, G, H, etc., mark the intersection of {100} on {111} in this plane.

Further points of intersection of the two forms are found by drawing through ABCD construction lines parallel to c which intersect the bipyramid edges at PQ, RS, etc.

The shape of the crystal can now be completed by joining points PE, EQ, QH, and HP; and FR, RJ, JS, SF, etc. The final shape is shown in heavy lines in Fig. 226.

These methods are applicable to all crystal systems; the only adjustment necessary is made when drawing the axial cross.

There is a general method described by Penfield for the construction of an edge between crystal faces. The edge can be drawn if two points that lie on it can be located. One such point can always be made the unit length of the *c* axis, for any plane can be constructed on the axial cross and its position adjusted (without change of attitude) so that it passes through this point. For example, a plane with the index (111) makes a unit intercept on all three axes and thus when constructed directly, passes through unity on the *c* axis. A plane with the index (221), however, has intercepts 1*a*, 1*b*, 2*c* and, in order that it shall pass through unity on

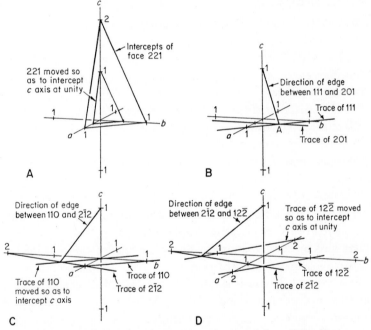

Fig. 227   Construction of edges between crystal faces (After Penfield).

c, needs to be 'moved in' so that it makes intercepts $\frac{1}{2}a$, $\frac{1}{2}b$, 1*c* (Fig. 227A).

The second point on an edge between two faces is the point of intersection of the two faces in the plane containing the *a* and *b* axes, the faces of course being drawn in the position at which they intersect the *c* axis at unity. Fig 227B illustrates the intersection at point A of faces

(111) and (201) The direction of the edge between these two faces is hence the line joining point A with unity on the *c* axis.

The following constructions should be noted:

(a) *To find the direction of the edge between an inclined face and a vertical face*. The vertical face, in order to pass through unity on the *c* axis, must be 'moved in' so that it coincides with the *c* axis, in the manner illustrated in Fig. 227C. The horizontal trace of the face must therefore pass through the point of intersection of the crystallographic axes. The intersection point of the two *faces* (110) and (2$\bar{1}$2) in the plane containing the *a* and *b* axes is found in the usual way and the direction of the edge constructed by joining this point to unity on *c*.

(b) *To find the direction of the edge between faces that intersect the c axis at opposite ends*, e.g. between faces (12$\bar{2}$) and (2$\bar{1}$2) (Fig. 227D). It is necessary in this case to move one of the faces (here (12$\bar{2}$)) beyond the point of intersection of the crystallographic axes so that it intersects the *c* axis in the same position as the other face. From Fig. 227D it is clear that this involves moving the face so that it has the same intercepts on the crystallographic axes but on the opposite side of their point of intersection.

The above two constructions give only the *direction* of the appropriate edge. The actual *position* of the edge necessarily runs from the point of intersection of the two faces in the plane containing *a* and *b* and this is determined by considerations involving the relative size that the faces are to assume on the finished drawing.

This method of construction is applicable to all crystal systems; variation of axial ratios and axial inclination are incorporated in the axial cross before construction commences.

Suggestions for further reading
Dana, E. S., *A Textbook of Mineralogy*, John Wiley & Sons, Inc., New York, Chapman and Hall Ltd., London, Fourth Edition, revised by W. E. Ford, 1932 (Appendix A).
Terpstra, P. and Codd, L. W., *Crystallometry*, Longmans, Green and Co. Ltd., London, 1961.

APPENDIX

CRYSTALLOGRAPHIC CONSTANTS OF SOME COMMON MINERALS

Mineral	System & Class	Axial ratios	Cell Dimensions (Å) a	b	c	Axial angles α	β	γ
Albite	Triclinic $\bar{1}$	0·637:1:0·560	8·14	12·79	7·16	94°20'	116°34'	87°39'
Almandine	Cubic m3m	1	11·526	—	—	—	—	—
Andalusite	Orthorhombic mmm	0·982:1:0·703	7·78	7·92	5·57	—	—	—
Anorthite	Triclinic $\bar{1}$	0·635:1:1·100	8·18	12·88	14·17	93°10'	115°51'	91°13'
Apatite	Hexagonal 6/m	0·735	9·38	—	6·89	—	—	—
Apophyllite	Tetragonal 4/mmm	1·761	8·960	—	15·78	—	—	—
Aragonite	Orthorhombic mmm	0·622:1:0·720	4·95	7·95	5·73	—	—	—
Augite	Monoclinic 2/m	1·092:1:0·589	9·73	8·9	5·25	—	105°50'	—
Axinite	Triclinic $\bar{1}$	0·779:1:0·978	7·15	9·16	5·25	88°4'	81°36'	77°42'
Barytes	Orthorhombic mmm	1·629:1:1·312	8·878	5·450	8·96	—	—	—
Beryl	Hexagonal 6/mmm	1·0001	9·188	—	7·152	—	—	—
Calcite	Trigonal $\bar{3}m$	0·8550 (morphological) 3·4099 (structural)	9·188	—	9·189	—	—	—
Cassiterite	Tetragonal 4/mmm	0·673	4·990	—	17·061	—	—	—
Celestite	Orthorhombic mmm	1·562:1:1·283	4·73	5·352	3·18	—	—	—
Chalcopyrite	Tetragonal $\bar{4}2m$	1·965	8·359	—	6·866	—	—	—
Corundum	Trigonal $\bar{3}m$	2·730	5·25	—	10·32	—	—	—
Dolomite	Trigonal $\bar{3}$	0·8235 (morphological) 3·330 (structural)	4·760	—	12·98	—	—	—
Epidote	Monoclinic 2/m	1·592:1:1·825	8·98	5·64	10·30	—	115°24'	—
Fluorite	Cubic m3m	1	5·463	—	—	—	—	—
Galena	Cubic m3m	1	5·94	—	—	—	—	—
Grossularite	Cubic m3m	1	11·851	—	—	—	—	—

CRYSTALLOGRAPHIC CONSTANTS OF SOME COMMON MINERALS contd.

Mineral	System & Class	Axial ratios	Cell Dimensions (Å)			Axial angles		
			a	b	c	α	β	γ
Gypsum	Monoclinic $2/m$	0·374:1:0·414	5·68	15·18	6·29	—	113°50'	—
Haematite	Trigonal $\bar{3}m$	2·7307	5·0345	—	13·749	—	—	—
Halite	Cubic $m3m$	1	5·639	—	—	—	—	—
Hornblende	Monoclinic $2/m$	0·547:1:0·295	9·9	18·0	5·3	—	105°31'	—
Idocrase	Tetragonal $4/mmm$	0·757	15·6	—	11·8	—	—	—
Kyanite	Triclinic $\bar{1}$	0·917:1:0·720	7·10	7·74	5·57	90°6'	101°2'	105°45'
Microcline	Triclinic $\bar{1}$	0·661:1:0·557	8·57	12·96	7·22	90°39'	115°56'	87°47'
Olivine (Forsterite)	Orthorhombic mmm	0·467:1:0·586	4·756	10·195	5·981	—	—	—
Orthoclase	Monoclinic $2/m$	0·659:1:0·554	8·562	12·996	7·193	—	116°1'	—
Pyrite	Cubic $m3$	1	5·417	—	—	—	—	—
Pyrope	Cubic $m3m$	1	11·459	—	—	—	—	—
Quartz	Trigonal 32	1·1001	4·913	—	5·405	—	—	—
Rutile	Tetragonal $4/mmm$	0·6439	4·594	—	2·958	—	—	—
Sphalerite	Cubic $\bar{4}3m$	1	5·41	—	—	—	—	—
Spinel	Cubic $m3m$	1	8·103	—	—	—	—	—
Staurolite	Monoclinic $2/m$ (Pseudo-orthorhombic)	0·471:1:0·340	7·83	16·62	5·65	—	90°	—
Tetrahedrite	Cubic $\bar{4}3m$	1	10·40	—	—	—	—	—
Topaz	Orthorhombic mmm	0·528:1:0·955	4·650	8·800	8·394	—	—	—
Tourmaline	Trigonal $3m$	0·448	15·84	—	7·10–7·25	—	—	—
Zircon	Tetragonal $4/mmm$	0·9054	6·604	—	5·979	—	—	—

INDEX

Figures in bold type refer to illustrations